12-25-71

Carly,

The guy who holds
a very SPECIAL
Part of our hearts.

Love ya!!

Russ & Maggie

the exorcist

William Peter Blatty

THE EXORCIST

1817

HARPER & ROW, PUBLISHERS

NEW YORK, EVANSTON, SAN FRANCISCO, LONDON

STANDARD BOOK NUMBER: 06-010365-5

LIBRARY OF CONGRESS CATALOG CARD NUMBER: 73-144189

for Beth

Now when [Jesus] stepped ashore, there met him a certain man who for a long time was possessed by a devil. . . . Many times it had laid hold of him and he was bound with chains. . . . but he would break the bonds asunder. . . . And Jesus asked him, saying, "What is thy name?" And he said, " Legion. . . ."

Luke 8:27–30

JAMES TORELLO: *Jackson was hung up on that meat hook. He was so heavy he bent it. He was on that thing three days before he croaked.*

FRANK BUCCIERI (giggling): *Jackie, you shoulda seen the guy. Like an elephant, he was, and when Jimmy hit him with that electric prod . . .*

TORELLO (excitedly): *He was floppin' around on that hook, Jackie. We tossed water on him to give the prod a better charge, and he's screamin'. . . .*

Excerpt from FBI wiretap of Cosa Nostra telephone conversation relating to murder of William Jackson

. . . There's no other explanation for some of the things the Communists did. Like the priest who had eight nails driven into his skull. . . . And there were the seven little boys and their teacher. They were praying the Our Father when soldiers came upon them. One soldier whipped out his bayonet and sliced off the teacher's tongue. The other took chopsticks and drove them into the ears of the seven little boys. How do you treat cases like that?

Dr. Tom Dooley

Dachau

Auschwitz

Buchenwald

prologue

Northern Iraq

The blaze of sun wrung pops of sweat from the old man's brow, yet he cupped his hands around the glass of hot sweet tea as if to warm them. He could not shake the premonition. It clung to his back like chill wet leaves.

The dig was over. The tell had been sifted, stratum by stratum, its entrails examined, tagged and shipped: the beads and pendants; glyptics; phalli; ground-stone mortars stained with ocher; burnished pots. Nothing exceptional. An Assyrian ivory toilet box. And man. The bones of man. The brittle remnants of cosmic torment that once made him wonder if matter was Lucifer upward-groping back to his God. And yet now he knew better. The fragrance of licorice plant and tamarisk tugged his gaze to poppied hills; to reeded plains; to the ragged, rock-strewn bolt of road that flung itself headlong into dread. Northwest was Mosul; east, Erbil; south was Baghdad and Kirkuk and the fiery furnace of Nebuchadnezzar. He

3

shifted his legs underneath the table in front of the lonely roadside chaykhana and stared at the grass stains on his boots and khaki pants. He sipped at his tea. The dig was over. What was beginning? He dusted the thought like a clay-fresh find but he could not tag it.

Someone wheezed from within the chaykhana: the withered proprietor shuffling toward him, kicking up dust in Russian-made shoes that he wore like slippers, groaning backs pressed under his heels. The dark of his shadow slipped over the table.

"*Kaman chay, chawaga?*"

The man in khaki shook his head, staring down at the laceless, crusted shoes caked thick with debris of the pain of living. The stuff of the cosmos, he softly reflected: matter; yet somehow finally spirit. Spirit and the shoes were to him but aspects of a stuff more fundamental, a stuff that was primal and totally other.

The shadow shifted. The Kurd stood waiting like an ancient debt. The old man in khaki looked up into eyes that were damply bleached as if the membrane of an eggshell had been pasted over the irises. Glaucoma. Once he could not have loved this man.

He slipped out his wallet and probed for a coin among its tattered, crumpled tenants: a few dinars; an Iraqi driver's license; a faded plastic calendar card that was twelve years out of date. It bore an inscription on the reverse: WHAT WE GIVE TO THE POOR IS WHAT WE TAKE WITH US WHEN WE DIE. The card had been printed by the Jesuit Missions. He paid for his tea and left a tip of fifty fils on a splintered table the color of sadness.

He walked to his jeep. The gentle, rippling click of key sliding into ignition was crisp in the silence. For a moment he waited, feeling at the stillness. Clustered on the summit of a towering mound, the fractured rooftops of Erbil hovered far in the distance, poised in the clouds like a rubbled, mud-

4

stained benediction. The leaves clutched tighter at the flesh of his back.

Something was waiting.

"*Allah ma'ak, chawaga.*"

Rotted teeth. The Kurd was grinning, waving farewell. The man in khaki groped for a warmth in the pit of his being and came up with a wave and a mustered smile. It dimmed as he looked away. He started the engine, turned in a narrow, eccentric U and headed toward Mosul. The Kurd stood watching, puzzled by a heart-dropping sense of loss as the jeep gathered speed. What was it that was gone? What was it he had felt in the stranger's presence? Something like safety, he remembered; a sense of protection and deep well-being. Now it dwindled in the distance with the fast-moving jeep. He felt strangely alone.

The painstaking inventory was finished by ten after six. The Mosul curator of antiquities, an Arab with sagging cheeks, was carefully penning a final entry into the ledger on his desk. For a moment he paused, looking up at his friend, as he dipped his penpoint into an inkpot. The man in khaki seemed lost in thought. He was standing by a table, hands in his pockets, staring down at some dry, tagged whisper of the past. The curator observed him, curious, unmoving; then returned to the entry, writing in a firm, very small neat script. Then at last he sighed, setting down the pen as he noted the time. The train to Baghdad left at eight. He blotted the page and offered tea.

The man in khaki shook his head, his eyes still fixed upon something on the table. The Arab watched him, vaguely troubled. What was in the air? There was something in the air. He stood up and moved closer; then felt a vague prickling at the base of his neck as his friend at last moved, reaching down for an amulet and cradling it pensively in his hand. It

5

was a green stone head of the demon Pazuzu, personification of the southwest wind. Its dominion was sickness and disease. The head was pierced. The amulet's owner had worn it as a shield.

"Evil against evil," breathed the curator, languidly fanning himself with a French scientific periodical, an olive-oil thumbprint smudged on the cover.

His friend did not move; he did not comment.

"Is something wrong?"

No answer.

"Father?"

The man in khaki still appeared not to hear, absorbed in the amulet, the last of his finds. After a moment he set it down, then lifted a questioning look to the Arab. Had he said something?

"Nothing."

They murmured farewells.

At the door, the curator took the old man's hand with an extra firmness. "My heart has a wish, Father: that you would not go."

His friend answered softly in terms of tea; of time; of something to be done.

"No, no, no, I meant home."

The man in khaki fixed his gaze on a speck of boiled chick-pea nestled in a corner of the Arab's mouth; yet his eyes were distant. "Home," he repeated. The word had the sound of an ending.

"The States," the Arab curator added, instantly wondering why he had.

The man in khaki looked into the dark of the other's concern. He had never found it difficult to love this man.

"Good-bye," he whispered; then quickly turned and stepped into the gathering gloom of the streets and a journey home whose length seemed somehow undetermined.

"I will see you in a year!" the curator called after him from

6

the doorway. But the man in khaki never looked back. The Arab watched his dwindling form as he crossed a narrow street at an angle, almost colliding with a swiftly moving droshky. Its cab bore a corpulent old Arab woman, her face a shadow behind the black lace veil draped loosely over her like a shroud. He guessed she was rushing to some appointment. He soon lost sight of his hurrying friend.

The man in khaki walked, compelled. Shrugging loose of the city, he breached the outskirts, crossing the Tigris. Nearing the ruins, he slowed his pace, for with every step the inchoate presentiment took firmer, more horrible form. Yet he had to know. He would have to prepare.

A wooden plank that bridged the Khosr, a muddy stream, creaked under his weight. And then he was there; he stood on the mound where once gleamed fifteen-gated Nineveh, feared nest of Assyrian hordes. Now the city lay sprawled in the bloody dust of its predestination. And yet he was here, the air was still thick with him, that Other who ravaged his dreams.

A Kurdish watchman, rounding a corner, unslung his rifle and began to run toward him, then abruptly stopped and grinned with a wave of recognition and proceeded on his rounds.

The man in khaki prowled the ruins. The Temple of Nabu. The Temple of Ishtar. He sifted vibrations. At the palace of Ashurbanipal he paused; then shifted a sidelong glance to a limestone statue hulking *in situ*: ragged wings; taloned feet; bulbous, jutting, stubby penis and a mouth stretched taut in feral grin. The demon Pazuzu.

Abruptly he sagged.

He knew.

It was coming.

He stared at the dust. Quickening shadows. He heard dim yappings of savage dog packs prowling the fringes of the city. The orb of the sun was beginning to fall below the rim of the world. He rolled his shirt sleeves down and buttoned them as a shivering breeze sprang up. Its source was southwest.

He hastened toward Mosul and his train, his heart encased in the icy conviction that soon he would face an ancient enemy.

I: The Beginning

one

Like the brief doomed flare of exploding suns that registers dimly on blind men's eyes, the beginning of the horror passed almost unnoticed; in the shriek of what followed, in fact, was forgotten and perhaps not connected to the horror at all. It was difficult to judge.

The house was a rental. Brooding. Tight. A brick colonial gripped by ivy in the Georgetown section of Washington, D.C. Across the street was a fringe of campus belonging to Georgetown University; to the rear, a sheer embankment plummeting steep to busy M Street and, beyond, the muddy Potomac. Early on the morning of April 1, the house was quiet. Chris MacNeil was propped in bed, going over her lines for the next day's filming; Regan, her daughter, was sleeping down the hall; and asleep downstairs in a room off the pantry were the middle-aged housekeepers, Willie and Karl. At approximately 12:25 A.M., Chris glanced from her script with a frown of puzzlement. She heard rapping sounds. They were odd. Muffled. Profound. Rhythmically clustered. Alien code tapped out by a dead man.

Funny.

She listened for a moment; then dismissed it; but as the rappings persisted she could not concentrate. She slapped down the script on the bed.

Jesus, that bugs me!

She got up to investigate.

She went out to the hallway and looked around. It seemed to be coming from Regan's bedroom.

What is she doing?

She padded down the hall and the rappings grew suddenly louder, much faster, and as she pushed on the door and stepped into the room, they abruptly ceased.

What the heck's going on?

Her pretty eleven-year-old was asleep, cuddled tight to a large stuffed round-eyed panda. Pookey. Faded from years of smothering; years of smacking, warm, wet kisses.

Chris moved softly to her bedside and leaned over for a whisper. "Rags? You awake?"

Regular breathing. Heavy. Deep.

Chris shifted her glance around the room. Dim light from the hall fell pale and splintered on Regan's paintings; on Regan's sculptures; on more stuffed animals.

Okay, Rags. Old mother's ass is draggin'. Say it. "April Fool!"

And yet Chris knew it wasn't like her. The child had a shy and very diffident nature. Then who was the trickster? A somnolent mind imposing order on the rattlings of heating pipes or plumbing? Once, in the mountains of Bhutan, she had stared for hours at a Buddhist monk who was squatting on the ground in meditation. Finally, she thought she had seen him levitate. Perhaps. Recounting the story to someone, she invariably added "perhaps." And perhaps her mind, that

12

untiring raconteur of illusion, had embellished the rappings.

Bullshit! I heard it!

Abruptly, she flicked a quick glance to the ceiling. There! Faint scratchings.

Rats in the attic, for pete's sake! Rats!

She sighed. *That's it. Big tails. Thump, thump.* She felt oddly relieved. And then noticed the cold. The room. It was icy.

She padded to the window. Checked it. Closed. She touched the radiator. Hot.

Oh, really?

Puzzled, she moved to the bedside and touched her hand to Regan's cheek. It was smooth as thought and lightly perspiring.

I must be sick!

She looked at her daughter, at the turned-up nose and freckled face, and on a quick, warm impulse leaned over the bed and kissed her cheek. "I sure do love you," she whispered, then returned to her room and her bed and her script.

For a while, Chris studied. The film was a musical comedy remake of *Mr. Smith Goes to Washington*. A subplot had been added dealing with campus insurrections. Chris was starring. She played a psychology teacher who sided with the rebels. And she hated it. *It's dumb! This scene is absolutely dumb!* Her mind, though untutored, never mistook slogans for truth, and like a curious bluejay she would peck relentlessly through verbiage to find the glistening, hidden fact. And so the rebel cause, to her, was "dumb." It didn't make sense. *How come?* she now wondered. *Generation gap? That's a crock; I'm thirty-two. It's just plain dumb, that's all, it's . . . !*

Cool it. One more week.

They'd completed the interiors in Hollywood. All that remained were a few exterior scenes on the campus of Georgetown University, starting tomorrow. It was Easter vacation and the students were away.

She was getting drowsy. Heavy lids. She turned to a page that was curiously ragged. Bemused, she smiled. Her English director. When especially tense, he would tear, with quivering, fluttering hands, a narrow strip from the edge of the handiest page and then chew it, inch by inch, until it was all in a ball in his mouth.

Dear Burke.

She yawned, then glanced fondly at the side of her script. The pages looked gnawed. She remembered the rats. *The little bastards sure got rhythm.* She made a mental note to have Karl set traps for them in the morning.

Fingers relaxing. Script slipping loose. She let it drop. *Dumb. It's dumb.* A fumbling hand groping out to the light switch. *There.* She sighed. For a time she was motionless, almost asleep; and then kicked off her covers with a lazy leg. *Too freaking hot.*

A mist of dew clung soft and gentle to the windowpanes.

Chris slept. And dreamed about death in the staggering particular, death as if death were still never yet heard of while something was ringing, she gasping, dissolving, slipping off into void, thinking over and over, *I am not going to be, I will die, I won't be, and forever and ever, oh, Papa, don't let them, oh, don't let them do it, don't let me be nothing forever and* melting, unraveling, ringing, the ringing—

The phone!

She leaped up with her heart pounding, hand to the phone and no weight in her stomach; a core with no weight and her telephone ringing.

She answered. The assistant director.

"In makeup at six, honey."

"Right."

"How ya feelin'?"

"If I go to the bathroom and it doesn't burn, then I figure I'm ahead."

He chuckled. "I'll see you."

"Right. And thanks."

She hung up. And for moments sat motionless, thinking of the dream. A dream? More like thought in the half life of waking. That terrible clarity. Gleam of the skull. Nonbeing. Irreversible. She could not imagine it. *God, it can't be!*

She considered. And at last bowed her head. *But it is.*

She went to the bathroom, put on a robe, and padded quickly down to the kitchen, down to life in sputtering bacon.

"Ah, good morning, Mrs. MacNeil."

Gray, drooping Willie, squeezing oranges, blue sacs beneath her eyes. A trace of accent. Swiss, Like Karl's. She wiped her hands on a paper towel and started moving toward the stove.

"I'll get it, Willie." Chris, ever sensitive, had seen her weary look, and as Willie now grunted and turned back to the sink, the actress poured coffee, then moved to the breakfast nook. Sat down. And warmly smiled as she looked at her plate. A blush-red rose. Regan. *That angel.* Many a morning, when Chris was working, Regan would quietly slip out of bed, come down to the kitchen and place a flower, then grope her way crusty-eyed back to her sleep. Chris shook her head; rueful; recalling: she had almost named her Goneril. *Sure. Right on. Get ready for the worst.* Chris chuckled at the memory. Sipped at her coffee. As her gaze caught the rose again, her expression turned briefly sad, large green eyes grieving in a waiflike face. She'd recalled another flower. A son. Jamie. He had died long ago at the age of three, when Chris was very young and an unknown chorus girl on Broadway. She had sworn she would not give herself ever again as she had to Jamie; as she had to his father, Howard MacNeil. She glanced quickly from the rose, and as her dream of death misted upward from the coffee, she quickly lit a cigarette. Willie brought juice and Chris remembered the rats. "Where's Karl?" she asked the servant.

15

"I am here, madam!"

Catting in lithe through a door off the pantry. Command-ing. Deferential. Dynamic. Crouching. A fragment of Kleenex pressed tight to his chin where he'd nicked himself shaving. "Yes?" Thickly muscled, he breathed by the table. Glitter-ing eyes. Hawk nose. Bald head.

"Hey, Karl, we've got rats in the attic. Better get us some traps."

"There are rats?"

"I just said that."

"But the attic is clean."

"Well, okay, we've got *tidy* rats!"

"No rats."

"Karl, I heard them last night," Chris said patiently, con-trolling.

"Maybe plumbing," Karl probed; "maybe boards."

"Maybe *rats!* Will you buy the damn traps and quit ar-guing?'

"Yes, madam!" Bustling away. "I go now!"

"No not *now*, Karl! The stores are all closed!"

"They are closed!" chided Willie.

"I will see."

He was gone.

Chris and Willie traded glances, and then Willie shook her head, turning back to the bacon. Chris sipped at her coffee. *Strange. Strange man.* Like Willie, hard-working; very loyal; discreet. And yet something about him made her vaguely uneasy. What was it? His subtle air of arrogance? Defiance? No. Something else. Something hard to pin down. The couple had been with her for almost six years, and yet Karl was a mask—a talking, breathing, untranslated hieroglyph running her errands on stilted legs. Behind the mask, though, some-thing moved; she could hear his mechanism ticking like a conscience. She stubbed out her cigarette; heard the front door creaking open, then shut.

"They are closed," muttered Willie.

Chris nibbled at bacon, then returned to her room, where she dressed in her costume sweater and skirt. She glanced in a mirror and solemnly stared at her short red hair, which looked perpetually tousled; at the burst of freckles on the small, scrubbed face; then crossed her eyes and grinned idiotically. *Hi, little wonderful girl next door! Can I speak to your husband? Your lover? Your pimp? Oh, your pimp's in the poorhouse? Avon calling!* She stuck out her tongue at herself. Then sagged. *Ah, Christ, what a life!* She picked up her wig box, slouched downstairs and walked out to the piquant, tree-lined street.

For a moment she paused outside the house and gulped at the morning. She looked to the right. Beside the house, a precipitous plunge of old stone steps fell away to M Street far below. A little beyond was the upper entry to the Car Barn, formerly used for the housing of streetcars: Mediterranean, tiled roof; rococo turrets; antique brick. She regarded it wistfully. *Fun. Fun street. Dammit, why don't I stay? Buy the house? Start to live?* From somewhere a bell began to toll. She glanced toward the sound. The tower clock on the Georgetown campus. The melancholy resonance echoed on the river; shivered; seeped through her tired heart. She walked toward her work; toward ghastly charade; toward the straw-stuffed, antic imitation of dust.

She entered the main front gates of the campus and her depression diminished; then grew even less as she looked at the row of trailer dressing rooms aligned along the driveway close to the southern perimeter wall; and by 8 A.M. and the day's first shot, she was almost herself: She started an argument over the script.

"Hey, Burke? Take a look at this damned thing, will ya?"

"Oh, you *do* have a script, I see! How nice!" Director Burke Dennings, taut and elfin, left eye twitching yet gleaming with mischief, surgically shaved a narrow strip from a page of her script with quivering fingers. "I believe I'll munch," he cackled.

They were standing on the esplanade that fronted the administration building and were knotted in the center of actors; lights; technicians; extras; grips. Here and there a few spectators dotted the lawn, mostly Jesuit faculty. Numbers of children. The cameraman, bored, picked up *Daily Variety* as Dennings put the paper in his mouth and giggled, his breath reeking faintly of the morning's first gin.

"Yes, I'm *terribly* glad you've been given a script."

A sly, frail man in his fifties, he spoke with a charmingly broad British accent so clipped and precise that it lofted even crudest obscenities to elegance, and when he drank, he seemed always on the verge of guffaw; seemed constantly struggling to retain his composure.

"Now then, tell me, my baby. What is it? What's wrong?"

The scene in question called for the dean of the mythical college in the script to address a gathering of students in an effort to squelch a threatened "sit-in." Chris would then run up the steps to the esplanade, tear the bullhorn away from the dean and then point to the main administration building and shout, "Let's tear it down!"

"It just doesn't make sense," said Chris.

"Well, it's perfectly plain," lied Dennings.

"Why the heck should they tear down the building, Burke? What for?"

"Are you sending me up?"

"No, I'm asking 'what for?' "

"Because it's *there*, love!"

"In the script?"

"No, on the *grounds!*"

"Well, it doesn't make sense, Burke. She just wouldn't do that."

"She would."

"No, she wouldn't."

"Shall we summon the writer? I believe he's in Paris!"

"Hiding?"

"*Fucking!*"

He'd clipped it off with impeccable diction, fox eyes glinting in a face like dough as the word rose crisp to Gothic spires. Chris fell weak to his shoulders, laughing. "Oh, Burke, you're impossible, dammit!"

"Yes." He said it like Caesar modestly confirming reports of his triple rejection of the crown. "Now then, shall we get on with it?"

Chris didn't hear. She'd darted a furtive, embarrassed glance to a nearby Jesuit, checking to see if he'd heard the obscenity. Dark, rugged face. Like a boxer's. Chipped. In his forties. Something sad about the eyes; something pained; and yet warm and reassuring as they fastened on hers. He'd heard. He was smiling. He glanced at his watch and moved away.

"I say, shall we get *on* with it!"

She turned, disconnected. "Yeah, sure, Burke; let's do it."

"Thank heaven."

"No, wait!"

"Oh, good Christ!"

She complained about the tag of the scene. She felt that the high point was reached with her line as opposed to her running through the door of the building immediately afterward.

"It adds nothing," said Chris. "It's dumb."

"Yes, it is, love, it is," agreed Burke sincerely. "However, the cutter insists that we do it," he continued, "so there we are. You see?"

"No, I don't."

"No, of course not. It's stupid. You see, since the following scene"—he giggled—"begins with Jed coming *at* us through a door, the cutter feels certain of a nomination if the scene preceding ends with you moving off through a door."

"That's dumb."

"Well, of course it is! It's vomit! It's simply cunting puk-

19

ing mad! Now then, why don't we shoot it and trust me to snip it from the final cut. It should make a rather tasty munch."

Chris laughed. And agreed. Burke glanced toward the cutter, who was known to be a temperamental egotist given to time-wasting argumentation. He was busy with the cameraman. The director breathed a sigh of relief.

Waiting on the lawn at the base of the steps while the lights were warming, Chris looked toward Dennings as he flung an obscenity at a hapless grip and then visibly glowed. He seemed to revel in his eccentricity. Yet at a certain point in his drinking, Chris knew, he would suddenly explode into temper, and if it happened at three or four in the morning, he was likely to telephone people in power and viciously abuse them over trifling provocations. Chris remembered a studio chief whose offense had consisted in remarking mildly at a screening that the cuffs of Dennings' shirt looked slightly frayed, prompting Dennings to awaken him at approximately 3 A.M. to describe him as a "cunting boor" whose father was "more than likely *mad!*" And on the following day, he would pretend to amnesia and subtly radiate with pleasure when those he'd offended described in detail what he had done. Although, if it suited him, he would remember. Chris thought with a smile of the night he'd destroyed his studio suite of offices in a gin-stoked, mindless rage, and how later, when confronted with an itemized bill and Polaroid photos detailing the damage, he'd archly dismissed them as "Obvious fakes, the damage was far, *far* worse than that!" Chris did not believe that Dennings was either an alcoholic or a hopeless problem drinker, but rather that he drank because it was expected of him: he was living up to his legend.

Ah, well, she thought; *I guess it's a kind of immortality.*

She turned, looking over her shoulder for the Jesuit who had smiled. He was walking in the distance, despondent, head lowered, a lone black cloud in search of the rain.

She had never liked priests. So assured. So secure. And yet this one . . .

"All ready, Chris?" Dennings.

"Yeah, ready."

"All right, absolute quiet!" The assistant director.

"Roll the film," ordered Burke.

"Speed."

"Now *action!*"

Chris ran up the steps while extras cheered and Dennings watched her, wondering what was on her mind. She'd given up the arguments far too quickly. He turned a significant look to the dialogue coach, who padded up to him dutifully and proffered his open script like an aging altar boy the missal to his priest at solemn Mass.

They worked with intermittent sun. By four, the overcast of roiling clouds was thick in the sky, and the assistant director dismissed the company for the day.

Chris walked homeward. She was tired. At the corner of Thirty-sixth and O she signed an autograph for an aging Italian grocery clerk who had hailed her from the doorway of his shop. She wrote her name and "Warm Best Wishes" on a brown paper bag. Waiting to cross, she glanced diagonally across the street to a Catholic church. Holy Something-or-other. Staffed by Jesuits. John F. Kennedy had married Jackie there, she had heard; had worshiped there. She tried to imagine it: John F. Kennedy among the votive lights and the pious, wrinkled women; John F. Kennedy bowed in prayer; *I believe* . . . a detente with the Russians; *I believe, I believe* . . . Apollo IV among the rattlings of the beads; *I believe* . . . *the resurrection and the life ever—*

That. That's it. That's the grabber.

She watched as a beer truck lumbered by with a clink of quivering warm, wet promises.

She crossed. As she walked down O and passed the grade-school auditorium, a priest rushed by from behind her, hands in the pockets of a nylon windbreaker. Young. Very tense. In need of a shave. Up ahead, he took a right, turning into an easement that opened to a courtyard behind the church.

Chris paused by the easement, watching him, curious. He seemed to be heading for a white frame cottage. An old screen door creaked open and still another priest emerged. He looked glum; very nervous. He nodded curtly toward the young man, and with lowered eyes, he moved quickly toward a door that led into the church. Once again the cottage door was pushed open from within. Another priest. It looked— *Hey, it is! The one who was smiling when Burke said "fuck"!* Only now he looked grave as he silently greeted the new arrival, his arm around his shoulder in a gesture that was gentle and somehow parental. He led him inside and the screen door closed with a slow, faint squeak.

Chris stared at her shoes. She was puzzled. *What's the drill?* She wondered if Jesuits went to confession.

Faint rumble of thunder. She looked up at the sky. Would it rain? . . . *the resurrection of the . . .*

Yeah. Yeah, sure. Next Tuesday. Flashes of lightning crackled in the distance. *Don't call us, kid, we'll call you.*

She tugged up her coat collar and slowly moved on. She hoped it would pour.

In a minute she was home. She made a dash for the bathroom. After that, she walked into the kitchen.

"Hi, Chris, how'd it go?"

Pretty blonde in her twenties sitting at the table. Sharon Spencer. Fresh. From Oregon. For the last three years, she'd been tutor to Regan and social secretary to Chris.

"Oh, the usual crock." Chris sauntered to the table and began to sift messages. "Anything exciting?"

"Do you want to have dinner next week at the White House?"

"Oh, I dunno, Marty; whadda you feel like doin'?"

"Eating candy and getting sick."

Chris chuckled. "Where's Rags, by the way?"

"Downstairs in the playroom."

"What doin'?"

"Sculpting. She's making a bird, I think. It's for you."

"Yeah, I need one," Chris murmured. She moved to the stove and poured a cup of hot coffee. "Were you kidding me about that dinner?" she asked.

"No, of course not," answered Sharon. "It's Thursday."

"Big party?"

"No, I gather it's just five or six people."

"No kidding!"

She was pleased but not really surprised. They courted her company: cab drivers; poets; professors; kings. What was it they liked about her? Life? Chris sat at the table. "How'd the lesson go?"

Sharon lit a cigarette, frowning. "Had a bad time with math again."

"Oh? Gee, that's funny."

"I know; it's her favorite subject," said Sharon.

"Oh, well, this 'new math.' Christ, I couldn't make change for the bus if—"

"Hi, Mom!"

She was bounding through the door, slim arms outstretched. Red ponytails. Soft, shining face full of freckles.

"Hi ya, stinkpot!" Beaming, Chris caught her in a bearhug, squeezing, then kissed the girl's cheek with smacking ardor. She could not repress the full flood of her love. "Mmum-mmum-mmum!" More kisses. Then she held Regan out and probed her face with eager eyes. "What'djya do today? Anything exciting?"

"Oh, stuff."

"So what *kinda* stuff?"

"Oh, lemme see." She had her knees against her mother's, swaying gently back and forth. "Well, of course, I studied."

"Uh-huh."

"An' I painted."

"Wha'djya paint?"

"Oh, well, flowers, ya know. Daisies? Only pink. An' then— Oh, yeah! This *horse!*" She grew suddenly excited, eyes widening. "This man had a *horse*, ya know, down by the river? We were walking, see, Mom, and then along came this *horse*, he was *beautiful!* Oh, Mom, ya should've seen him, and the man let me *sit* on him! *Really!* I mean, practically a minute!"

Chris twinkled at Sharon with secret amusement. "Himself?" she asked, lifting an eyebrow. On moving to Washington for the shooting of the film, the blonde secretary, who was now virtually one of the family, had lived in the house, occupying an extra bedroom upstairs. Until she'd met the "horseman" at a nearby stable. Sharon needed a place to be alone, Chris then decided, and had moved her to a suite in an expensive hotel and insisted on paying the bill.

"Himself." Sharon smiled in response to Chris.

"It was a *gray* horse!" added Regan. "Mother, can't we get a horse? I mean, *could* we?"

"We'll see, baby."

"When could I have one?"

"We'll see. Where's the bird you made?"

Regan looked blank for a moment; then turned around to Sharon and grinned, her mouth full of braces and shy rebuke. "You told." Then, "It was surprise," she snickered to her mother.

"You mean . . . ?"

"With the long funny nose, like you wanted!"

"Oh, Rags, that's sweet. Can I see it?"

"No, I still have to paint it. When's dinner, Mom?"

"Hungry?"

"I'm starving."

"Gee, it's not even five. When was lunch?" Chris asked Sharon.

"Oh, twelvish," Sharon answered.

"When are Willie and Karl coming back?"

She had given them the afternoon off.

"I think seven," said Sharon.

"Mom, can't we go Hot Shoppe?" Regan pleaded. "Could we?"

Chris lifted her daughter's hand; smiled fondly; kissed it. "Run upstairs and get dressed and we'll go."

"Oh, I *love* you!"

Regan ran from the room.

"Honey, wear the new dress!" Chris called out after her.

"How would you like to be eleven?" mused Sharon.

"That an offer?"

Chris reached for her mail, began listlessly sorting through scrawled adulation.

"Would you take it?" asked Sharon.

"With the brain I've got now? All the memories?"

"Sure."

"No deal."

"Think it over."

"I'm thinking." Chris picked up a script with a covering letter clipped neatly to the front of it. Jarris. Her agent. "Thought I told them no scripts for a while."

"You should read it," said Sharon.

"Oh, yeah?"

"Yes, I read it this morning."

"Pretty good?"

"It's great."

"And I get to play a nun who discovers she's a lesbian, right?"

"No, you get to play nothing."

"Shit, movies are better than ever. What the hell are you talking about, Sharon? What's the grin for?"

"They want you to direct," Sharon exhaled coyly with the smoke from her cigarette.

"What!"

"Read the letter."

"My God, Shar, you're kidding!"

Chris pounced on the letter with eager eyes snapping up the words in hungry chunks: ". . . new script . . . a triptych . . . studio wants Sir Stephen Moore . . . accepting role provided—"

"I direct his segment!"

Chris flung up her arms, letting loose a hoarse, shrill cry of joy. Then with both her hands she cuddled the letter to her chest. "Oh, Steve, you angel, you remembered!" Filming in Africa. Drunk. In camp chairs. Watching the blood-hush end of day. *"Ah, the business is bunk! For the actor it's crap, Steve!" "Oh, I like it." "It's crap! Don't you know where it's at in this business? Directing!" "Ah, yes." "Then you've done something, something that's yours; I mean, something that lives!" "Well, then do it." "I've tried; they won't buy it." "Why not?" "Oh, come on, you know why: they don't think I can cut it."* Warm remembrance. Warm smile. Dear Steve . . .

"Mom, I can't find the dress!" Regan called from the landing.

"In the closet!" Chris answered.

"I looked!"

"I'll be up in a second!" Chris called. For a moment she examined the script. Then gradually wilted. "So it's probably crap."

"Oh, come on, now. I really think it's good."

"Oh, you thought *Psycho* needed a laugh track."

Sharon laughed.

"Mommy?"

"I'm coming!"

Chris got up slowly. "Got a date, Shar?"

"Yes."

Chris motioned at the mail. "You go on, then. We can catch all this stuff in the morning."

Sharon got up.

"Oh, no, wait," Chris amended, remembering something. "There's a letter that's got to go out tonight."

"Oh, okay." The secretary reached for her dictation pad.

"Moth-therrr!" A whine of impatience.

"Wait'll I come down," Chris told Sharon. She started to leave the kitchen, but stopped as Sharon eyed her watch.

"Gee, it's time for me to meditate, Chris," she said.

Chris looked at her narrowly with muted exasperation. In the last six months, she had watched her secretary suddenly turn "seeker after serenity." It had started in Los Angeles with self-hypnosis, which then yielded to Buddhistic chanting. During the last few weeks that Sharon was quartered in the room upstairs, the house had reeked of incense, and lifeless dronings of "Nam myoho renge kyo" ("See, you just keep on chanting that, Chris, just that, and you get your wish, you get everything you want . . .") were heard at unlikely and untimely hours, usually when Chris was studying her lines. "You can turn on TV," Sharon had generously told her employer on one of these occasions. "It's fine. I can chant when there's all kinds of noise. It won't bother me a bit." Now it was transcendental meditation.

"You really think that kind of stuff is going to do you any good, Shar?" Chris asked tonelessly.

"It gives me peace of mind," responded Sharon.

"Right," Chris said dryly. She turned away and said good-night. She said nothing about the letter, and as she left the kitchen, she murmured, "Nam myoho renge kyo."

"Keep it up about fifteen or twenty minutes," said Sharon. "Maybe for you it would work."

Chris halted and considered a measured response. Then gave it up. She went upstairs to Regan's bedroom, moving

27

immediately to the closet. Regan was standing in the middle of the room staring up at the ceiling.

"What's doin'?" Chris asked her, hunting for the dress. It was a pale-blue cotton. She'd bought it the week before, and remembered hanging it in the closet.

"Funny noises," said Regan.

"I know. We've got friends."

Regan looked at her. "Huh?"

"Squirrels, honey; squirrels in the attic." Her daughter was squeamish and terrified of rats. Even mice upset her.

The hunt for the dress proved fruitless.

"See, Mom, it's not there."

"Yes, I see. Maybe Willie picked it up with the cleaning."

"It's gone."

"Yeah, well, put on the navy. It's pretty."

They went to the Hot Shoppe. Chris ate a salad while Regan had soup, four rolls, fried chicken, a chocolate shake, and a helping and a half of blueberry pie with coffee ice cream. *Where does she put it,* Chris wondered fondly, *in her wrists?* The child was slender as a fleeting hope.

Chris lit a cigarette over her coffee and looked through the window on her right. The river was dark and currentless waiting.

"I enjoyed my dinner, Mom."

Chris turned to her, and as often happened, caught her breath and felt again that ache on seeing Howard's image in Regan's face. It was the angle of the light. She dropped her glance to Regan's plate.

"Going to leave that pie?" Chris asked her.

Regan lowered her eyes. "I ate some candy."

Chris stubbed out her cigarette and chuckled. "Let's go."

They were back before seven. Willie and Karl had already returned. Regan made a dash for the basement playroom, eager to finish the sculpture for her mother. Chris headed for the kitchen to pick up the script. She found Willie brewing coffee; coarse; open pot. She looked irritable and sullen.

"Hi, Willie, how'd it go? Have a real nice time?"

"Do not ask." She added an eggshell and a pinch of salt to the bubbling contents of the pot. They had gone to a movie, Willie explained. She had wanted to see the Beatles, but Karl had insisted on an art-house film about Mozart. "Terrible," she simmered as she lowered the flame. "That dumbhead!"

"Sorry 'bout that." Chris tucked the script underneath her arm. "Oh, Willie, have you seen that dress that I got for Rags last week? The blue cotton?"

"Yes, I see it in her closet. This morning."

"Where'd you put it?"

"It is there."

"You didn't maybe pick it up by mistake with the cleaning?"

"It is there."

"With the cleaning?"

"In the closet."

"No, it isn't. I looked."

About to speak, Willie tightened her lips and scowled at the coffee. Karl had walked in.

"Good evening, madam." He went to the sink for a glass of water.

"Did you set those traps?" asked Chris.

"No rats."

"Did you set them?"

"I set them, of course, but the attic is clean."

"Tell me, how was the movie, Karl?"

"Exciting." His back, like his face, was a resolute blank.

Chris started from the kitchen, humming a song made famous by the Beatles. But then she turned. *Just one more shot!*

"Did you have any trouble getting the traps, Karl?"

29

"No; no trouble."

"At six in the morning?"

"All-night market."

Jesus!

Chris took a long and luxurious bath, and when she went to the closet in her bedroom for her robe, she discovered Regan's missing dress. It lay crumpled in a heap on the floor of the closet.

Chris picked it up. *What's it doing in here?*

The tags were still on it. For a moment, Chris thought back. Then remembered that the day that she'd purchased the dress, she had also bought two or three items for herself. *Must've put 'em all together.*

Chris carried the dress into Regan's bedroom, put it on a hanger and slipped it on the rack. She glanced at Regan's wardrobe. *Nice. Nice clothes. Yeah, Rags, look here, not there at the daddy who never writes.*

As she turned from the closet, she stubbed her toe against the base of a bureau. *Oh, Jesus, that smarts!* As she lifted her foot and massaged her toe, she noticed that the bureau was out of position by about three feet. *No wonder I bumped it. Willie must have vacuumed.*

She went down to the study with the script from her agent.

Unlike the massive double living room with its large bay windows and view, the study had a feeling of whispered density; of secrets between rich uncles. Raised brick fireplace; oak paneling; crisscrossed beams of a wood that implied it had once been a drawbridge. The room's few hints of a time that was present were the added bar, a few bright pillows, and a leopardskin rug that belonged to Chris and was spread on the pinewood floor by the fire where she now stretched out with her head and shoulders propped on the front of a downy sofa.

She took another look at the letter from her agent. *Faith,*

Hope and Charity: three distinct segments, each with a different cast and director. Hers would be *Hope*. She liked the idea. And she liked the title. Possibly dull, she thought; but refined. *They'll probably change it to something like "Rock Around the Virtues."*

The doorbell chimed. Burke Dennings. A lonely man, he dropped by often. Chris smiled ruefully, shaking her head, as she heard him rasp an obscenity at Karl, whom he seemed to detest and continually baited.

"Yes, hullo, where's a drink!" he demanded crossly, entering the room and moving to the bar with eyes averted, hands in the pockets of his wrinkled raincoat.

He sat on a barstool. Irritable. Shifty-eyed. Vaguely disappointed.

"On the prowl again?" Chris asked.

"What the hell do you mean?" he sniffed.

"You've got that funny look." She had seen it before when they'd worked on a picture together in Lausanne. On their first night there, at a staid hotel overlooking Lake Geneva, Chris had difficulty sleeping. At 5 A.M., she flounced out of bed and decided to dress and go down to the lobby in search of either coffee or some company. Waiting for an elevator out in the hall, she glanced through a window and saw the director walking stiffly along the lakeside, hands deep in the pockets of his coat against the glacial winter cold. By the time she reached the lobby, he was entering the hotel. "Not a hooker in sight!" he snapped bitterly, passing her with eyes cast down; and then entered the elevator and went up to bed. When she'd laughingly mentioned the incident later, the director had grown furious and accused her of promulgating "gross hallucinations" that people were "likely to believe just because you're a star!" He had also referred to her as "simply cunting mad," but then pointed out soothingly, in an effort to assuage her feelings, that "perhaps" she had seen someone after all, and had simply mistaken him for Dennings.

"After all," he'd pointed out at the time, "my great-great-grandmother happens to have been Swiss."

Chris moved behind the bar now and reminded him of the incident.

"Oh, now, don't be so silly!" snapped Dennings. "It so happens that I've spent the entire evening at a bloody *tea*, a faculty *tea!*"

Chris leaned on the bar. "You were just at a tea?"

"Oh, yes, go ahead; smirk!"

"You got smashed at a tea," she said dryly, "with some Jesuits."

"No, the Jesuits were sober."

"They don't drink?"

"Are you out of your cunting *mind?*" he shouted. "They *swilled!* Never seen such capacities in all my *life!*"

"Hey, come on, hold it down, Burke! Regan!"

"Yes, Regan," Dennings whispered. "Where the hell is my *drink?*"

"Will you tell me what you were doing at a faculty tea?"

"Bloody public relations; something *you* should be doing."

Chris handed him a gin on the rocks.

"God, the way we've been mucking their grounds," the director muttered; pious; the glass to his lips. "Oh, yes, go ahead, laugh! That's all that you're good for, laughing and showing a bit of bum."

"I'm just smiling."

"Well, *someone* had to make a good show."

"And how many times did you say 'fuck,' Burke?"

"Darling, that's crude," he rebuked her gently. "Now tell me, how are you?"

She answered with a despondent shrug.

"Are you glum? Come on, tell me."

"I dunno."

"Tell your uncle."

"Shit, I think I'll have a drink," she said, reaching for a glass.

"Yes, it's good for the stomach. Now, then, what?"

She was slowly pouring vodka. "Ever think about dying?"

"I beg your—"

"Dying," she interrupted. "Ever think about it, Burke? What it means? I mean, *really* what it means?"

Faintly edgy, he answered, "I don't know. No, I don't. I don't think about it at all. I just *do* it. What the hell'd you bring it up for?"

She shrugged. "I don't know," she answered softly. She plopped ice into her glass; eyed it thoughtfully. "Yeah . . . yeah, I do," she amended. "I sort of . . . well, I thought about it this morning . . . like a dream . . . waking up. I don't know. I mean, it just sort of hit me . . . what it means. I mean, the end—*the end!*—like I'd never even heard of it before." She shook her head. "Oh, Jesus, did that spook me! I felt like I was falling off the goddam planet at a hundred million miles an hour."

"Oh, rubbish. Death's a comfort," Dennings sniffed.

"Not for *me* it isn't, Charlie."

"Well, you live through your children."

"Oh, come off it! My children aren't me."

"Yes, thank heaven. One's entirely enough."

"I mean, think about it, Burke! Not existing—forever! It's—"

"*Oh,* for heaven sakes! Show your bum at the faculty tea next week and perhaps those priests can give you comfort!"

He banged down his glass. "Let's another."

"You know, I didn't know they drank?"

"Well, you're stupid."

His eyes had grown mean. Was he reaching the point of no return? Chris wondered. She had the feeling she had touched a nerve. Had she?

"Do they go to confession?" she asked him.

"How would I know!" he suddenly bellowed.

"Well, weren't you studying to be a—"

"Where's the bloody drink!"

"Want some coffee?"

"Don't be fatuous. I want another drink."

"Have some coffee."

"Come along, now. One for the road."

"The Lincoln Highway?"

"That's ugly, and I loathe an ugly drunk. Come along, dammit, fill it!"

He shoved his glass across the bar and she poured more gin.

"I guess maybe I should ask a couple of them over," Chris murmured.

"Ask who?"

"Well, whoever." She shrugged. "The big wheels; you know, priests."

"They'll never leave; they're fucking plunderers," he rasped, and gulped his gin.

Yeah, he's starting to blow, thought Chris and quickly changed the subject: she explained about the script and her chance to direct.

"Oh, good," Dennings muttered.

"It scares me."

"Oh, twaddle. My baby, the difficult thing about directing is making it seem as if the damned thing were difficult. I hadn't a clue my first time out, but here I am, you see. It's child's play."

"Burke, to be honest with you, now that they've offered me my chance, I'm really not sure I could direct my grandmother across the street. I mean, all of that technical stuff."

"Come along; leave all that to the editor, the cameraman and the script girl, darling. Get good ones and they'll see you through. What's important is handling the cast, and you'd be marvelous, just marvelous at that. You could not only tell

34

them how to move and read a line, my baby, you could show them. Just remember Paul Newman and *Rachel, Rachel* and don't be so hysterical."

She still looked doubtful. "Well, about this technical stuff," she worried. Drunk or sober, Dennings was the best director in the business. She wanted his advice.

"For instance," he asked her.

For almost an hour she probed to the barricades of minutiae. The data were easily found in texts, but reading tended to fray her patience. Instead, she read people. Naturally inquisitive, she juiced them; wrung them out. But books were unwringable. Books were glib. They said "therefore" and "clearly" when it wasn't clear at all, and their circumlocutions could never be challenged. They could never be stopped for a shrewdly disarming, "Hold it, I'm dumb. Could I have that again?" They could never be pinned; made to wriggle; dissected. Books were like Karl.

"Darling, all you really need is a brilliant cutter," the director cackled, rounding it off. "I mean someone who really knows his doors."

He'd grown charming and bubbly, and seemed to have passed the threatened danger point.

"Beg pardon, madam. You wish something?"

Karl stood attentively at the door to the study.

"Oh, hullo, Thorndike," Dennings giggled. "Or is it Heinrich? I can't keep it straight."

"It is Karl."

"Yes, of course it is. Damn. I'd forgotten. Tell me, Karl, was it public relations you told me you did for the Gestapo, or was it community relations? I believe there's a difference."

Karl spoke politely. "Neither one, sir. I am Swiss."

"Oh, yes, of course." The director guffawed. "And you never went bowling with Goebbels, I suppose."

Karl, impervious, turned to Chris.

"And never went flying with Rudolph *Hess!*"

35

"Madam wishes?"

"Oh, *I* don't know. Burke, you want coffee?"

"*Fuck it!*"

The director stood up abruptly and strode belligerently from the room and the house.

Chris shook her head, and then turned to Karl. "Unplug the phones," she ordered expressionlessly.

"Yes, madam. Anything else?"

"Oh, maybe some Sanka. Where's Rags?"

"Down in playroom. I call her?"

"Yeah, it's bedtime. Oh, no, wait a second, Karl. Never mind. I'd better go see the bird. Just get me the Sanka, please."

"Yes, madam."

"And for the umpty-eighth time, I apologize for Burke."

"I pay no attention."

"I know. That's what bugs him."

Chris walked to the entry hall of the house, pulled open the door to the basement staircase and started downstairs.

"Hi ya, stinky, whatchya doin' down there? Got the bird?"

"Oh, yes, come see! Come on down, it's all finished!"

The playroom was paneled and brightly decorated. Easels. Paintings. Phonograph. Tables for games and a table for sculpting. Red and white bunting left over from a party for the previous tenant's teen-aged son.

"Hey, that's great!" exclaimed Chris as her daughter handed her the figure. It was not quite dry and looked something like a "worry bird," painted orange, except for the beak, which was laterally striped in green and white. A tuft of feathers was glued to the head.

"Do you like it?" asked Regan.

"Oh, honey, I do, I really do. Got a name for it?"

"Uh-uh."

"What's a good one?"

"I dunno," Regan shrugged.

"Let me see, let me see." Chris tapped fingertips to teeth.

"I don't know. Whaddya think? Whaddya think about 'Dumb-bird'? Huh? Just 'Dumbbird.' "

Regan was snickering, hand to her mouth to conceal the braces. Nodding.

" 'Dumbbird' by a landslide! I'll leave it here to dry and then I'll put him in my room."

Chris was setting down the bird when she noticed the Ouija board. Close. On the table. She'd forgotten she had it. Almost as curious about herself as she was about others, she'd originally bought it as a possible means of exposing clues to her subconscious. It hadn't worked. She'd used it a time or two with Sharon, and once with Dennings, who had skillfully steered the plastic planchette ("Are you the one who's moving it, ducky?") so that all of the "messages" were obscene, and then afterward blamed it on the "fucking *spirits!*"

"You playin' with the Ouija board?"

"Yep."

"You know how?"

"Oh, well, sure. Here, I'll show you." She was moving to sit by the board.

"Well, I think you need *two* people, honey."

"No ya don't, Mom; I do it all the time."

Chris was pulling up a chair. "Well, let's both play, okay?"

Hesitation. "Well, okay." She had her fingertips positioned on the white planchette and as Chris reached out to position hers, the planchette made a swift, sudden move to the position on the board marked NO.

Chris smiled at her slyly. "Mother, I'd rather do it myself? Is that it? You don't want me to play?"

"No, I *do!* Captain *Howdy* said 'no.' "

"Captain who?"

"Captain Howdy."

"Honey, who's Captain Howdy?"

"Oh, ya know. I make questions and he does the answers."

"Oh?"

"Oh, he's nice."

Chris tried not to frown as she felt a dim and sudden concern. The child had loved her father deeply, yet never had reacted visibly to her parents' divorce. And Chris didn't like it. Maybe she cried in her room; she didn't know. But Chris was fearful she was repressing and that her emotions might one day erupt in some harmful form. A fantasy playmate. It didn't sound healthy. Why "Howdy"? For Howard? Her father? *Pretty close.*

"So how come you couldn't even come up with a name for a dum-dum bird, and then you hit me with something like 'Captain Howdy'? Why do you call him 'Captain Howdy'?"

" 'Cause that's his *name*, of course," Regan snickered.

"Says who?"

"Well, *him.*"

"Of course."

"Of course."

"And what else does he say to you?"

"Stuff."

"What stuff?"

Regan shrugged. "Just stuff."

"For instance."

"I'll show you. I'll ask him some questions."

"You do that."

Her fingertips on the planchette, Regan stared at the board with eyes drawn tight in concentration. "Captain Howdy, don't you think my mom is pretty?"

A second . . . five . . . ten . . . twenty . . .

"Captain Howdy?"

More seconds. Chris was surprised. She'd expected her daughter to slide the planchette to the section marked YES. *Oh, for pete's sake, what now? An unconscious hostility? Oh, that's crazy.*

"Captain Howdy, that's *really* not very *polite,*" chided Regan.

"Honey, maybe he's sleeping."

"Do you think?"

"I think you should be sleeping."

"Already?"

"C'mon, babe! Up to bed!" Chris stood up.

"He's a poop," muttered Regan, then followed her mother up the stairs.

Chris tucked her into bed and then sat on the bedside. "Honey, Sunday's no work. You want to do somethin'?"

"What?"

When they'd first come to Washington, Chris had made an effort to find playmates for Regan. She'd uncovered only one, a twelve-year-old girl named Judy. But Judy's family was away for Easter, and Chris was concerned now that Regan might be lonely.

"Oh, well, I don't know," Chris replied. "Somethin'. You want to go see the sights? Hey, the cherry blossoms, maybe! That's right, they're out early! You want to go see 'em?"

"Oh, yeah, Mom!"

"And tomorrow night a movie! How's that?"

"Oh, I love you!"

Regan gave her a hug and Chris hugged her back with an extra fervor, whispering, "Oh, Rags, honey, I love you."

"You can bring Mr. Dennings if you like."

Chris pulled back for an appraisal. "Mr. Dennings?"

"Well, I mean, it's okay."

Chris chuckled. "No, it isn't okay. Honey, why would I want to bring Mr. Dennings?"

"Well, you like him."

"Oh, well, sure I like him, honey; don't you?"

She made no answer.

"Baby, what's going on?" Chris prodded her daughter.

"You're going to marry him, Mommy, aren't you." It wasn't a question, but a sullen statement.

Chris exploded into a laugh. "Oh, my baby, of course not!

What on earth are you *talking* about? Mr. Dennings? Where'd you get that idea?"

"But you like him."

"I like pizzas, but I wouldn't ever marry one! Honey, he's a friend, just a crazy old friend!"

"You don't like him like Daddy?"

"I *love* your daddy, honey; I'll always love your daddy. Mr. Dennings comes by here a lot 'cause he's lonely, that's all; he's a friend."

"Well, I heard . . ."

"You heard what? Heard from who?"

Whirling slivers of doubt in the eyes; hesitation; then a shrug of dismissal. "I don't know. I just thought."

"Well, it's silly, so forget it."

"Okay."

"Now go to sleep."

"Can I read? I'm not sleepy."

"Sure. Read your new book, hon, until you get tired."

"Thanks, Mommy."

"Good night, hon."

"Good night."

Chris blew her a kiss from the door and then closed it. She walked down the stairs. *Kids! Where do they get their ideas!* She wondered if Regan connected Dennings to her filing for divorce. *Oh, come on, that's dumb.* Regan knew only that Chris had filed. Yet Howard had wanted it. Long separations. Erosion of ego as the husband of a star. He'd found someone else. Regan didn't know that. *Oh, quit all this amateur psychoanalyzing and try to spend a little more time with her!*

Back to the study. The script. Chris read. Halfway through, she saw Regan coming toward her.

"Hi, honey. What's wrong?"

"There's these real funny noises, Mom."

"In your room?"

"It's like knocking. I can't go to sleep."

Where the hell are those traps!

"Honey, sleep in my bedroom and I'll see what it is."

Chris led her to the bedroom and tucked her in.

"Can I watch TV for a while till I sleep?"

"Where's your book?"

"I can't find it. Can I watch?"

"Sure; okay." Chris tuned in a channel on the bedroom portable. "Loud enough?"

"Yes, Mom."

"Try to sleep."

Chris turned out the light and went down the hall. She climbed the narrow, carpeted stairs that led to the attic. She opened the door and felt for the light switch; found it; flicked it, stooping as she entered.

She glanced around. Cartons of clippings and correspondence on the pinewood flood. Nothing else, except the traps. Six of them. Baited. The room was spotless. Even the air smelled clean and cool. The attic was unheated. No pipes. No radiator. No little holes in the roof.

"There is nothing."

Chris jumped from her skin. *"Oh, good Jesus!"* she gasped, turning quickly with her hand to a fluttering heart. "Jesus Christ, Karl, don't *do* that!"

He was standing on the steps.

"Very sorry. But you see? It is clean."

"Yeah, it's clean. Thanks a lot."

"Maybe cat better."

"What?"

"To catch rats."

Without waiting for an answer, he nodded and left.

For a moment, Chris stared at the doorway. Either Karl hadn't any sense of humor whatever, or he had one so sly it escaped her detection. She couldn't decide which one it was.

She considered the rappings again, then glanced at the

angled roof. The street was shaded by various trees, most of them gnarled and intertwined with vines; and the branches of a mushrooming, massive basswood umbrellaed the entire front third of the house. Was it squirrels after all? *It must be. Or branches. Right. Could be branches.* The nights had been windy.

"Maybe cat better."

Chris glanced at the doorway again. *Pretty smart-ass?* Abruptly she smiled, looking pertly mischievous.

She went downstairs to Regan's bedroom, picked something up, brought it back to the attic, and then after a minute went back to her bedroom. Regan was sleeping. She returned her to her room, tucked her into her bed, then went back to her own bedroom, turned off the television set and went to sleep.

The house was quiet until morning.

Eating her breakfast, Chris told Karl in an offhand way that she thought she'd heard a trap springing shut during the night.

"Like to go and take a look?" Chris suggested, sipping coffee and pretending to be engrossed in the morning paper. Without any comment, he went up to investigate.

Chris passed him in the hall on the second floor as he was returning, staring expressionlessly at the large stuffed mouse he was holding. He'd found it with its snout clamped tight in a trap.

As she walked toward her bedroom, Chris lifted an eyebrow at the mouse.

"Someone is funny," Karl muttered as he passed her. He returned the stuffed animal to Regan's bedroom.

"Sure a lot of things goin' on," Chris murmured, shaking her head as she entered her bedroom. She slipped off her robe and prepared to go to work. *Yeah, maybe cat better, old buddy.*

Much better. Whenever she grinned, her entire face appeared to crinkle.

The filming went smoothly that day. Later in the morning, Sharon came by the set and during breaks between scenes, in her portable dressing room, she and Chris handled items of business: a letter to her agent (she would think about the script); "okay" to the White House; a wire to Howard reminding him to telephone on Regan's birthday; a call to her business manager asking if she could afford to take off for a year; plans for a dinner party April twenty-third.

Early in the evening, Chris took Regan out to a movie, and the following day they drove around to points of interest in Chris's Jaguar XKE. The Lincoln Memorial. The Capitol. The cherry blossom lagoon. A bite to eat. Then across the river to Arlington Cemetery and the Tomb of the Unknown Soldier. Regan turned solemn, and later, at the grave of John F. Kennedy, seemed to grow distant and a little sad. She stared at the "eternal flame" for a time; then mutely reached for Chris's hand. "Mom, why do people have to die?"

The question pierced her mother's soul. *Oh, Rags, you too? You too? Oh, no!* And yet what could she tell her? Lies? She couldn't. She looked at her daughter's upturned face, eyes misting with tears. Had she sensed her own thoughts? She had done it so often . . . so often before. "Honey, people get tired," she answered Regan tenderly.

"Why does God let them?"

For a moment, Chris stared. She was puzzled. Disturbed. An atheist, she had never taught Regan religion. She thought it dishonest. "Who's been telling you about God?" she asked.

"Sharon."

"Oh." She would have to speak to her.

"Mom, why does God *let* us get tired?"

Looking down at those sensitive eyes and that pain, Chris

surrendered; couldn't tell her what she believed. "Well, after a while God gets lonesome for us, Rags. He wants us back."

Regan folded herself into silence. She stayed quiet during the drive home, and her mood persisted all the rest of the day and through Monday.

On Tuesday, Regan's birthday, it seemed to break. Chris took her along to the filming, and when the shooting day was over, the cast and crew sang "Happy Birthday" and brought out a cake. Always a kind and gentle man when sober, Dennings had the lights rewarmed and filmed her as she cut it. He called it a "screen test," and afterwards promised to make her a star. She seemed quite gay.

But after dinner and the opening of presents, the mood seemed to fade. No word from Howard. Chris placed a call to him in Rome, and was told by a clerk at his hotel that he hadn't been there for several days and couldn't be reached. He was somewhere on a yacht.

Chris made excuses.

Regan nodded, subdued, and shook her head to her mother's suggestion that they go to the Hot Shoppe for a shake. Without a word, she went downstairs to the basement playroom, where she remained until time for bed.

The following morning when Chris opened her eyes, she found Regan in bed with her, half awake.

"Well, what in the . . . . What are you doing *here?*" Chris chuckled.

"My bed was shaking."

"You nut." Chris kissed her and pulled up her covers. "Go to sleep. It's still early."

What looked like morning was the beginning of endless night.

two

He stood at the edge of the lonely subway platform, listening for the rumble of a train that would still the ache that was always with him. Like his pulse. Heard only in silence. He shifted his bag to the other hand and stared down the tunnel. Points of light. They stretched into dark like guides to hopelessness.

A cough. He glanced to the left. The gray-stubbled derelict numb on the ground in a pool of his urine was sitting up. With yellowed eyes he stared at the priest with the chipped, sad face.

The priest looked away. He would come. He would whine. *Couldjya help an old altar boy, Father? Wouldjya?* The vomit-flaked hand pressing down on the shoulder. The fumbling for the medal. The reeking of the breath of a thousand confessions with the wine and the garlic and the stale mortal sins belching out all together, and smothering . . . smothering . . .

The priest heard the derelict rising.

Don't come!

Heard a step.

Ah, my God, let me be!

"Hi ya, Faddah."

He winced. Sagged. Couldn't turn. He could not bear to search for Christ again in stench and hollow eyes; for the Christ of pus and bleeding excrement, the Christ who could not be. In absent gesture, he felt at his sleeve as if for an unseen band of mourning. He dimly remembered another Christ.

"Hey, *Faddah!*"

The hum of an incoming train. Then sounds of stumbling. He looked to the tramp. He was staggering. Fainting. With a blind, sudden rush, the priest was to him; caught him; dragged him to the bench against the wall.

"I'm a Cat'lic," the derelict mumbled. "I'm Cat'lic."

The priest eased him down; stretched him out; saw his train. He quickly pulled a dollar from out of his wallet and placed it in the pocket of the derelict's jacket. Then decided he would lose it. He plucked out the dollar and stuffed it into a urine-damp trouser pocket, then he picked up his bag and boarded the train.

He sat in a corner and pretended to sleep. At the end of the line he walked to Fordham University. The dollar had been meant for his cab.

When he reached the residence hall for visitors, he signed his name on the register. *Damien Karras,* he wrote. Then examined it. Something was wrong. Wearily he remembered and added, *S.J.*

He took a room in Weigel Hall and, after an hour, was able to sleep.

The following day he attended a meeting of the American Psychiatric Association. As principal speaker, he delivered a paper entitled "Psychological Aspects of Spiritual Development." At the end of the day, he enjoyed a few drinks and a bite to eat with some other psychiatrists. They paid. He left them early. He would have to see his mother.

He walked to the crumbling brownstone apartment building on Manhattan's East Twenty-first Street. Pausing by the steps that led up to the door, he eyed the children on the stoop. Unkempt. Ill-clothed. No place to go. He remembered evictions: humiliations: walking home with a seventh-grade sweetheart and encountering his mother as she hopefully rummaged through a garbage can on the corner. He climbed the steps and opened the door as if it were a tender wound. An odor like cooking. Like rotted sweetness. He remembered the visits to Mrs. Choirelli and her tiny apartment with the eighteen cats. He gripped the banister and climbed, overcome by a sudden, draining weariness that he knew was caused by guilt. He should never have left her. Not alone.

Her greeting was joyful. A shout. A kiss. She rushed to make coffee. Dark. Stubby, gnarled legs. He sat in the kitchen and listened to her talk, the dingy walls and soiled floor seeping into his bones. The apartment was a hovel. Social Security. Each month, a few dollars from a brother.

She sat at the table. Mrs. This. Uncle That. Still in immigrant accents. He avoided those eyes that were wells of sorrow, eyes that spent days staring out of a window.

He should never have left her.

He wrote a few letters for her later. She could neither read nor write any English. Then he spent time repairing the tuner on a crackling, plastic radio. Her world. The news. Mayor Lindsay.

He went to the bathroom. Yellowing newspaper spread on the tile. Stains of rust in the tub and the sink. On the floor, an old corset. Seeds of vocation. From these he had fled into love. Now the love had grown cold. In the night, he heard it whistling through the chambers of his heart like a lost, crying wind.

At a quarter to eleven, he kissed her good-bye; promised to return just as soon as he could. He left with the radio tuned to the news.

Once back in his room in Weigel Hall, he gave some thought to writing a letter to the Jesuit head of the Maryland province. He'd covered the ground with him once before: request for a transfer to the New York province in order to be closer to his mother; request for a teaching post and relief from his duties. In requesting the latter, he'd cited as a reason "unfitness" for the work.

The Maryland Provincial had taken it up with him during the course of his annual inspection tour of Georgetown University, a function that closely paralleled that of an army inspector general in the granting of confidential hearings to those who had grievances or complaints. On the point of Damien Karras' mother, the Provincial had nodded and expressed his sympathy; but the question of the priest's "unfitness" he thought contradictory on its face. But Karras had pursued it:

"Well, it's more than psychiatry, Tom. You know that. Some of their problems come down to vocation, to the meaning of their lives. Hell, it isn't always sex that's involved, it's their faith, and I just can't cut it, Tom, it's too much. I need out. I'm having problems of my own. I mean, doubts."

"What thinking man doesn't, Damien?"

A harried man with many appointments, the Provincial had not pressed him for the reasons for his doubt. For which Karras was grateful. He knew that his answers would have sounded insane: *The need to rend food with the teeth and then defecate. My mother's nine First Fridays. Stinking socks. Thalidomide babies. An item in the paper about a young altar boy waiting at a bus stop; set on by strangers; sprayed with kerosene; ignited.* No. Too emotional. Vague. Existential. More rooted in logic was the silence of God. In the world there was evil. And much of the evil resulted from doubt; from an honest confusion among men of good will. Would a reasonable God refuse to end it? Not reveal Himself? Not speak?

"Lord, give us a sign. . . ."

The raising of Lazarus was dim in the distant past. No one now living had heard his laughter.

Why not a sign?

At various times the priest would long to have lived with Christ: to have seen; to have touched; to have probed His eyes. *Ah, my God, let me see You! Let me know! Come in dreams!*

The yearning consumed him.

He sat at the desk now with pen above paper. Perhaps it wasn't time that had silenced the Provincial. Perhaps he understood that faith was finally a matter of love.

The Provincial had promised to consider the requests, but thus far nothing had been done. Karras wrote the letter and went to bed.

He sluggishly awakened at 5 A.M. and went to the chapel in Weigel Hall, secured a Host, then returned to his room and said Mass.

" *'Et clamor meus ad te veniat,'* " he prayed with murmured anguish. " 'Let my cry come unto Thee. . . .' "

He lifted the Host in consecration with an aching remembrance of the joy it once gave him; felt once again, as he did each morning, the pang of an unexpected glimpse from afar and unnoticed of a long-lost love.

He broke the Host above the chalice.

" 'Peace I leave you. My peace I give you. . . .' "

He tucked the Host inside his mouth and swallowed the papery taste of despair.

When the Mass was over, he polished the chalice and carefully placed it in his bag. He rushed for the seven-ten train back to Washington, carrying pain in a black valise.

three

Early on the morning of April 11, Chris made a telephone call to her doctor in Los Angeles and asked him for a referral to a local psychiatrist for Regan.

"Oh? What's wrong?"

Chris explained. Beginning on the day after Regan's birthday—and following Howard's failure to call—she had noticed a sudden and dramatic change in her daughter's behavior and disposition. Insomnia. Quarrelsome. Fits of temper. Kicked things. Threw things. Screamed. Wouldn't eat. In addition, her energy seemed abnormal. She was constantly moving, touching, turning; tapping; running and jumping about. Doing poorly with schoolwork. Fantasy playmate. Eccentric attention-getting tactics.

"Such as what?" the physician inquired.

She started with the rappings. Since the night she'd investigated the attic, she'd heard them again on two occasions.

In both of these instances, she'd noticed, Regan was present in the room; and the rappings would cease at the moment Chris entered. Secondly, she told him, Regan would "lose" things in the room: a dress; her toothbrush; books; her shoes. She complained about "somebody moving" her furniture. Finally, on the morning following the dinner at the White House, Chris saw Karl in Regan's bedroom pulling a bureau back into place from a spot that was halfway across the room. When Chris had inquired what he was doing, he repeated his former "Someone is funny," and refused to elaborate any further, but shortly thereafter Chris had found Regan in the kitchen complaining that someone had moved all her furniture during the night when she was sleeping.

This was the incident, Chris explained, that had finally crystallized her suspicions. It was clearly her daughter who was doing it all.

"You mean somnambulism? She's doing it in her sleep?"

"No, Marc, she's doing it when she's awake. To get attention."

Chris mentioned the matter of the shaking bed, which had happened twice more and was always followed by Regan's insistence that she sleep with her mother.

"Well, that could be physical," the internist ventured.

"No, Marc, I didn't say the bed *is* shaking. I said that she *says* that it's shaking."

"Do you know that it *isn't* shaking?"

"No."

"Well, it might be clonic spasms," he murmured.

"*Who?*"

"Any temperature?"

"No. Listen, what do you think?" she asked. "Should I take her to a shrink or what?"

"Chris, you mentioned her schoolwork. How is she doing with her math?"

"Why'd you ask?"

"How's she doing?" he persisted.

"Just rotten. I mean, *suddenly* rotten."

He grunted.

"Why'd you ask?" she repeated.

"Well, it's part of the syndrome."

"Of what?"

"Nothing serious. I'd rather not guess about it over the phone. Got a pencil?"

He wanted to give her the name of a Washington internist.

"Marc, can't you come out here and check her yourself?" Jamie. A lingering infection. Chris's doctor at that time had prescribed a new, broad-spectrum antibiotic. Refilling a prescription at a local drugstore, the pharmacist was wary. "I don't want to alarm you, ma'am, but this . . . Well, it's quite new on the market, and they've found that in Georgia it's been causing aplastic anemia in . . ." Jamie. Jamie. Dead. And ever since, Chris had never trusted doctors. Only Marc. And that had taken years. "Marc, *can't* you?" Chris pleaded.

"No, I can't, but don't worry. This man is brilliant. The best. Now get a pencil."

Hesitation. Then, "Okay."

She wrote down the name.

"Have him look her over and then tell him to call me," the internist advised. "And forget the psychiatrist for now."

"Are you sure?"

He delivered a blistering statement regarding the readiness of the general public to recognize psychosomatic illness, while failing to recognize the reverse: that illness of the body was often the cause of seeming illness of the mind.

"Now what would you say," he proposed as an instance, "if you were my internist, God forbid, and I told you I had headaches, recurring nightmares, nausea, insomnia and blurring of the vision; and also that I generally felt unglued and was worried to death about my job? Would you say I was neurotic?"

"I'm a bad one to ask, Marc; I know that you're crazy."

"Those symptoms I gave you are the same as for brain tumor, Chris. Check the body. That's first. Then we'll see."

Chris telephoned the internist and made an appointment for that afternoon. Her time was her own now. The filming was over, at least for her. Burke Dennings continued, loosely supervising the work of the "second unit," a generally less expensive crew that was filming scenes of lesser importance, mostly helicopter shots of various exteriors around the city; also stunt work; scenes without any of the principal actors. But he wanted each foot of film to be perfect.

The doctor was in Arlington. Samuel Klein. While Regan sat crossly in an examining room, Klein seated her mother in his office and took a brief case history. She told him the trouble. He listened; nodded; made copious notes. When she mentioned the shaking of the bed, he appeared to frown. But Chris continued:

"Marc seemed to think it was kind of significant that Regan's doing poorly with her math. Now why was that?"

"You mean schoolwork?"

"Yes, schoolwork, but math in particular, though. What's it mean?"

"Well, let's wait until I've looked at her, Mrs. MacNeil."

He then excused himself and gave Regan a complete examination that included taking samples of her urine and her blood. The urine was for testing of her liver and kidney functions; the blood for a number of checks: diabetes; thyroid function; red-cell blood count looking for possible anemia, white-cell blood count looking for exotic diseases of the blood.

After he finished, he sat for a while and talked to Regan, observing her demeanor, and then returned to Chris and started writing a prescription.

"She appears to have a hyperkinetic behavior disorder."

"A what?"

"A disorder of the nerves. At least we think it is. We don't know yet exactly how it works, but it's often seen in early adolescence. She shows all the symptoms: the hyperactivity; the temper; her performance in math."

"Yeah, the math. Why the math?"

"It affects concentration." He ripped the prescription from the small blue pad and handed it over. "Now this is for Ritalin."

"What?"

"Methylphenidate."

"Oh."

"Ten milligrams, twice a day. I'd recommend one at eight A.M., and the other at two in the afternoon."

She was eyeing the prescription.

"What is it? A tranquilizer?"

"A stimulant."

"*Stimulant?* She's higher'n a kite right *now.*"

"Her condition isn't quite what it seems," explained Klein. "It's a form of overcompensation. An overreaction to depression."

"Depression?"

Klein nodded.

"Depression . . ." Chris murmured. She was thoughtful.

"Well, you mentioned her father," said Klein.

Chris looked up. "Do you think I should take her to see a psychiatrist?"

"Oh, no. I'd wait and see what happens with the Ritalin. I think that's the answer. Wait two or three weeks."

"So you think it's all nerves."

"I suspect so."

"And those lies she's been telling? This'll stop it?"

His answer puzzled her. He asked her if she'd ever known Regan to swear or use obscenities.

"Never," Chris answered.

54

"Well, you see, that's quite similar to things like her lying —uncharacteristic, from what you tell me, but in certain disorders of the nerves it can—"

"Wait a minute," Chris interrupted, perplexed. "Where'd you ever get the notion she uses obscenities? I mean, is that what you were saying or did I misunderstand?"

For a moment, he eyed her rather curiously; considered; then cautiously ventured, "Yes, I'd say that she uses obscenities. Weren't you aware of it?"

"I'm *still* not aware of it! What are you talking about?"

"Well, she let loose quite a string while I was examining her, Mrs. MacNeil."

"You're kidding! Like what?"

He looked evasive. "Well, I'd say her vocabulary's rather extensive."

"Well, what, for instance? I mean, give me an example!"

He shrugged.

"You mean 'shit'? Or 'fuck'?"

He relaxed. "Yes, she used those words," he said.

"And what else did she say? Specifically."

"Well, specifically, Mrs. MacNeil, she advised me to keep my goddam fingers away from her cunt."

Chris gasped with shock. "She used *those* words?"

"Well, it isn't unusual, Mrs. MacNeil, and I really wouldn't worry about it at all. It's a part of the syndrome."

She was shaking her head, looking down at her shoes. "It's just hard to believe."

"Look, I doubt that she even understood what she was saying," he soothed.

"Yeah, I guess," murmured Chris. "Maybe not."

"Try the Ritalin," he advised her, "and we'll see what develops. And I'd like to take a look at her again in two weeks."

He consulted a calendar pad on his desk. "Let's see; let's

55

make it Wednesday the twenty-seventh. Would that be convenient?" he asked, glancing up.

"Yeah, sure," she murmured, getting up from the chair. She crumpled the prescription in a pocket of her coat. "The twenty-seventh would be fine."

"I'm quite a big fan of yours," Klein said, smiling, as he opened the door leading into the hall.

She paused in the doorway, preoccupied, a fingertip pressed to her lip. She glanced to the doctor.

"You don't think a psychiatrist, huh?"

"I don't know. But the best explanation is always the simplest one. Let's wait. Let's wait and see." He smiled encouragingly. "In the meantime, try not to worry."

"How?"

She left him.

As they drove back home, Regan asked her what the doctor had said.

"That you're nervous."

Chris had decided not to talk about her language. *Burke. She picked it up from Burke.*

But she did speak to Sharon about it later, asking if she'd ever heard Regan use that kind of obscenity.

"Why, no," replied Sharon. "I mean, not even lately. But you know, I think her art teacher made a remark." A special tutor who came to the house.

"You mean recently?" Chris asked.

"Yes, it was just last week. But you know *her*. I just figured maybe Regan said 'damn' or 'crap.' You know, something like that."

"By the way, have you been talking to her much about religion, Shar?"

Sharon flushed.

"Well, a little; that's all. I mean, it's hard to avoid. You see, she asks so many questions, and—well . . . " She gave a helpless little shrug. "It's just hard. I mean, how do I answer without telling what I think is a great big lie?"

"Give her multiple choice."

In the days that preceded her scheduled dinner party, Chris was extremely diligent in seeing that Regan took her dosage of Ritalin. By the night of the party, however, she had failed to observe any noticeable improvement. There were subtle signs, in fact, of a gradual deterioration: increased forgetfulness; untidiness; and one complaint of nausea. As for attention-getting tactics, although the familiar ones failed to recur, there appeared to be a new one: reports of a foul, unpleasant "smell" in Regan's bedroom. At Regan's insistence, Chris took a whiff one day and smelled nothing.

"You don't?"

"You mean, you smell it right now?" Chris had asked her.

"Well, sure!"

"What's it smell like?"

She'd wrinkled her nose. "Well, like something burny."

"Yeah?" Chris had sniffed.

"Don't you smell it?"

"Well, yes, hon," she'd lied. "Just a little. Let's open up the window for a while, get some air in."

In fact, she'd smelled nothing, but had made up her mind that she would temporize, at least until the appointment with the doctor. She was also preoccupied with a number of other concerns. One was arrangements for the dinner party. Another had to do with the script. Although she was very enthusiastic about the prospect of directing, a natural caution had prevented her from making a prompt decision. In the meantime, her agent was calling her daily. She told him she'd given the script to Dennings for an opinion, and hoped he was reading and not consuming it.

The third, and the most important, of Chris's concerns

was the failure of two financial ventures: a purchase of convertible debentures through the use of prepaid interest; and an investment in an oil-drilling project in southern Libya. Both had been entered upon for the sheltering of income that would have been subject to enormous taxation. But something even worse had developed: the wells had come up dry and rocketing interest rates had prompted a sell-off in bonds.

These were the problems that her gloomy business manager flew into town to discuss. He arrived on Thursday. Chris had him charting and explaining through Friday. At last, she decided on a course of action that the manager thought wise. He nodded approval. But he frowned when she brought up the subject of buying a Ferrari.

"You mean, a new one?"

"Why not? You know, I drove one in a picture once. If we write to the factory, maybe, and remind them, it could be they'd give us a deal. Don't you think?"

He didn't. And cautioned that he thought a new car was improvident.

"Ben, I made eight hundred *thou* last year and you're saying I can't get a freaking *car!* Don't you think that's ridiculous? Where did it go?"

He reminded her that most of her money was in shelters. Then he listed the various drains on her gross: federal income tax; projected federal income tax; her state tax; tax on her real estate holdings; ten percent commission to her agent; five to him; five to her publicist; one and a quarter taken out as donation to the Motion Picture Welfare Fund; an outlay for wardrobe in tune with the fashion; salaries to Willie and Karl and Sharon and the caretaker of the Los Angeles home; various travel costs; and, finally, her monthly expenses.

"Will you do another picture this year?" he asked her.

She shrugged. "I don't know. Do I have to?"

"Yes, I think you'd better."

She cupped her face in both her hands and eyed him moodily. "What about a Honda?"

He made no reply.

Later that evening, Chris tried to put all of her worries aside; tried to keep herself busy with making preparations for the next night's party.

"Let's serve the curry buffet instead of sit-down," she told Willie and Karl. "We can set up a table at the end of the living room. Right?"

"Very good, madam," Karl answered quickly.

"So what do you think, Willie? A fresh fruit salad for dessert?"

"Yes, excellent!" said Karl.

"Thanks, Willie."

She'd invited an interesting mixture. In addition to Burke ("Show up sober, dammit!") and the youngish director of the second unit, she expected a senator (and wife); an Apollo astronaut (and wife); two Jesuits from Georgetown; her next-door neighbors; and Mary Jo Perrin and Ellen Cleary.

Mary Jo Perrin was a plump and gray-headed Washington seeress whom Chris had met at the White House dinner and liked immensely. She'd expected to find her austere and forbidding, but "You're not like that at *all!*" she'd been able to tell her. Bubbly-warm and unpretentious.

Ellen Cleary was a middle-aged State Department secretary who'd worked in the U.S. Embassy in Moscow when Chris toured Russia. She had gone to considerable effort and trouble to rescue Chris from a number of difficulties and encumbrances encountered in the course of her travels, not the least of which had been caused by the redheaded actress' outspokenness. Chris had remembered her with affection over the years, and had looked her up on coming to Washington.

"Hey, Shar," she asked, "which priests are coming?"

"I'm not sure yet. I invited the president and the dean of the college, but I think that the president's sending an alternate. His secretary called me late this morning and said that he might have to go out of town."

"Who's he sending?" Chris asked with guarded interest.

"Let me see." Sharon rummaged through scraps of notes. "Yes, here it is, Chris. His assistant—Father Joseph Dyer."

"You mean from the campus?"

"Well, I'm not sure."

"Oh, okay."

She seemed disappointed.

"Keep an eye on Burke tomorrow night," she instructed.

"I will."

"Where's Rags?"

"Downstairs."

"You know, maybe you should start to keep your typewriter there; don't you think? I mean, that way you can watch her when you're typing. Okay? I don't like her being alone so much."

"Good idea."

"Okay, later. Go home. Meditate. Play with horses."

The planning and preparations at an end, Chris again found herself turning worried thoughts toward Regan. She tried to watch television. Could not concentrate. Felt uneasy. There was a strangeness in the house. Like settling stillness. Weighted dust.

By midnight, all in the house were asleep.

There were no disturbances. That night.

four

She greeted her guests in a lime-green hostess costume with long, belled sleeves and pants. Her shoes were comfortable. They reflected her hope for the evening.

The first to arrive was Mary Jo Perrin, who came with Robert, her teen-age son. The last was pink-faced Father Dyer. He was young and diminutive, with fey eyes behind steel-rimmed spectacles. At the door, he apologized for his lateness. "Couldn't find the right necktie," he told Chris expressionlessly. For a moment, she stared at him blankly, then burst into laughter. Her day-long depression began to lift.

The drinks did their work. By a quarter to ten, they were scattered about the living room eating their dinners in vibrant knots of conversation.

Chris filled her plate from the steaming buffet and scanned the room for Mary Jo Perrin. There. On a sofa with Father

Wagner, the Jesuit dean. Chris had spoken to him briefly. He had a bald, freckled scalp and a dry, soft manner. Chris drifted to the sofa and folded to the floor in front of the coffee table as the seeress chuckled with mirth.

"Oh, come on, Mary Jo!" the dean said, smiling as he lifted a forkful of curry to his mouth.

"Yeah, come on, Mary Jo," echoed Chris.

"Oh, hi! Great curry!" said the dean.

"Not too hot?"

"Not at all; it's just right. Mary Jo has been telling me there used to be a Jesuit who was also a medium."

"And he doesn't believe me!" chuckled the seeress.

"Ah, *distinguo*," corrected the dean. "I just said it was *hard* to believe."

"You mean *medium* medium?" asked Chris.

"Why, of course," said Mary Jo. "Why, he even used to levitate!"

"Oh, I do it every morning," said the Jesuit quietly.

"You mean he held séances?" Chris asked Mrs. Perrin.

"Well, yes," she answered. "He was very, very famous in the nineteenth century. In fact, he was probably the only spiritualist of his time who wasn't ever clearly convicted of fraud."

"As I said, he wasn't a Jesuit," commented the dean.

"Oh, my, but *was* he!" She laughed. "When he turned twenty-two, he joined the Jesuits and promised not to work anymore as a medium, but they threw him out of France"— she laughed even harder—"right after a séance that he held at the Tuileries. Do you know what he *did*? In the middle of the séance he told the empress she was about to be touched by the hands of a spirit child who was about to fully materialize, and when they suddenly turned all of the lights on"—she guffawed—"they caught him sitting with his naked *foot* on the empress' *arm!* Now, can you imagine?"

The Jesuit was smiling as he set down his plate. "Don't

come looking for discounts any more on indulgences, Mary Jo."

"Oh, come on, every family's got one black sheep."

"We were pushing our quota with the Medici popes."

"Y'know, I had an experience once," began Chris.

But the dean interrupted. "Are you making this a matter of confession?"

Chris smiled and said, "No, I'm not a Catholic."

"Oh, well, neither are the Jesuits." Mrs. Perrin chuckled.

"Dominican slander," retorted the dean. Then to Chris he said, "I'm sorry, my dear. You were saying?"

"Well, just that I thought I saw somebody levitate once. In Bhutan."

She recounted the story.

"Do you think that's possible?" she ended. "I mean, really, seriously."

"Who knows?" He shrugged. "Who knows what gravity is. Or matter, when it comes to that."

"Would you like my opinion?" interjected Mrs. Perrin.

The dean said, "No, Mary Jo; I've taken a vow of poverty."

"So have I," Chris muttered.

"What was that?" asked the dean, leaning forward.

"Oh, nothing. Say, there's something I've been meaning to ask you. Do you know that little cottage that's back of the church over there?" She pointed in the general direction.

"Holy Trinity?" he asked.

"Yes, right. Well, what goes on in there?"

"Oh, well, that's where they say Black Mass," said Mrs. Perrin.

"Black who?"

"Black Mass."

"What's that?"

"She's kidding," said the dean.

"Yes, I know," said Chris, "but I'm dumb. I mean, what's a Black Mass?"

"Oh, basically, it's a travesty on the Catholic Mass," explained the dean. "It's connected to witchcraft. Devil worship."

"Really? You mean, there really *is* such a thing?"

"I really couldn't say. Although I heard a statistic once about something like possibly fifty thousand Black Masses being said every year in the city of Paris."

"You mean *now?*" marveled Chris.

"It's just something I heard."

"Yes, of course, from the Jesuit secret service," twitted Mrs. Perrin.

"Not at all. I hear voices," responded the dean.

"You know, back in L.A.," mentioned Chris, "you hear an awful lot of stories about witch cults being around. I've often wondered if it's true."

"Well, as I said, I wouldn't know," said the dean. "But I'll tell you who might—Joe Dyer. Where's Joe?"

The dean looked around.

"Oh, over there," he said, nodding toward the other priest, who was standing at the buffet with his back to them. He was heaping a second helping onto his plate. "Hey, Joe?"

The young priest turned, his face impassive. "You called, great dean?"

The other Jesuit beckoned with his fingers.

"All right, just a second," answered Dyer, and resumed his attack on the curry and salad.

"That's the only leprechaun in the priesthood," said the dean with an edge of fondness. He sipped at his wine. "They had a couple of cases of desecration in Holy Trinity last week, and Joe said something about one of them reminding him of some things they used to do at Black Mass, so I expect he knows something about the subject."

"What happened at the church?" asked Mary Jo Perrin.

"Oh, it's really too disgusting," said the dean.

"Come on, we're all through with our dinners."

"No, please. It's too much," he demurred.

"Oh, come on!"

"You mean you can't read my mind, Mary Jo?" he asked her.

"Oh, I could," she responded, "but I really don't think that I'm worthy to enter that Holy of Holies!" She chuckled.

"Well, it really is sick," began the dean.

He described the desecrations. In the first of the incidents, the elderly sacristan of the church had discovered a mound of human excrement on the altar cloth directly before the tabernacle.

"Oh, that really is sick." Mrs. Perrin grimaced.

"Well, the other's even worse," remarked the dean; then employed indirection and one or two euphemisms to explain how a massive phallus sculpted in clay had been found glued firmly to a statue of Christ on the left side altar.

"Sick enough?" he concluded.

Chris noticed that Mary Jo seemed genuinely disturbed as she said, "Oh, that's enough, now. I'm sorry that I asked. Let's change the subject, please."

"No, I'm fascinated," said Chris.

"Yes, of course. I'm a fascinating human."

It was Father Dyer. He was hovering over her with his plate. "Listen, give me just a minute, and then I'll be back. I think I've got something going over there with the astronaut."

"Like what?" asked the dean.

Father Dyer raised his eyebrows in deadpan surmise. "Would you believe," he asked, "first missionary on the moon?"

They burst into laughter.

"You're just the right size," said Mrs. Perrin. "They could stow you in the nose cone."

"No, not me," he corrected her solemnly, and then turned to the dean to explain: "I've been trying to fix it up for Emory."

"That's our disciplinarian on campus," Dyer explained in an aside to the women. "Nobody's up there and that's what he likes, you see; he sort of likes things quiet."

"And so who would he convert?" Mrs. Perrin asked.

"What do you mean?" Dyer frowned at her earnestly. "He'd convert the astronauts. That's it. I mean, that's what he likes: You know, one or two people. No groups. Just a couple."

With deadpan gaze, Dyer glanced toward the astronaut. "Excuse me," he said and walked away.

"I like him," said Mrs. Perrin.

"Me too," Chris agreed. Then she turned to the dean. "You haven't told me what goes on in that cottage," she reminded him. "Big secret? Who's that priest I keep seeing there? You know, sort of dark? Do you know the one I mean?"

"Father Karras," said the dean in a lowered tone; with a trace of regret.

"What's he do?"

"He's a counselor." He put down his wineglass and turned it by the stem. "Had a pretty rough knock last night, poor guy."

"Oh, what?" asked Chris with a sudden concern.

"Well, his mother passed away."

Chris felt a melting sensation of grief that she couldn't explain. "Oh, I'm sorry," she said.

"He seems to be taking it pretty hard," resumed the Jesuit. "She was living by herself, and I guess she was dead for a couple of days before they found her."

"Oh, how awful," Mrs. Perrin murmured.

"Who found her?" Chris asked solemnly.

"The superintendent of her apartment building. I guess they wouldn't have found her even now except . . . Well, the next-door neighbors complained about her radio going all the time."

"That's sad," Chris murmured.

"Excuse me, please, madam."

66

She looked up at Karl. He held a tray filled with glasses and liqueurs.

"Sure, set it down here, Karl; that'll be fine."

Chris liked to serve the liqueurs to her guests herself. It added an intimacy, she felt, that might otherwise be lacking.

"Well, let's see now, I'll start with you," she told the dean and Mrs. Perrin; and served them. Then she moved about the room, taking orders and fetching for each of her guests, and by the time she had made the rounds, the various clusters had shifted to new combinations, except for Dyer and the astronaut, who seemed to be getting thicker. "No, I'm really not a priest," Chris heard Dyer say solemnly, his arm on the astronaut's chuckle-heaved shoulder. "I'm actually a terribly avant-garde rabbi." And not long after, she overheard Dyer inquiring of the astronaut: "What is space?" and when the astronaut shrugged and said he really didn't know, Father Dyer had fixed him with an earnest frown and said, "You should."

Chris was standing with Ellen Cleary afterward, reminiscing about Moscow, when she heard a familiar, strident voice ringing angrily through from the kitchen.

Oh, Jesus! Burke!

He was shrieking obscenities at someone.

Chris excused herself and went quickly to the kitchen, where Dennings was railing viciously at Karl while Sharon made futile attempts to hush him.

"Burke!" exclaimed Chris. "Knock it off!"

The director ignored her, continued to rage, the corners of his mouth flecked foamy with saliva, while Karl leaned mutely against the sink with folded arms and stolid expression, his eyes fixed unwaveringly on Dennings.

"Karl!" Chris snapped. "Will you get out of here? Get *out!* Can't you see how he *is?*"

But the Swiss would not budge until Chris began actually to shove him toward the door.

67

"Naa-zi *pig!*" Dennings screamed at his back. And then he turned genially to Chris and rubbed his hands together. "What's dessert?" he asked mildly.

"Dessert!" Chris thumped at her brow with the heel of her hand.

"Well, I'm hungry," he whined.

Chris turned to Sharon. "Feed him! I've got to get Regan up to bed. And, Burke, for *chrissakes,*" she asked the director, "will you behave yourself! There are priests out there!" She pointed.

He creased his brow as his eyes grew intense with a sudden and apparently genuine interest. "Oh, you noticed that too?" he asked without guile.

Chris left the kitchen and went down to check Regan in the basement playroom, where her daughter had spent the entire day. She found her playing with the Ouija board. She seemed sullen; abstracted; remote. *Well, at least she isn't feisty,* Chris reflected, and hopeful of diverting her, she brought her to the living room and began to introduce her to her guests.

"Oh, isn't she darling!" said the wife of the senator.

Regan was strangely well behaved, except for a moment with Mrs. Perrin when she would neither speak nor accept her hand. But the seeress made a joke of it.

"Knows I'm a fake." She winked at Chris. But then, with a curious air of scrutiny, she reached forward and gripped Regan's hand with a gentle pressure, as if checking her pulse. Regan quickly shook her off and glared malevolently.

"Oh, dear, dear, dear, she must be tired," Mrs. Perrin said casually; yet she continued to watch Regan with a probing fixity, an anxiety unexplained.

"She's been feeling kind of sick," Chris murmured in apology. She looked down at Regan. "Haven't you, honey?"

Regan did not answer. She kept her eyes on the floor.

There was no one left for Regan to meet except the senator

and Robert, Mrs. Perrin's son, and Chris thought it best to pass them up. She took Regan up to bed and tucked her in.

"Do you think you can sleep?" Chris asked.

"I don't know," she answered dreamily. She'd turned on her side and was staring at the wall with a distant expression.

"Would you like me to read to you for a while?"

A shake of the head.

"Okay, then. Try to sleep."

She leaned over and kissed her, and then walked to the door and flicked the light switch.

"Night, my baby."

Chris was almost out the door when Regan called out to her very softly:

"Mother, what's wrong with me?"

So haunted. The tone so despairing. So disproportionate to her condition. For a moment the mother felt shaken and confused. But quickly she righted herself.

"Well, it's just like I said, hon; it's nerves. All you need is those pills for a couple of weeks and I know you'll be feeling just fine. Now then, try to go to sleep, hon, okay?"

No response. Chris waited.

"Okay?" she repeated.

"Okay," whispered Regan.

Chris abruptly noticed goose pimples rising on her forearm. She rubbed it. *Good Christ, it gets cold in this room. Where's the draft coming in from?*

She moved to the window and checked along the edges. Found nothing. Turned to Regan. "You warm enough, baby?"

No answer.

Chris moved to the bedside. "Regan? You asleep?" she whispered.

Eyes closed. Deep breathing.

Chris tiptoed from the room.

From the hall she heard singing, and as she walked down the stairs, she saw with pleasure that the young Father

Dyer was playing the piano near the living-room picture window and was leading a group that had gathered around him in cheerful song. As she entered the living room, they had just finished "Till We Meet Again."

Chris started forward to join the group, but was quickly intercepted by the senator and his wife, who had their coats across their arms. They seemed edgy.

"Are you leaving so soon?" Chris asked.

"Oh, I'm really so sorry, and my dear, we've had a marvelous evening," the senator effused. "But poor Martha's got a headache."

"Oh, I am so sorry, but I do feel terrible," moaned the senator's wife. "Will you excuse us, Chris? It's been such a lovely party."

"I'm really sorry you have to go," said Chris.

She accompanied them to the door and she could hear Father Dyer in the background asking, "Does anyone else know the words to 'I'll Bet You're Sorry Now, Tokyo Rose'?"

She bade them good night. On her way back to the living room, Sharon stepped quietly out from the study.

"Where's Burke?" Chris asked her.

"In there," Sharon answered with a nod toward the study. "He's sleeping it off. Say, what did the senator say to you? Anything?"

"What do you mean?" asked Chris. "They just left."

"Well, I guess it's as well."

"Sharon, what do you mean?"

"Oh, Burke," sighed Sharon. In a guarded tone, she described an encounter between the senator and the director. Dennings had remarked to him, in passing, said Sharon, that there appeared to be "an alien pubic hair floating round in my gin." Then he'd turned to the senator and added in a tone that was vaguely accusatory, "Never seen it before in my life! Have you?"

Chris giggled as Sharon went on to describe how the senator's embarrassed reaction had triggered one of Dennings' quixotic rages, in which he'd expressed his "boundless gratitude" for the existence of politicians, since without them "one couldn't distinguish who the *statesmen* were, you see."

When the senator had moved away in a huff, the director turned to Sharon and said proudly, "There, you see? I didn't curse. Now then, don't you think I handled that rather demurely?"

Chris couldn't help laughing. "Oh, well, let him sleep. But you'd better stay in there in case he wakes up. Would you mind?"

"Not at all." Sharon entered the study.

In the living room, Mary Jo Perrin sat alone and thoughtful in a corner chair. She looked edgy; disturbed. Chris started to join her, but changed her mind when one of the neighbors drifted over to the corner.

Chris headed for the piano instead. Dyer broke off his playing of chords and looked up to greet her. "Yes, young lady, and what can we do for you today? We're running a special on novenas."

Chris chuckled with the others. "I thought I'd get the scoop on what goes on at Black Mass," she said. "Father Wagner said you were the expert."

The group at the piano fell silent with interest.

"No, not really," said Dyer, lightly touching some chords. "Why'd you mention Black Mass?" he asked her soberly.

"Oh, well, some of us were talking before about—well . . . about those things that they found at Holy Trinity, and—"

"Oh, you mean the desecrations?" Dyer interrupted.

"Hey, somebody give us a clue what's going on," demanded the astronaut.

"Me too," said Ellen Cleary. "I'm lost."

"Well, they found some desecrations at the church down the street," explained Dyer.

"Well, like what?" asked the astronaut.

"Forget it," Father Dyer advised him. "Let's just say obscenities, okay?"

"Father Wagner says you told him it was like at Black Mass," prompted Chris, "and I wondered what went on at those things?"

"Oh, I really don't know all that much," he protested. "In fact, most of what I know is what I've heard from another Jeb."

"What's a Jeb?" Chris asked.

"Short for Jesuit. Father Karras is the expert on all this stuff."

Chris was suddenly alert. "Oh, the dark priest at Holy Trinity?"

"You know him?" asked Dyer.

"No, I just heard him mentioned, that's all."

"Well, I think he did a paper on it once. You know, just from the psychiatric side."

"Whaddya mean?" asked Chris.

"Whaddya *mean*, whaddya mean?"

"Are you telling me he's a psychiatrist?"

"Oh, well, sure. Gee, I'm sorry. I just assumed that you knew."

"Listen, somebody *tell* me something!" the astronaut demanded impatiently. "What *does* go on at Black Mass?"

"Let's just say perversions." Dyer shrugged. "Obscenities. Blasphemies. It's an evil parody of the Mass, where instead of God they worshiped Satan and sometimes offered human sacrifice."

Ellen Cleary shook her head and walked away. "This is getting too creepy for me." She smiled thinly.

Chris paid her no notice. The dean joined the group unobtrusively. "But how can you *know* that?" she asked the young Jesuit. "Even if there was such a thing as Black Mass, who's to say what went on there?"

"Well, I guess they got most of it," answered Dyer, "from the people who were caught and then confessed."

"Oh, come on," said the dean. "Those confessions were worthless, Joe. They were tortured."

"No, only the snotty ones," Dyer said blandly.

There was a ripple of vaguely nervous laughter. The dean eyed his watch. "Well, I really should be going," he said to Chris. "I've got the six-o'clock Mass in Dahlgren Chapel."

"I've got the banjo Mass." Dyer beamed. Then his eyes shifted to a point in the room behind Chris, and he sobered abruptly. "Well, now, I think we have a visitor, Mrs. Mac-Neil," he cautioned, motioning with his head.

Chris turned. And gasped on seeing Regan in her nightgown, urinating gushingly onto the rug. Staring fixedly at the astronaut, she intoned in a lifeless voice, "You're going to die up there."

"*Oh, my God!*" cried Chris in pain, rushing to her daughter. "Oh, God, oh, my baby, oh, come on, come with me!"

She took Regan by the arms and led her quickly away with a tremulous apology over her shoulder to the ashen astronaut: "Oh, I'm so sorry! She's been sick, she must be walking in her sleep! She didn't know what she was saying!"

"Gee, maybe we should go," she heard Dyer say to someone.

"No, no, stay," Chris protested, turning around for a moment. "Please, stay! It's okay! I'll be back in just a minute!"

Chris paused by the kitchen, instructing Willie to see to the rug before the stain became indelible, and then she walked Regan upstairs to her bathroom, bathed her and changed her nightgown. "Honey, why did you say that?" Chris asked her repeatedly, but Regan appeared not to understand and mumbled non sequiturs. Her eyes were vacant and clouded.

Chris tucked her into bed, and almost immediately Regan appeared to fall asleep. For a time Chris waited, listening to her breathing. Then left the room.

At the bottom of the stairs, she encountered Sharon and the young director of the second unit assisting Dennings out of the study. They had called a cab and were going to shepherd him back to his suite at the Sheraton-Park.

"Take it easy," Chris advised as they left the house with Dennings between them.

Barely conscious, the director said, "Fuck it," and slipped into fog and the waiting cab.

Chris returned to the living room, where the guests who still remained expressed their sympathy as she gave them a brief account of Regan's illness. When she mentioned the rappings and the other "attention-getting" phenomena, Mrs. Perrin stared at her intently. Once Chris looked at her, expecting her to comment, but she said nothing and Chris continued.

"Does she walk in her sleep quite a bit?" asked Dyer.

"No, tonight's the first time. Or at least, the first time I know of, so I guess it's this hyperactivity thing. Don't you think?"

"Oh, I really wouldn't know," said the priest. "I've heard sleepwalking's common at puberty, except that—" Here he shrugged and broke off. "I don't know. Guess you'd better ask your doctor."

Throughout the remainder of the discussion, Mrs. Perrin sat quietly, watching the dance of flames in the living-room fireplace. Almost as subdued, Chris noticed, was the astronaut, who was scheduled for a flight to the moon within the year. He stared at his drink with a now-and-then grunt meant to signify interest and attention. As if by tacit understanding, no one made reference to what Regan had said to him.

"Well, I do have that Mass," said the dean at last, rising to leave.

It triggered a general departure. They all stood up and expressed their thanks for dinner and the evening.

At the door, Father Dyer took Chris's hand and probed her

74

eyes earnestly. "Do you think there's a part in one of your movies for a very short priest who can play the piano?" he asked.

"Well, if there isn't"—Chris laughed—"then I'll have one written in for you, Father."

"I was thinking of my brother," he told her solemnly.

"Oh, you!" she laughed again, and bade him a fond and warm good night.

The last to leave were Mary Jo Perrin and her son. Chris held them at the door with idle chatter. She had the feeling that Mary Jo had something on her mind, but was holding it back. To delay her departure, Chris asked her opinion on Regan's continued use of the Ouija board and her Captain Howdy fixation. "Do you think there's any harm in it?" she asked.

Expecting an airily perfunctory dismissal, Chris was surprised when Mrs. Perrin frowned and looked down at the doorstep. She seemed to be thinking, and still in this posture, she stepped outside and joined her son, who was waiting on the stoop.

When at last she lifted her head, her eyes were in shadow.

"I would take it away from her," she said quietly.

She handed ignition keys to her son. "Bobby, start up the motor," she instructed. "It's cold."

He took the keys, told Chris that he'd loved her in all her films, and then walked shyly away toward an old, battered Mustang parked down the street.

Mrs. Perrin's eyes were still in shadow.

"I don't know what you think of me," she said, speaking slowly. "Many people associate me with spiritualism. But that's wrong. Yes, I think I have a gift," she continued quietly. "But it isn't occult. In fact, to me it seems natural; perfectly natural. Being a Catholic, I believe that we all have a foot in two worlds. The one that we're conscious of is time. But now and then a freak like me gets a flash from the other foot;

and that one, I think . . . is in eternity. Well, eternity has no time. There the future is present. So now and again when I feel that other foot, I believe that I get to see the future. Who knows? Maybe not. Maybe all of it's coincidence." She shrugged. "But I think I do. And if that's so, why, I still say it's natural, you see. But now the occult . . ." She paused, picking words. "The occult is something different. I've stayed away from that. I think dabbling with that can be dangerous. And that includes fooling around with a Ouija board."

Until now, Chris had thought her a woman of eminent sense. And yet something in her manner now was deeply disturbing. She felt a creeping foreboding that she tried to dispel.

"Oh, come on, Mary Jo." Chris smiled. "Don't you know how those Ouija boards work? It isn't anything at all but a person's subconscious, that's all."

"Yes, perhaps," she answered quietly. "Perhaps. It could all be suggestion. But in story after story that I've heard about séances, Ouija boards, all of that, they always seem to point to the opening of a door of some sort. Oh, not to the spirit world, perhaps; you don't believe in that. Perhaps, then, a door in what you call the subconscious. I don't know. All I know is that things seem to happen. And, my dear, there are lunatic asylums all over the world filled with people who dabbled in the occult."

"Are you kidding?"

There was momentary silence. Then again the soft voice began droning out of darkness. "There was a family in Bavaria, Chris, in nineteen twenty-one. I don't remember the name, but they were a family of eleven. You could check it in the newspapers, I suppose. Just a short time following an attempt at a séance, they went out of their minds. All of them. All eleven. They went on a burning spree in their house, and when they'd finished with the furniture, they started on the three-month-old baby of one of the younger daughters. And that is when the neighbors broke in and stopped them.

76

"The entire family," she ended, "was put in an asylum."

"Oh, boy!" breathed Chris as she thought of Captain Howdy. He had now assumed a menacing coloration. Mental illness. Was that it? Something. "I *knew* I should take her to see a psychiatrist!"

"Oh, for heaven sakes," said Mrs. Perrin, stepping into the light, "you never mind about me; you just listen to your doctor." There was attempted reassurance in her voice that was not convincing. "I'm great at the future"—Mrs. Perrin smiled—"but in the present I'm absolutely helpless." She was fumbling in her purse. "Now then, where are my glasses? There, you see? I've mislaid them. Oh, here they are right here." She had found them in a pocket of her coat. "Lovely home," she remarked as she put on the glasses and glanced up at the upper façade of the house. "Gives a feeling of warmth."

"God almighty, I'm relieved! For a second, there, I thought you were going to tell me it's haunted!"

Mrs. Perrin glanced down to her. "Why would I tell you a thing like that?"

Chris was thinking of a friend, a noted actress in Beverly Hills who had sold her home because of her insistence that it was inhabited by a poltergeist. "I don't know." She grinned wanly. "On account of who you are, I guess. I was kidding."

"It's a very fine house," Mrs. Perrin reassured her in an even tone. "I've been here before, you know; many times."

"Have you really?"

"Yes, an admiral had it; a friend of mine. I get a letter from him now and then. They've shipped him to sea again, poor dear. I don't know if it's really him that I miss or this house." She smiled. "But then maybe you'll invite me back."

"Mary Jo, I'd *love* to have you back. I mean it. You're a fascinating person."

"Well, at least I'm the *nerviest* person you know."

"Oh, come on. Listen, call me. Please. Will you call me next week?"

"Yes, I would like to hear how your daughter's coming on."

"Got the number?"

"Yes, at home in my book."

What was off? wondered Chris. There was something in her tone that was slightly off-center.

"Well, good night," said Mrs. Perrin, "and thanks again for a marvelous evening." And before Chris could answer her, she was walking rapidly down the street.

For a moment, Chris watched her; and then closed the front door. A heavy lassitude overcame her. *Quite a night,* she thought; *some night . . . some night . . .*

She went to the living room and stood over Willie, who was kneeling by the urine stain. She was brushing up the nap of the rug.

"White vinegar I put on," muttered Willie. "Twice."

"Comin' out?"

"Maybe now," answered Willie. "I do not know. We will see."

"No, you can't really tell until the damned thing dries."

Yeah, that's brilliant there, punchy. That's really a brilliant observation. Judas priest, kid, go to bed!

"C'mon, leave it alone for now, Willie. Get to sleep."

"No, I finish."

"Okay, then. And thanks. Good night."

"Good night, madam."

Chris started up the stairs with weary steps. "Great curry, there, Willie. Everybody loved it."

"Yes, thank you, madam."

Chris looked in on Regan and found her still asleep. Then she remembered the Ouija board. Should she hide it? Throw it away? *Boy, Perrin's really dingy when it comes to that stuff.* Yet Chris was aware that the fantasy playmate was morbid and unhealthy. *Yeah, maybe I should chuck it.*

Still, Chris was hesitant. Standing by the bedside and looking at Regan, she remembered an incident when her daughter was only three: the night that Howard had decided she was much too old to continue to sleep with her baby bottle, on which she had grown dependent. He'd taken it away from her that night, and Regan had screamed until four in the morning, then acted hysterical for days. And now Chris feared a similar reaction. *Better wait until I talk it all out with a shrink.* Moreover, the Ritalin, she reflected, hadn't had a chance to take effect.

At the last, she decided to wait and see.

Chris retired to her room, settled wearily into bed, and almost instantly fell asleep. Then awakened to fearful, hysterical screaming at the rim of her consciousness.

"Mother, come *here*, come *here*, I'm *afraid!*"

"Yes, I'm coming, all right, hon, I'm coming!"

Chris raced down the hall to Regan's bedroom. Whimpering. Crying. Sounds like bedsprings.

"Oh, my baby, what's wrong?" Chris exclaimed as she reached out and flicked on the lights.

Good Christ almighty!

Regan lay taut on her back, face stained with tears and contorted with terror as she gripped at the sides of her narrow bed.

"Mother, why is it *shaking?*" she cried. "Make it *stop!* Oh, I'm *scared!* Make it *stop!* Mother, please make it *stop!*"

The mattress of the bed was quivering violently back and forth.

II: The Edge

. . . In our sleep, pain, which cannot forget, falls drop by drop upon the heart until, in our own despair, against our will, comes wisdom through the awful grace of God. . . .

Aeschylus

one

They brought her to an ending in a crowded cemetery where the gravestones cried for breath.

The Mass had been lonely as her life. Her brothers from Brooklyn. The grocer on the corner who'd extended her credit. Watching them lower her into the dark of a world without windows, Damien Karras sobbed with a grief he had long misplaced.

"Ah, Dimmy, Dimmy . . ."

An uncle with an arm around his shoulder.

"Never mind, she's in heaven now, Dimmy, she's happy."

Oh, God, let it be! Ah, God! Ah, please! Oh, God, please be!

They waited in the car while he lingered by the grave. He could not bear the thought of her being alone.

Driving to Pennsylvania Station, he listened to his uncles speak of their illnesses in broken, immigrant accents.

" . . . emphysema . . . gotta quit smokin' . . . I ohmos' died las' year, you know that?"

Spasms of rage fought to break from his lips, but he pressed them back and felt ashamed. He looked out the window: they were passing by the Home Relief Station where on Saturday mornings in the dead of winter she would pick up the milk and the sacks of potatoes while he lay in his bed; the Central Park Zoo, where she left him in summer while she begged by the fountain in front of the Plaza. Passing the hotel, Karras burst into sobs, and then choked back the memories, wiped at the wetness of stinging regrets. He wondered why love had waited for this distance, waited for the moment when he need not touch, when the limits of contact and human surrender had dwindled to the size of a printed Mass card tucked in his wallet: *In Memoriam* . . .

He knew. This grief was old.

He arrived at Georgetown in time for dinner, but had no appetite. He paced inside his cottage. Jesuit friends came by with condolences. Stayed briefly. Promised prayers.

Shortly after ten, Joe Dyer appeared with a bottle of Scotch. He displayed it proudly: "Chivas Regal!"

"Where'd you get the money for it—out of the poor-box?"

"Don't be an asshole, that would be breaking my vow of poverty."

"Where did you get it, then?"

"I stole it."

Karras smiled and shook his head as he fetched a glass and a pewter coffee mug. He rinsed them out in his tiny bathroom sink and said, "I believe you."

"Greater faith I have never seen."

Karras felt a stab of familiar pain. He shook it off and returned to Dyer, who was sitting on his cot breaking open the seal. He sat beside him.

"Would you like to absolve me now or later?"

"Just pour," said Karras, "and we'll absolve each other."

Dyer poured deep into glass and cup. "College presidents

84

shouldn't drink," he murmured. "It sets a bad example. I figure I relieved him of a terrible temptation."

Karras swallowed Scotch, but not the story. He knew the president's ways too well. A man of tact and sensitivity, he always gave through indirection. Dyer had come, he knew, as a friend, but also as the president's personal emissary. So when Dyer made a passing comment about Karras possibly needing "a rest," the Jesuit psychiatrist took it as hopeful omen of the future and felt a momentary flood of relief.

Dyer was good for him; made him laugh; talked about the party and Chris MacNeil; purveyed new anecdotes about the Jesuit Prefect of Discipline. He drank very little, but continually replenished Karras' glass, and when he thought he was numb enough for sleep, he got up from the cot and made Karras stretch out, while he sat at the desk and continued to talk until Karras' eyes were closed and his comments were mumbled grunts.

Dyer stood up and undid the laces of Karras' shoes. He slipped them off.

"Gonna steal my shoes now?" Karras muttered thickly.

"No, I tell fortunes by reading the creases. Now shut up and go to sleep."

"You're a Jesuit cat burglar."

Dyer laughed lightly and covered him with a coat that he took from a closet. "Listen, someone's got to worry about the bills around this place. All you other guys do is rattle beads and pray for the hippies down on M Street."

Karras made no answer. His breathing was regular and deep. Dyer moved quietly to the door and flicked out the light.

"Stealing is a sin," muttered Karras in the darkness.

"*Mea culpa,*" Dyer said softly.

For a time he waited, then at last decided that Karras was asleep. He left the cottage.

In the middle of the night, Karras awakened in tears. He had dreamed of his mother. Standing at a window high in

Manhattan, he'd seen her emerging from a subway kiosk across the street. She stood at the curb with a brown paper shopping bag, searching for him. He waved. She didn't see him. She wandered the street. Buses. Trucks. Unfriendly crowds. She was growing frightened. She returned to the subway and began to descend. Karras grew frantic, ran to the street and began to weep as he called her name; as he could not find her; as he pictured her helpless and bewildered in the maze of tunnels beneath the ground.

He waited for his sobbing to subside, and then fumbled for the Scotch. He sat on the cot and drank in darkness. Wet came the tears. They would not cease. This was like childhood, this grief.

He remembered a telephone call from his uncle:

"Dimmy, da edema's affected her brain. She won't let a doctor come anywhere near her. Jus' keeps screamin' things. Even talks ta da goddam radio. I figure she's got ta go ta Bellevue, Dimmy. A regular hospital won't put up wit' dat. I jus' figure a coupla months an' she's good as new; den we take her out again. Okay? Lissen, Dimmy, I tell you: we awready done it. Dey give her a shot an' den take her in da ambulance dis mornin'. We didn' wanna bodda you, excep' dere is a hearin' and you gotta sign da papers. Now . . . What? . . . Private hospital? Who's got da money, Dimmy? You?"

He didn't remember falling asleep.

He awakened in torpor, with memory of loss draining blood from his stomach. He reeled to the bathroom; showered; shaved; dressed in a cassock. It was five-thirty-five. He unlocked the door to Holy Trinity, put on his vestments, and offered up Mass at the left side altar.

"Memento etiam . . ." he prayed with bleak despair. "Remember thy servant, Mary Karras. . . ."

In the tabernacle door he saw the face of the nurse at Bellevue Receiving; heard again the screams from the isolation room.

"You her son?"

"Yes, I'm Damien Karras."

"Well, I wouldn't go in there. She's pitchin' a fit."

He'd looked through the port at the windowless room with the naked light bulb hanging from the ceiling; padded walls; stark; no furniture save for the cot on which she raved.

". . . grant her, we pray Thee, a place of refreshment, light and peace. . . ."

As she met his gaze, she'd grown suddenly silent; moved to the port with a baffled look.

"Why you do this, Dimmy? Why?"

The eyes had been meeker than a lamb's.

"Agnus Dei . . ." he murmured as he bowed and struck his breast. "Lamb of God, who takest away the sins of the world, grant her rest. . . ."

As he closed his eyes and held the Host, he saw his mother in the hearing room, her hands clasped gentle in her lap, her expression docile and confused as the judge explained to her the Bellevue psychiatrist's report.

"Do you understand that, Mary?"

She'd nodded; wouldn't open her mouth; they had taken her dentures.

"Well, what do you say about that, Mary?"

She'd proudly answered him:

"My boy, he speak for me."

An anguished moan escaped from Karras as he bowed his head above the Host. He struck his breast as if it were time and murmured, "Domine, non sum dignus. . . . I am not worthy . . . say but the word and my soul shall be healed."

Against all reason, against all knowledge, he prayed there was Someone to hear his prayer.

He did not think so.

After the Mass, he returned to the cottage and tried to sleep. Without success.

Later in the morning, a youngish priest that he'd never

seen came by unexpectedly. He knocked and looked in the door.

"You busy? Can I see you for a while?"

In the eyes, the restless burden; in the voice, the tugging plea.

For a moment, Karras hated him.

"Come in," he said gently. And inwardly raged at this portion of his being that rendered him helpless; that he could not control; that lay coiled within him like a length of rope, always ready to fling itself unbidden at the cry of someone else's need. It gave him no peace. Not even in sleep. At the edge of his dreams, there was often a sound like a faint, brief cry of someone in distress. It was almost inaudible in the distance. Always the same. And for minutes after waking, he would feel the anxiety of some duty unfulfilled.

The young priest fumbled; faltered; seemed shy. Karras led him patiently. Offered cigarettes. Instant coffee. Then forced a look of interest as the moody young visitor gradually unfolded a familiar problem: the terrible loneliness of priests.

Of all the anxieties that Karras encountered among the community, this one had lately become the most prevalent. Cut off from their families as well as from women, many of the Jesuits were also fearful of expressing affection for fellow priests; of forming deep and loving friendships.

"Like I'd like to put my arm around another guy's shoulder, but right away I'm scared he's going to think I'm queer. I mean, you hear all these theories about so many latents attracted to the priesthood. So I just don't do it. I won't even go to somebody's room just to listen to records; or talk; or smoke. It's not that I'm afraid of *him*; I'm just worried about *him* getting worried about *me*."

Karras felt the weight easing slowly from the other and onto him. He let it come; let the young priest talk. He knew he would return again and again; find relief from aloneness; make Karras his friend; and when he'd realized he had done so without fear and suspicion, perhaps he would go on to make friends among the others.

The psychiatrist grew weary; found himself drifting into private sorrow. He glanced at a plaque that someone had given him the previous Christmas. MY BROTHER HURTS. I SHARE HIS PAIN. I MEET GOD IN HIM, he read. A failed encounter. He blamed himself. He had mapped the streets of his brother's torment, yet never had walked them; or so he believed. He thought that the pain which he felt was his own.

At last the visitor looked at his watch. It was time for lunch in the campus refectory. He rose and started to leave. Then paused to glance at a current novel on Karras' desk.

"Have you read it?" asked Karras.

The other shook his head. "No, I haven't. Should I?"

"I don't know. I just finished it and I'm not at all sure that I really understand it," Karras lied. He picked up the book and handed it over. "Want to take it along? You know, I'd really like to hear someone else's opinion."

"Well, sure," said the Jesuit, examining the copy on the flap of the dust jacket. "I'll try to get it back to you in a couple of days."

His mood seemed brighter.

As the screen door creaked with his departure, Karras felt momentary peace. He picked up his breviary and stepped out to the courtyard, where he slowly paced and said his Office.

In the afternoon, he had still another visitor, the elderly pastor of Holy Trinity, who took a chair by the desk and offered condolences on the passing of Karras' mother.

"Said a couple of Masses for her, Damien. And one for you," he wheezed with the barest trace of a brogue.

"That was thoughtful of you, Father. Thank you very much."

"How old was she?"

"Seventy."

"A good old age."

Karras fixed his gaze on an altar card that the pastor had carried in with him. One of three employed in the Mass, it was covered in plastic and inscribed with a portion of the prayers that were said by the priest. The psychiatrist wondered what he was doing with it.

"Well, Damien, we've had another one of those things here today. In the church, y'know. Another desecration."

A statue of the Virgin at the back of the church had been painted like a harlot, the pastor told him. Then he handed the altar card to Karras. "And this one the morning after you'd gone, y'know, to New York. Was it Saturday? Saturday. Yes. Well, take a look at that. I just had a talk with a sergeant of police, and—well . . . well, look at this card, would you, Damien?"

As Karras examined it, the pastor explained that someone had slipped in a typewritten sheet between the original card and its cover. The ersatz text, though containing some strike-overs and various typographical errors, was in basically fluent and intelligible Latin and described in vivid, erotic detail an imagined homosexual encounter involving the Blessed Virgin Mary and Mary Magdalene.

"That's enough, now, you don't have to read it all," said the pastor, snapping back the card as if fearing that it might be an occasion of sin. "Now that's excellent Latin; I mean, it's got style, a church Latin style. Well, the sergeant says he talked to some fellow, a psychologist, and he says that the person's been doin' this all—well, he could be a priest, y'know, a very sick priest. Do you think?"

The psychiatrist considered for a while. Then nodded. "Yes. Yes, it could. Acting out a rebellion, perhaps, in a state of complete somnambulism. I don't know. It could be. Maybe so."

"Can you think of any candidates, Damien?"

"I don't get you."

"Well, now, sooner or later they come and see you, wouldn't

you say? I mean, the sick ones, if there are any, from the campus. Do y'know any *like* that? I mean with that kind of illness, y'know."

"No, I don't."

"No, I didn't think you'd tell me."

"Well, I wouldn't know anyway, Father. Somnambulism is a way of resolving any number of possible conflict situations, and the usual form of resolution is symbolic. So I really wouldn't know. And if it is a somnambulist, he's probably got a complete posterior amnesia about what he's done, so that even *he* wouldn't have a clue."

"What if you were to tell him?" the pastor asked cagily. He plucked at an earlobe, a habitual gesture, Karras had noticed, whenever he thought he was being wily.

"I really don't know," repeated the psychiatrist.

"No. No, I really didn't think that you'd tell me." He rose and moved for the door. "Y'know what you're like, you people? Like priests!" he complained.

As Karras laughed gently, the pastor returned and dropped the altar card on his desk. "I suppose you should study this thing," he mumbled. "Something might come to you."

The pastor moved for the door.

"Did they check it for fingerprints?" asked Karras.

The pastor stopped and turned slightly. "Oh, I doubt it. After all, it's not a criminal we're after, now, is it? More likely it's only a demented parishioner. What do you think of that, Damien? Do you think that it could be someone in the parish? You know, I think so. It wasn't a priest at all, it was someone among the parishioners." He was pulling at his earlobe again. "Don't you think?"

"I really wouldn't know," he said again.

"No, I didn't think you'd tell me."

Later that day, Father Karras was relieved of his duties as counselor and assigned to the Georgetown University Medical School as lecturer in psychiatry. His orders were to "rest."

two

Regan lay on her back on Klein's examining table, arms and legs bowed outward. Taking her foot in both his hands, the doctor flexed it toward her ankle. For moments he held it there in tension, then suddenly released it. The foot relaxed into normal position.

He repeated the procedure several times but without any variance in the result. He seemed dissatisfied. When Regan abruptly sat up and spat in his face, he instructed a nurse to remain in the room and returned to his office to talk to Chris.

It was April 26. He'd been out of the city both Sunday and Monday and Chris hadn't reached him until this morning to relate the happening at the party and the subsequent shaking of the bed.

"It was actually moving?"

"It was moving."

"How long?"

"I don't know. Maybe ten, maybe fifteen seconds. I mean, that's all I saw. Then she sort of went stiff and wet the bed. Or maybe she'd wet it before. I don't know. But then all of a sudden she was dead asleep and never woke up till the next afternoon."

Dr. Klein entered thoughtfully.

"Well, what is it?" Chris asked in an anxious tone.

When she'd first arrived, he'd reported his suspicion that the shaking of the bed had been caused by a seizure of clonic contractions, an alternating tensing and relaxing of the muscles. The chronic form of such a condition, he'd told her, was clonus, and usually indicated a lesion in the brain.

"Well, the test was negative," he told her, and described the procedure, explaining that in clonus the alternate flexing and releasing of the foot would have triggered a run of clonic contractions. As he sat at his desk, he still seemed worried, however. "Has she ever had a fall?"

"Like on the head?" Chris asked.

"Well, yes."

"No, not that I know of."

"Childhood diseases?"

"Just the usual. Measles and mumps and chicken pox."

"Sleepwalking history?"

"Not until now."

"What do you mean? She was walking in her sleep at the party?"

"Well, yes. She still doesn't know what she did that night. And there's other stuff, too, that she doesn't remember."

"Lately?"

Sunday. Regan still sleeping. An overseas telephone call from Howard.

"How's Rags?"

"Thanks a lot for the call on her birthday."

"I was stuck on a yacht. Now for chrissakes lay off me. I called her the minute I was back in the hotel."

"Oh, sure."

"She didn't tell you?"

"You talked to her?"

"Yes. That's why I thought I'd better call you. What the hell's going on with her?"

"What are you getting at?"

"She just called me a 'cocksucker' and hung up the phone."

Recounting the incident to Dr. Klein, Chris explained that when Regan had finally awakened, she had no memory whatever of either the telephone call or of what had happened on the night of the dinner.

"Then perhaps she wasn't lying about the moving of the furniture," Klein hypothesized.

"I don't get you."

"Well, she moved it herself, no doubt, but perhaps while in one of those states where she didn't really know what she was doing. It's known as automatism. Like a trance state. The patient doesn't know or remember what he's doing."

"But something just occurred to me, doc, you know that? There's a great big heavy bureau in her room made out of teakwood. It must weigh half a ton. I mean, how could she have moved that?"

"Extraordinary strength is pretty common in pathology."

"Oh, really? How come?"

The doctor shrugged. "No one knows."

"Now, besides what you've told me," he continued, "have you noticed any other bizarre behavior?"

"Well, she's gotten real sloppy."

"Bizarre," he repeated.

"For her, that's bizarre. Oh, now wait! There's this! You remember that Ouija board she's been playing with? Captain Howdy?"

"The fantasy playmate." The internist nodded.

"Well, now she can hear him," Chris revealed.

The doctor leaned forward, folding his arms atop the desk.

As Chris continued, his eyes were alert and had narrowed to dart points of speculation.

"Yesterday morning," said Chris, "I could hear her talking to Howdy in her bedroom. I mean, she'd talk, and then seem to wait, as if she were playing with the Ouija board. When I peeked inside the room, though, there wasn't any Ouija board there; just Rags; and she was nodding her head, doc, just like she was agreeing with what he was saying."

"Did she see him?"

"I don't think so. She sort of had her head to the side, the way she does when she listens to records."

The doctor nodded thoughtfully. "Yes. Yes, I see. Any other phenomena like that? Does she see things? Smell things?"

"Smell," Chris remembered. "She keeps smelling something bad in her bedroom."

"Something burning?"

"Hey, that's right!" Chris exclaimed. "How'd you know that?"

"It's sometimes the symptom of a type of disturbance in the chemicoelectrical activity of the brain. In the case of your daughter, in the temporal lobe, you see." He put a hand to the front of his skull. "Up here, in the forward part of the brain. Now it's rare but it does cause bizarre hallucinations and usually just before a convulsion. I suppose that's why it's taken for schizophrenia so often; but it isn't schizophrenia. It's produced by a lesion in the temporal lobe. Now the test for clonus isn't conclusive, Mrs. MacNeil, so I think I'd like to give her an EEG."

"What's that?"

"Electroencephalograph. It will show us the pattern of her brain waves. That's usually a pretty good indication of abnormal functioning."

"But you think that's it, huh? Temporal lobe?"

"Well, she does have the syndrome, Mrs. MacNeil. For

95

example, the untidiness; the pugnacity; behavior that's socially embarrassing; the automatism, as well. And of course, the seizures that made the bed shake. Usually, that's followed by either wetting the bed or vomiting, or both, and then sleeping very deeply."

"You want to test her right now?" asked Chris.

"Yes, I think we should do it immediately, but she's going to need sedation. If she moves or jerks it will void the results, so may I give her, say, twenty-five milligrams of Librium?"

"Jesus, do what you have to," she told him, shaken.

She accompanied him to the examining room, and when Regan saw him readying the hypodermic, she screamed and filled the air with a torrent of obscenities.

"Oh, honey, it's to *help* you!" Chris pleaded in distress. She held Regan still while Dr. Klein gave the injection.

"I'll be back," the doctor said, nodding, and while a nurse wheeled the EEG apparatus into the room, he left to attend another patient. When he returned a short time later, the Librium still had not taken effect.

Klein seemed surprised. "That was quite a strong dose," he remarked to Chris.

He injected another twenty-five milligrams; left; came back; found Regan tractable and docile.

"What are you doing?" Chris asked him as Klein applied the saline-tipped electrodes to Regan's scalp.

"We put four on each side," he explained. "That enables us to take a brain-wave reading from the left and right side of the brain and then compare them."

"Why compare them?"

"Well, deviations could be significant. For example, I had a patient who used to hallucinate," said Klein. "He'd see things, he'd hear things, things that weren't actually there, of course. Well, I found a discrepancy in comparing the left and right readings of his brain waves and discovered that actually the man was hallucinating on just one side of his head."

"That's wild."

"The left eye and ear functioned normally; only the right side had visions and heard things.

"Well, all right, now, let's see." He had turned the machine on. He pointed to the waves on the fluorescent screen. "Now that's both sides together," he explained. "What I'm looking for now are spiky waves"—he patterned in the air with his index finger—"especially waves of very high amplitude coming at four to eight per second. That's temporal lobe," he told her.

He studied the pattern of the brain wave carefully, but discovered no dysrhythmia. No spikes. No flattened domes. And when he switched to comparison readings, the results were also negative.

Klein frowned. He couldn't understand it. He repeated the procedure. And found no change.

He brought in a nurse to attend to Regan and returned to his office with her mother.

"So what's the story?" Chris inquired.

The doctor sat pensively on the edge of his desk. "Well, the EEG would have proved that she had it, but the lack of dysrhythmia doesn't prove to me conclusively that she doesn't. It might be hysteria, but the pattern before and after her convulsion was much too striking."

Chris furrowed her brow. "You know, you keep on saying that, doc—'convulsion.' What exactly is the name of this disease?"

"Well, it isn't a disease," he said quietly.

"Well, what do you call it? I mean, specifically."

"You know it as epilepsy, Mrs. MacNeil."

"Oh, my God!"

Chris sank to a chair.

"Now, let's hold it," soothed Klein. "I can see that like most of the general public your impression of epilepsy is exaggerated and probably largely mythical."

"Isn't it hereditary?" Chris said, wincing.

"That's one of the myths," Klein told her calmly. "At least, most doctors seem to think so. Look, practically anyone can be made to convulse. You see, most of us are born with a pretty high threshold of resistance to convulsions; some with a low one; so the difference between you and an epileptic is a matter of degree. That's all. Just degree. It is not a disease."

"Then what is it—a freaking hallucination?"

"A disorder: a controllable disorder. And there are many, many types of it, Mrs. MacNeil. For example, you're sitting here now and for a second you seem to go blank, let's say, and you miss a little bit of what I'm saying. Well, now that's a kind of epilepsy, Mrs. MacNeil. That's right. It's a true epileptic attack."

"Yeah, well, that isn't Regan," Chris rebutted. "And how come it's happening just all of a sudden?"

"Look, we still aren't sure that's what she's got, and I grant you that maybe you were right in the first place; very possibly it's psychosomatic. However, I doubt it. And to answer your question, any number of changes in the function of the brain can trigger a convulsion in the epileptic: worry; fatigue; emotional stress; a particular note on a musical instrument. I once had a patient, for instance, who never used to have a seizure except on a bus when he was a block away from home. Well, we finally discovered what was causing it: flickering light from a white slat fence reflected in the window of the bus. Now at another time of day, or if the bus had been going at a different speed, he wouldn't have convulsed, you see. He had a lesion, a scar in the brain that was caused by some childhood disease. In the case of your daughter, the scar would be forward—up front in the temporal lobe—and when it's hit by a particular electrical impulse of a certain wavelength and periodicity, it triggers a sudden burst of abnormal reactions from deep within a focus in the lobe. Do you see?"

"I guess," Chris sighed, dejected. "But I'll tell you the

truth, doc, I don't understand how her whole personality could be changed."

"In temporal lobe, that's extremely common, and can last for days or even weeks. It isn't rare to find destructive and even criminal behavior. There's such a big change, in fact, that two or three hundred years ago people with temporal lobe disorders were often considered to be possessed by a devil."

"They were *what?*"

"Taken over by the mind of a demon. You know, something like a superstitious version of split personality."

Chris closed her eyes and lowered her forehead onto a fist. "Listen, tell me something good," she murmured.

"Well, now, don't be alarmed. If it *is* a lesion, in a way she's fortunate. Then all we have to do is remove the scar."

"Oh, swell."

"Or it could be just pressure on the brain. Look, I'd like to have some X rays taken of her skull. There's a radiologist here in the building, and perhaps I can get him to take you right away. Shall I call him?"

"God, yes; go ahead; let's do it."

Klein called and set it up. They would take her immediately, they told him.

He hung up the phone and began writing a prescription. "Room twenty-one on the second floor. Then I'll probably call you tomorrow or Thursday. I'd like a neurologist in on this. In the meantime, I'm taking her off the Ritalin. Let's try her on Librium for a while."

He ripped the prescription sheet from the pad and handed it over. "I'd try to stay close to her, Mrs. MacNeil. In these walking trance states, if that's what it is, it's always possible for her to hurt herself. Is your bedroom close to hers?"

"Yeah, it is."

"That's fine. Ground floor?"

"No, second."

"Big windows in her bedroom?"

"Well, one. What's the deal?"

"Well, I'd try to keep it closed, maybe even put a lock on it. In a trance state, she might go through it. I once had a—"

"—Patient," Chris finished with a trace of a wry, weary smile.

He grinned. "I guess I do have a lot of them, don't I?"

"A couple."

She propped her face on her hand and leaned thoughtfully forward. "You know, I thought of something else just now."

"And what was that?"

"Well, like after a fit, you were saying, she'd right away fall dead asleep. Like on Saturday night. I mean, didn't you say that?"

"Well, yes." Klein nodded. "That's right."

"Well, then, how come those other times she said that her bed was shaking, she was always wide awake?"

"You didn't tell me that."

"Well, it's so. She looked just fine. She'd just come to my room and then ask to get in bed with me."

"Bed wetting? Vomiting?"

Chris shook her head. "She was fine."

Klein frowned and gently chewed on his lip for a moment. "Well, let's look at those X rays," he finally told her.

Feeling drained and numb, Chris shepherded Regan to the radiologist; stayed at her side while the X rays were taken; took her home. She'd been strangely mute since the second injection, and Chris made an effort now to engage her.

"Want to play some Monopoly or somethin'?"

Regan shook her head and then stared at her mother with unfocused eyes that seemed to be retracted into infinite remoteness. "I'm feeling sleepy," Regan said in a voice that belonged to the eyes. Then, turning, she climbed up the stairs to her bedroom.

Must be the Librium, Chris reflected as she watched her.

Then at last she sighed and went into the kitchen. She poured some coffee and sat down at the breakfast-nook table with Sharon.

"How'd it go?"

"Oh, Christ!"

Chris fluttered the prescription slip onto the table. "Better call and get that filled." she said, and then explained what the doctor had told her. "If I'm busy or out, keep a real good eye on her, would you, Shar? He—" Dawning. Sudden. "That reminds me."

She got up from the table and went up to Regan's bedroom, found her under the covers and apparently asleep.

Chris moved to the window and tightened the latch. She stared below. The window, facing out from the side of the house, directly overlooked the precipitous public staircase that plunged to M Street far below.

Boy, I'd better call a locksmith right away.

Chris returned to the kitchen and added the chore to the list from which Sharon sat working, gave Willie the dinner menu, and returned a call from her agent.

"What about the script?" he wanted to know.

"Yeah, it's great, Ed; let's do it," she told him. "When's it go?"

"Well, your segment's in July, so you'll have to start preparing right away."

"You mean now?"

"I mean now. This isn't acting, Chris. You're involved in a lot of the preproduction. You've got to work with the set designer, the costume designer, the makeup artist, the producer. And you'll have to pick a cameraman and a cutter and block out your shots. C'mon, Chris, you know the drill."

"Oh, shit."

"You've got a problem?"

"Yeah, I do; I've got a problem."

"What's the problem?"

"Well, Regan's pretty sick."

"Oh, I'm sorry. What's wrong?"

"They don't know yet. I'm waiting for some tests. Listen, Ed, I can't leave her."

"So who says to leave her?"

"No, you don't understand, Ed. I need to be at home with her. She needs my attention. Look, I just can't explain it, Ed, it's too complicated, so why don't we just hold off for a while?"

"We can't. They want to try for the Music Hall over Christmas, Chris, and I think that they're pushing it *now*."

"Oh, for chrissakes, Ed, they can wait two weeks. Now come on!"

"Look, you've bugged me that you want to direct, and now all of a—"

"Right, Ed, I know," she interrupted. "Look, I want it; I really want it bad, but you'll just have to tell 'em that I need some more time!"

"And if I do, we're going to blow it. Now that's my opinion. Look, they don't want you anyway, that's not news. They're just doing this for Moore, and I think if they go back to him now and say she isn't too sure she wants to do it yet, *he'll* have an out. Now come on, Chris, talk sense. Look, you do what you want. I don't care. There's no money in this thing unless it hits. But if you want it, I'm telling you: I ask for a delay and I think we're going to blow it. Now then, what should I tell them?"

"Ahh, boy," sighed Chris.

"It's not easy. I know."

"No, it isn't. Well, listen . . ."

She thought. Then shook her head. "Ed, they'll just have to wait," she said wearily.

"Your decision."

"Okay, Ed. Let me know."

"I will. I'll be calling. Take it easy."

"You too, Ed. Good-bye."

She hung up the phone in a state of depression and lit up a cigarette. "I talked to Howard, by the way, did I tell you?" she said to Sharon.

"Oh, when? Did you tell him what's happening with Rags?"

"I told him. I told him he ought to come see her."

"Is he coming?"

"I don't know. I don't think so," Chris answered.

"You'd think he'd make the effort."

"Yeah, I know." Chris sighed. "But you've got to understand his hang-up, Shar. That's it. I know that's it."

"What's it?"

"Oh, the whole 'Mr. Chris MacNeil' thing. Rags was a part of it. She was in and he was out. Always me and Rags together on the magazine covers; me and Rags in the layouts; mother and daughter, pixie twins." She tipped ash from her cigarette with a moody finger. "Ah, nuts, who knows. It's all mixed up. But it's hard to get hacked with him, Shar; I just can't."

She reached out for a book by Sharon's elbow. "So what are you reading?"

"What do you mean? Oh, *that*. That's for you. I forgot. Mrs. Perrin dropped it by."

"She was here?"

"Yes, this morning. Said she's sorry she missed you and she's going out of town, but she'll call you as soon as she's back."

Chris nodded and glanced at the title of the book: A *Study of Devil Worship and Related Occult Phenomena*. She opened it and found a penned note from Mary Jo Perrin:

Dear Chris: I happened by the Georgetown University Library and picked this up for you. It has some chapters about Black Mass. You should read it *all*, however; I think you'll find the other sections particularly interesting. See you soon.

Mary Jo

"Sweet lady," said Chris.

"Yes, she is," agreed Sharon.

Chris riffled through the pages of the book. "What's the scoop on Black Mass? Pretty hairy?"

"I don't know," answered Sharon. "I haven't read it."

"No good for serenity?"

Sharon stretched and yawned. "Oh, that stuff turns me off."

"What happened to your Jesus complex?"

"Oh, come on."

Chris slid the book across the table to Sharon. "Here, read it and tell me what happens."

"And get nightmares?"

"What do you think you get paid for?"

"Throwing up."

"I can do that myself," Chris muttered as she picked up the evening paper. "All you have to do is stick your business manager's advice down your throat and you're vomiting blood for a week." Irritably, she put the paper aside. "Would you turn on the radio, Shar? Get the news."

Sharon had dinner at the house with Chris, and then left for a date. She forgot the book. Chris saw it on the table and thought about reading it, but finally she felt too weary. She left it on the table and walked upstairs.

She looked in on Regan, who still seemed to be asleep under the covers, and apparently sleeping through. She checked the window again. Leaving the room, Chris made sure to leave the door wide open and then did the same with her own before getting into bed. She watched part of a movie on television. Then slept.

The following morning, the book about devil worship had vanished from the table.

No one noticed.

three

The consulting neurologist pinned up the X rays again and searched for indentations that would look as if the skull had been pounded like copper with a tiny hammer. Dr. Klein stood behind him with folded arms. They had both looked for lesions and collections of fluid; for a possible shifting of the pineal gland. Now they probed for Lückenshadl Skull, the telltale depressions that would indicate chronic intracranial pressure.

They did not find it. The date was Thursday, April 28.

The consulting neurologist removed his glasses and carefully tucked them into the left breast pocket of his jacket. "There's just nothing there, Sam. Nothing I can see."

Klein frowned at the floor with a shake of the head. "Doesn't figure."

"Want to run another series?"

"I don't think so. I'll try an LP."

"Good idea."

"In the meantime, I'd like you to see her."

"How's today?"

"Well, I'm—" Telephone buzzer. "Excuse me." He picked up the telephone. "Yes?"

"Mrs. MacNeil on the phone. Says it's urgent."

"What line?"

"She's on twelve."

He punched the extension button. "Dr. Klein, Mrs. MacNeil. What's the trouble?"

Her voice was distraught and on the brim of hysteria. "Oh, God, doc, it's Regan! Can you come right away?"

"Well, what's wrong?"

"I don't know, doc, I just can't describe it! Oh, for God's sake, come over! Come now!"

"Right away!"

He disconnected and buzzed his receptionist. "Susan, tell Dresner to take my appointments." He hung up the phone and started taking off his jacket. "That's her. You want to come? It's only just across the bridge."

"I've got an hour."

"Let's go."

They were there within minutes, and at the door, where Sharon greeted them, they heard moans and screams of terror from Regan's bedroom. She looked frightened. "I'm Sharon Spencer," she said. "Come on. She's upstairs."

She led them to the door of Regan's bedroom, where she cracked it open and called in, "Doctors, Chris!"

Chris immediately came to the door, her face contorted in a vise of fear. "Oh, my God, come on in!" she quavered. "Come on in and take a look at what she's doing!"

"This is Dr.—"

In the middle of the introduction, Klein broke off as he stared at Regan. Shrieking hysterically, she was flailing her arms as her body seemed to fling itself up horizontally into the air above her bed and then slammed down savagely onto the mattress. It was happening rapidly and repeatedly.

"Oh, Mother, make him *stop!*" she was screeching. "*Stop* him. He's trying to kill me! *Stop* him! *Stooopppppp hiiiiiimmmmmmmmmm, Motherrrrrrrrrrrrrrr!*"

"Oh, my baby!" Chris whimpered as she jerked up a fist to her mouth and bit it. She turned a beseeching look to Klein. "Doc, what is it? What's happening?"

He shook his head, his gaze fixed on Regan as the odd phenomenon continued. She would lift about a foot each time and then fall with a wrenching of her breath, as if unseen hands had picked her up and thrown her down.

Chris shaded her eyes with a trembling hand. "Oh, Jesus, Jesus!" she said hoarsely. "Doc, what *is* it?"

The up and down movements ceased abruptly and the girl twisted feverishly from side to side with her eyes rolled upward into their sockets so that only the whites were exposed.

"Oh, he's burning me . . . *burning* me!" Regan was moaning. "Oh, I'm burning! I'm burning! . . ."

Her legs began rapidly crossing and uncrossing.

The doctors moved closer, one on either side of the bed. Still twisting and jerking, Regan arched her head back, disclosing a swollen, bulging throat. She began to mutter something incomprehensible in an oddly guttural tone.

". . . nowonmai . . . nowonmai . . ."

Klein reached down to check her pulse.

"Now, let's see what the trouble is, dear," he said gently.

And abruptly was reeling, stunned and staggering, across the room from the force of a vicious backward swing of Regan's arm as the girl sat up, her face contorted with a hideous rage.

"The sow is *mine!*" she bellowed in a coarse and powerful voice. "She is *mine!* Keep away from her! She is *mine!*"

A yelping laugh gushed up from her throat, and then she fell on her back as if someone had pushed her. She pulled up her nightgown, exposing her genitals. "*Fuck* me! *Fuck* me!" she screamed at the doctors, and with both her hands began masturbating frantically.

Moments later, Chris ran from the room with a stifled sob when Regan put her fingers to her mouth and licked them.

As Klein approached the bedside, Regan seemed to hug herself, her hands caressing her arms.

"Ah, yes, my pearl . . ." she crooned in that strangely coarsened voice. Her eyes were closed as if in ecstasy. "My child . . . my flower . . . my pearl . . ."

Then again she was twisting from side to side, moaning meaningless syllables over and over. And abruptly sat up with eyes staring wide with helpless terror.

She mewed like a cat.

Then barked.

Then neighed.

And then, bending at the waist, started whirling her torso around in rapid, strenuous circles. She gasped for breath. "Oh, *stop* him!" she wept. "Please, *stop* him! It hurts! Make him *stop!* Make him *stop!* I can't *breathe!*"

Klein had seen enough. He fetched his medical bag to the window and quickly began to prepare an injection.

The neurologist remained beside the bed and saw Regan fall backward as if from a shove. Her eyes rolled upward into their sockets again, and rolling from side to side, she began to mutter rapidly in guttural tones. The neurologist leaned closer and tried to make it out. Then he saw Klein gently beckoning. He moved to him.

"I'm giving her Librium," Klein told him guardedly, holding the syringe to the light of the window. "But you're going to have to hold her."

The neurologist nodded. He seemed preoccupied. He inclined his head to the side as if listening to the muttering from the bed.

"What's she saying?" Klein whispered.

"I don't know. Just gibberish. Nonsense syllables." Yet his own explanation seemed to leave him unsatisfied. "She says it as if it means something, though. It's got cadence."

Klein nodded toward the bed and they approached quietly from either side. As they came, she went rigid, as if in the stiffening grip of tetany, and the doctors looked at each other significantly. Then looked again to Regan as she started to arch her body upward into an impossible position, bending it backward like a bow until the brow of her head had touched her feet. She was screaming in pain.

The doctors eyed each other with questioning surmise. Then Klein gave a signal to the neurologist. But before the consultant could seize her, Regan fell limp in a faint and wet the bed.

Klein leaned over and rolled up her eyelid. Checked her pulse. "She'll be out for a while," he murmured. "I think she convulsed. Don't you?"

"Yes, I think so."

"Well, let's take some insurance," said Klein.

Deftly he administered the injection.

"Well, what do you think?" Klein asked the consultant as he pressed a circle of sterile tape against the puncture.

"Temporal lobe. Sure, maybe schizophrenia's a possibility, Sam, but the onset's much too sudden. She hasn't any history of it, right?"

"No, she hasn't."

"Neurasthenia?"

Klein shook his head.

"Then hysteria, maybe," offered the consultant.

"I've thought of that."

"Sure. But she'd have to be a freak to get her body twisted up like she did voluntarily, now, wouldn't you say?" He shook his head. "No, I think it's pathological, Sam—her strength; the paranoia; the hallucinations. Schizophrenia, okay; those symptoms it covers. But temporal lobe would also cover the

convulsions. There's one thing that bothers me, though. . . ."
He trailed off with a puzzled frown.

"What's that?"

"Well, I'm really not sure but I thought I heard signs of dissociation: 'my pearl' . . . 'my child' . . . 'my flower' . . . 'the sow.' I had the feeling she was talking about herself. Was that your impression too, or am I reading something into it?"

Klein stroked his lip as he mulled the question. "Well, frankly, at the time it never occurred to me, but then now that you point it out . . ." He grunted thoughtfully. "Could be. Yes. Yes, it could."

Then he shrugged off the notion. "Well, I'll do an LP right now while she's out and then maybe we'll know something."

The neurologist nodded.

Klein poked around in his medical bag, found a pill and tucked it in his pocket. "Can you stay?"

The neurologist checked his watch. "Maybe half an hour."

"Let's talk to the mother."

They left the room and entered the hallway.

Chris and Sharon were leaning, heads lowered, against the balustrade by the staircase. As the doctors approached them, Chris wiped her nose with a balled, moist handkerchief. Her eyes were red from crying.

"She's sleeping," Klein told her.

"Thank God," Chris sighed.

"And she's heavily sedated. She'll probably sleep right through until tomorrow."

"That's good," Chris said weakly. "Doc, I'm sorry about being such a baby."

"You're doing just fine," he assured her. "It's a frightening ordeal. By the way, this is Dr. David."

"Hello," said Chris with a bleak smile.

"Dr. David's a neurologist."

"What do you think?" she asked them both.

"Well, we still think it's temporal lobe," Klein answered, "and—"

"Jesus, what in the hell are you *talking* about!" Chris erupted. "She's been acting like a psycho, like a split personality! What do you—"

Abruptly she pulled herself together and lowered her forehead into a hand.

"Guess I'm all up-tight." She exhaled wearily. "I'm sorry." She lifted a haggard look to Klein. "You were saying?"

It was David who responded. "There haven't been more than a hundred authenticated cases of split personality, Mrs. MacNeil. It's a rare condition. Now I know the temptation is to leap to psychiatry, but any responsible psychiatrist would exhaust the somatic possibilities first. That's the safest procedure."

"Okay, so what's next?" Chris sighed.

"A lumbar tap," answered David.

"A spinal?"

He nodded. "What we missed in the X rays and the EEG could turn up there. At the least, it would exhaust certain other possibilities. I'd like to do it now, right here, while she's sleeping. I'll give her a local, of course, but it's movement I'm trying to eliminate."

"How could she jump off the bed like that?" Chris asked, her face squinting up in anxiety.

"Well, I think we discussed that before," said Klein. "Pathological states can induce abnormal strength and accelerated motor performance."

"But you don't know why," said Chris.

"Well, it seems to have something to do with motivation," commented David. "But that's all we know."

"Well, now, what about the spinal?" Klein asked Chris. "May we?"

She exhaled, sagging, staring at the floor.

"Go ahead," she murmured. "Do whatever you have to. Just make her well."

"We'll try," said Klein. "May I use your phone?"

"Sure, come on. In the study."

"Oh, incidentally," said Klein as she turned to lead them, "she needs to have her bedding changed."

"I'll do it," said Sharon. She moved toward Regan's bedroom.

"Can I make you some coffee?" asked Chris as the doctors followed down the stairs. "I gave the housekeepers the afternoon off, so it'll have to be instant."

They declined.

"I see you haven't fixed that window yet," noted Klein.

"No, we called," Chris told him. "They're coming out tomorrow with shutters you can lock."

He nodded approval.

They entered the study, where Klein called his office and instructed an assistant to deliver the necessary equipment and medication to the house.

"And set up the lab for a spinal workup," Klein instructed. "I'll run it myself right after the tap."

When he'd finished the call, he turned to Chris and asked what had happened since last he saw Regan.

"Well, Tuesday"—Chris pondered—"there was nothing at all. She went straight up to bed and slept right through until late the next morning, then—"

"Oh, no, no, wait," she amended. "No, she didn't. That's right. Willie mentioned that she'd heard her in the kitchen awfully early. I remember feeling glad that she'd gotten her appetite back. But she went back to bed then, I guess, because she stayed there the rest of the day."

"She was sleeping?" Klein asked her.

"No, I think she was reading," Chris answered. "Well, I started feeling a little better about it all. I mean, it looked as if the Librium was just what she needed. She was sort of far away, I noticed, and that bothered me a little, but still it was a pretty big improvement. Well, last night, again, nothing," Chris continued. "Then this morning it started."

She inhaled deeply.

"Boy, did it start!" She shook her head.

She'd been sitting in the kitchen, Chris told the doctors, when Regan ran screaming down the stairs and to her mother, cowering defensively behind her chair as she clutched Chris's arms and explained in a terrified voice that Captain Howdy was chasing her; had been pinching her; punching her; shoving her; mouthing obscenities; threatening to kill her. "There he is!" she had shrieked at last, pointing to the kitchen door. Then she'd fallen to the floor, her body jerking in spasms as she gasped and wept that Howdy was kicking her. Then suddenly, Chris recounted, Regan had stood in the middle of the kitchen with arms extended and had begun to spin rapidly "like a top," continuing the movements for several minutes, until she had fallen to the floor in exhaustion.

"And then all of a sudden," Chris finished distressfully, "I saw there was this . . . *hate* in her eyes, this *hate*, and she told me . . ."

She was choking up.

"She called me a . . . Oh, Jesus!"

She burst into sobs, and shielded her eyes as she wept convulsively.

Klein moved quietly to the bar; poured a glass of water from the tap. He walked toward Chris.

"Oh, shit, where's a cigarette?" Chris sighed tremulously as she wiped at her eyes with the back of a finger.

Klein gave her the water and a small green pill. "Try this instead," he advised.

"That a tranquilizer?"

"Yes."

"I'll have a double."

"One's enough."

"Big spender," Chris murmured with a wan smile.

She swallowed the pill and then handed the empty glass to the doctor. "Thanks," she said softly, and rested her brow on quivering fingertips. She shook her head gently. "Yeah, then it started," she picked up moodily. "All of that other stuff. It was like she was someone else."

"Like Captain Howdy, perhaps?" asked David.

Chris looked up at him in puzzlement. He was staring so intently. "What do you mean?" she asked.

"I don't know." He shrugged. "Just a question."

She turned to the fireplace with absent, haunted eyes. "I don't know," she said dully. "Just somebody else."

There was a moment of silence. Then David stood up and explained he had to leave for another appointment, and after some reassuring statements, said good-bye.

Klein walked him to the door. "You'll check the sugar?" David asked him.

"No, I'm the Rosslyn village idiot."

David smiled thinly. "I'm a little up-tight about this myself," he said. He looked away in thought. "Strange case."

For a moment he stroked his chin and seemed to brood. Then he looked up at Klein. "Let me know what you find."

"You'll be home?"

"Yes, I will. Give a call." He waved a good-bye and left.

A short time later, after the arrival of the equipment, Klein anesthetized Regan's spinal area with Novocain, and as Chris and Sharon watched, extracted the spinal fluid, keeping watch on the manometer. "Pressure's normal," he murmured.

When he'd finished, he went to the window to see if the fluid was clear or hazy.

It was clear.

He carefully stowed the tubes of fluid in his bag.

"I doubt that she will," Klein told the women, "but in case she awakens in the middle of the night and creates a disturbance, you might want a nurse here to give her sedation."

"Can't I do it myself?" Chris asked worriedly.

"Why not a nurse?"

She did not want to mention her deep distrust of doctors and nurses. "I'd rather do it myself," she said simply. "Couldn't I?"

"Well, injections are tricky," he answered. "An air bubble's very dangerous."

"Oh, I know how to do it," interjected Sharon. "My mother ran a nursing home up in Oregon."

"Gee, would you do that, Shar? Would you stay here tonight?" Chris asked her.

"Well, beyond tonight," interjected Klein. "She may need intravenous feeding, depending on how she comes along."

"Could you teach me how to do it?" Chris asked him anxiously.

He nodded. "Yes, I guess I could."

He wrote a prescription for soluble Thorazine and disposable syringes. He gave it to Chris. "Have this filled right away."

Chris handed it to Sharon. "Honey, do that for me, would you? Just call and they'll send it. I'd like to go with the doctor while he makes those tests. . . . Do you mind?" she asked him.

He noted the tightness around her eyes; the look of confusion and of helplessness. He nodded.

"I know how you feel." He smiled at her gently. "I feel the same way when I talk to mechanics about my car."

They left the house at precisely 6:18 P.M.

In his laboratory in the Rosslyn medical building, Klein ran a number of tests. First he analyzed protein content.

Normal.

Then a count of blood cells.

"Too many red," Klein explained, "means bleeding. And too many white would mean infection."

He was looking in particular for a fungus infection that was often the cause of chronic bizarre behavior. And again drew a blank.

At the last, Klein tested the fluid's sugar content.

"How come?" Chris asked him intently.

"Well, now, the spinal sugar," he told her, "should measure two-thirds of the amount of blood sugar. Anything significantly under that ratio would mean a disease in which the bacteria eat the sugar in the spinal fluid. And if so, it could account for her symptoms."

But he failed to find it.

Chris shook her head and folded her arms. "Here we are again, folks," she murmured bleakly.

For a while Klein brooded. Then at last he turned and looked to Chris. "Do you keep any drugs in your house?" he asked her.

"Huh?"

"Amphetamines? LSD?"

"Gee, no. Look, I'd tell you. No, there's nothing like that."

He nodded and stared at his shoes, then looked up and said, "Well—I guess that it's time we consulted a psychiatrist, Mrs. MacNeil."

She was back in the house at exactly 7:21 P.M., and at the door she called, "Sharon?"

Sharon wasn't there.

Chris went upstairs to Regan's bedroom. Still heavily asleep. Not a ruffle in her covers. Chris noticed that the window was open wide. An odor of urine. *Sharon must've opened it to air out the room,* she thought. She closed it. *Where did she go?*

Chris returned downstairs just as Willie came in.

"Hi ya, Willie. Any fun today?"

"Shopping. Movies."

"Where's Karl?"

Willie made a gesture of dismissal. "He lets me see the Beatles this time. By myself."

"Good work."

Willie held up her fingers in a V. The time was 7:35.

At 8:01, while Chris was in the study talking to her agent on the phone, Sharon walked through the door with several packages, and then flopped in a chair and waited.

"Where've you been?" asked Chris when she'd finished.

"Oh, didn't he tell you?"

"Oh, didn't *who* tell me?"

"Burke. Isn't he here? Where is he?"

"He was here?"

"You mean he wasn't when you got home?"

"Listen, start all over," said Chris.

"Oh, that nut," Sharon chided with a headshake. "I couldn't get the druggist to deliver, so when Burke came around, I thought, fine, he can stay here with Regan while I go get the Thorazine." She shrugged. "I should have known."

"Yeah, you should've. And so what did you buy?"

"Well, since I thought I had the time, I went and bought a rubber drawsheet for her bed." She displayed it.

"Did you eat?"

"No, I thought I'd fix a sandwich. Would you like one?"

"Good idea. Let's go and eat."

"What happened with the tests?" Sharon asked as they walked slowly to the kitchen.

"Not a thing. All negative. I'm going to have to get her a shrink," Chris answered dully.

After sandwiches and coffee, Sharon showed Chris how to give an injection.

"The two main things," she explained, "are to make sure that there aren't any air bubbles, and then you make sure that you haven't hit a vein. See, you aspirate a little, like this" —she was demonstrating—"and see if there's blood in the syringe."

For a time, Chris practiced the procedure on a grapefruit,

and seemed to grow proficient. Then at 9:28, the front door-bell rang. Willie answered. It was Karl. As he passed through the kitchen, en route to his room, he nodded a good evening and remarked he'd forgotten to take his key.

"I can't believe it," Chris said to Sharon. "That's the first time he's ever admitted a mistake."

They passed the evening watching television in the study.

At 11:46, Chris answered the phone. The young director of the second unit. He sounded grave.

"Have you heard the news yet, Chris?"

"No, what?"

"Well, it's bad."

"What is it?" she asked.

"Burke's dead."

He'd been drunk. He had stumbled. He had fallen down the steep flight of steps beside the house, fallen far to the bottom, where a passing pedestrian on M Street watched as he tumbled into night without end. A broken neck. This bloody, crumpled scene, his last.

As the telephone fell from Chris's fingers, she was silently weeping, standing unsteadily. Sharon ran and caught her, supported her, hung up the phone and led her to the sofa.

"Burke's dead," Chris sobbed.

"Oh, my God!" gasped Sharon. "What happened?"

But Chris could not speak yet. She wept.

Then, later, they talked. For hours. They talked. Chris drank. Reminisced about Dennings. Now laughed. Now cried. "Ah, my God," she kept sighing. "Poor Burke . . . poor Burke . . ."

Her dream of death kept coming back to her.

At a little past five in the morning, Chris was standing moodily behind the bar, her elbows propped, head lowered, eyes sad. She was waiting for Sharon to return from the kitchen with a tray of ice.

She heard her coming.

"I still can't believe it," Sharon was sighing as she entered the study.

Chris looked up and froze.

Gliding spiderlike, rapidly, close behind Sharon, her body arched backward in a bow with her head almost touching her feet, was Regan, her tongue flicking quickly in and out of her mouth while she hissed sibilantly like a serpent.

"Sharon?" Chris said numbly, still staring at Regan.

Sharon stopped. So did Regan. Sharon turned and saw nothing. And then screamed as she felt Regan's tongue snaking out at her ankle.

Chris whitened. "Call that doctor and get him out of bed! Get him *now!*"

Wherever Sharon moved, Regan would follow.

four

Friday, April 29. While Chris waited in the hall outside the bedroom, Dr. Klein and a noted neuropsychiatrist were examining Regan.

The doctors observed for half an hour. Flinging. Whirling. Tearing at the hair. She occasionally grimaced and pressed her hands against her ears as if blotting out sudden, deafening noise. She bellowed obscenities. Screamed in pain. Then at last she flung herself face downward onto the bed and tucked her legs up under her stomach. She moaned incoherently.

The psychiatrist motioned Klein away from the bed.

"Let's get her tranquilized," he whispered. "Maybe I can talk to her."

The internist nodded and prepared an injection of fifty milligrams of Thorazine. When the doctors approached the bed, however, Regan seemed to sense them and quickly turned over, and as the neuropsychiatrist attempted to hold her, she began to shriek in malevolent fury. Bit him. Fought him. Held him off. It was only when Karl was called in to assist that they managed to keep her sufficiently rigid for Klein to administer the injection.

The dosage proved inadequate. Another fifty milligrams was injected. They waited.

Regan grew tractable. Then dreamy. Then stared at the doctors in sudden bewilderment. "Where's Mom? I want my Mom!" she wept.

At a nod from the neuropsychiatrist, Klein left the room to go and get Chris.

"Your mother will be here in just a second, dear," the psychiatrist told Regan. He sat on the bed and stroked her head. "There, there, it's all right, dear, I'm a doctor."

"*I want Mom!*" wept Regan.

"She's coming. Do you hurt, dear?"

She nodded, the tears streaming down.

"Where?"

"Just every place!" sobbed Regan. "I feel all achy!"

"Oh, my baby!"

"*Mom!*"

Chris ran to the bed and hugged her. Kissed her. Comforted and soothed. Then Chris herself began to weep. "Oh, Rags, you're back! It's really you!"

"Oh, Mom, he hurt me!" Regan sniffled. "Make him stop hurting me! Please? Okay?"

Chris looked puzzled for a moment, then glanced to the doctors with a pleading question in her eyes.

"She's heavily sedated," the psychiatrist said gently.

"You mean . . . ?"

He cut her off. "We'll see." Then he turned to Regan. "Can you tell me what's wrong, dear?"

"I don't *know*," she answered. "I don't know why he does it to me." Tears rolled down from her eyes. "He was always my friend before!"

"Who's that?"

"Captain Howdy! And then it's like somebody else is inside me! Making me do things!"

"Captain Howdy?"

"I don't know!"

"A person?"

She nodded.

"Who?"

"I don't *know!*"

"Well, all right, then; let's try something, Regan. A game." He was reaching in his pocket for a shining bauble attached to a silvery length of chain. "Have you ever seen movies where someone gets hypnotized?"

She nodded.

"Well, I'm a hypnotist. Oh, yes! I hypnotize people all the time. That's, of course, if they let me. Now I think if I hypnotize you, Regan, it will help you get well. Yes, that person inside you will come right out. Would you like to be hypnotized? See, your mother's right here, right beside you."

Regan looked questioningly to Chris.

"Go ahead, honey, do it," Chris urged her. "Try it."

Regan turned to the psychiatrist and nodded. "Okay," she said softly. "But only a little."

The psychiatrist smiled and glanced abruptly to the sound of pottery breaking behind him. A delicate vase had fallen to the floor from the top of a bureau where Dr. Klein was now resting his forearm. He looked at his arm and then down at the shards with an air of puzzlement; then stooped to pick them up.

"Never mind, doc, Willie'll get it," Chris told him.

"Would you close those shutters for me, Sam?" the psychiatrist asked him. "And pull the drapes?"

When the room was dark, the psychiatrist gripped the chain in his fingertips and began to swing the bauble back and forth with an easy movement. He shone a penlight on it. It glowed.

He began to intone the hypnotic ritual. "Now watch this, Regan, keep watching, and soon you'll feel your eyelids growing heavier and heavier. . . ."

Within a very short time, she seemed to be in trance.

"Extremely suggestible," the psychiatrist murmured. Then he spoke to the girl. "Are you comfortable, Regan?"

"Yes." Her voice was soft and whispery.

"How old are you, Regan?"

"Twelve."

"Is there someone inside you?"

"Sometimes."

"When?"

"Different times."

"It's a person?"

"Yes."

"Who is it?"

"I don't know."

"Captain Howdy?"

"I don't know."

"A man?"

"I don't know."

"But he's there."

"Yes, sometimes."

"Now?"

"I don't know."

"If I ask him to tell me, will you let him answer?"

"No!"

"Why not?"

"I'm afraid!"

"Of what?"

"I don't know!"

"If he talks to me, Regan, I think he will leave you. Do you want him to leave you?"

"Yes."

"Let him speak, then. Will you let him speak?"

A pause. Then, "Yes."

"I am speaking to the person inside of Regan now," the psychiatrist said firmly. "If you are there, you *too* are hypnotized and must answer all my questions." For a moment, he paused to allow the suggestion to enter her bloodstream. Then he repeated it: "If you are there, then you are hypnotized and must answer all my questions. Come forward and answer, now: Are you there?"

Silence. Then something curious happened: Regan's breath turned suddenly foul. It was thick, like a current. The psychiatrist smelled it from two feet away. He shone the penlight on Regan's face.

Chris stifled a gasp. Her daughter's features were contorting into a malevolent mask: lips pulling tautly into opposite directions, tumefied tongue lolling wolfish from her mouth.

"Oh, my God!" breathed Chris.

"Are you the person in Regan?" the psychiatrist asked.

She nodded.

"Who are you?"

"Nowonmai," she answered gutturally.

"That's your name?"

She nodded.

"You're a man?"

She said, "Say."

"Did you answer?"

"Say."

"If that's 'yes,' nod your head."

She nodded.

"Are you speaking in a foreign language?"

"Say."

"Where do you come from?"

"Dog."

"You say that you come from a dog?"

"Dogmorfmocion," Regan replied.

The psychiatrist thought for a moment, then attempted another approach. "When I ask you questions now, you will answer by moving your head: a nod for 'yes,' and a shake for 'no.' Do you understand that?"

Regan nodded.

"Did your answers have meaning?" he asked her.   Yes.

"Are you someone whom Regan has known?"   No.

"That she knows of?"   No.

"Are you someone she's invented?"   No.

"You're real?"   Yes.

"Part of Regan?"   No.

"Were you ever a part of Regan?"   No.

"Do you like her?"   No.

"Dislike her?"   Yes.

"Do you hate her?"   Yes.

"Over something she's done?"   Yes.

"Do you blame her for her parents' divorce?"   No.

"Has it something to do with her parents?"   No.

"With a friend?"   No.

"But you hate her."   Yes.

"Are you punishing Regan?"   Yes.

"You wish to harm her?"   Yes.

"To kill her?"   Yes.

"If she died, wouldn't you die too?"   No.

The answer seemed to disquiet him and he lowered his eyes in thought. The bed springs squeaked as he shifted his weight. In the smothering stillness, Regan's breathing rasped as from a rotted, putrid bellows. Here. Yet far. Distantly sinister.

The psychiatrist lifted his glance again to that hideous, twisted face. His eyes gleamed sharply with speculation.

"Is there something she can do that would make you leave her?"   Yes.

"Can you tell me what it is?"   Yes.

"Will you tell me?"   No.

"But—"

Abruptly the psychiatrist gasped in startled pain as he realized with horrified incredulity that Regan was squeezing his scrotum with a hand that had gripped him like an iron talon. Eyes wide-staring, he struggled to free himself. He couldn't. "Sam! Sam, help me!" he croaked.

Agony. Bedlam.

Chris looking up and then leaping for the light switch.

Klein running forward.

Regan with her head back, cackling demonically, then howling like a wolf.

Chris slapped at the light switch. Turned. Saw grainy, flickering film of a slow-motion nightmare: Regan and the doctors writhing on the bed in a tangle of shifting arms and legs, in a melee of grimaces, gasps and curses, and the howling and the yelping and the hideous laughter, with Regan oinking, Regan neighing, then the film racing faster and the bedstead shaking, violently quivering from side to side as Chris watched helplessly while her daughter's eyes rolled upward into their sockets and she wrenched up a keening shriek of terror torn raw and bloody from the base of her spine.

Regan crumpled and fell unconscious. Something unspeakable left the room.

For a breathless moment, no one moved. Then slowly and carefully, the doctors untangled themselves; stood up. They stared at Regan. After a time, the expressionless Klein took Regan's pulse. Satisfied, he slowly pulled up her blanket and nodded to the others. They left the room and went down to the study.

For a time, no one spoke. Chris was on the sofa. Klein and the psychiatrist sat near her in facing chairs. The psychiatrist was pensive, pinching at his lip as he stared at the coffee table; then he sighed and looked up at Chris. She turned her burned-out gaze to his. "What the hell's going on?" she asked in a mournful, haggard whisper.

"Did you recognize the language she was speaking?" he asked her.

Chris shook her head.

"Have you any religion?"

"No."

"Your daughter?"

"No."

And now the psychiatrist asked her a lengthy series of questions relating to Regan's psychological history. When at last he had finished, he seemed disturbed.

"What is it?" Chris asked him, white-knuckled fingers clenching and unclenching on a balled-up handkerchief. "What has she got?"

"Well, it's somewhat confusing," the psychiatrist evaded. "And frankly, it would be quite irresponsible of me to attempt a diagnosis after so brief an examination."

"Well, you must have some idea," she insisted.

The psychiatrist sighed, fingering his brow. "Well, I know you're quite anxious, so I will mention one or two tentative impressions."

Chris leaned forward, nodding tensely. Fingers in her lap started fumbling with the handkerchief, telling the stitches in the hem as if they were wrinkled linen rosary beads.

"To begin with," he told her, "it's highly improbable that she's faking."

Klein was nodding in agreement. "We think so for a number of reasons," the psychiatrist continued. "For example, the abnormal and painful contortions; and most dramatically, I suppose, from the change in her features when we were talking to the so-called person she thinks is inside her. You see, a psychic effect like that is unlikely unless she *believed* in this person. Do you follow?"

"I think I do," Chris answered, squinting her eyes in puzzlement. "But one thing I don't understand is where this person comes from. I mean, you keep hearing about 'split personality' but I've never really known any explanation."

"Well, neither does anyone else, Mrs. MacNeil. We use

concepts like 'consciousness'—'mind'—'personality,' but we don't really know yet what these things are." He was shaking his head. "Not really. Not at all. So when I start talking about something like multiple or split personality, all we have are some theories that raise more questions than they give answers. Freud thought that certain ideas and feelings are somehow repressed by the conscious mind, but remain alive in a person's subconscious; remain quite strong, in fact, and continue to seek expression through various psychiatric symptoms. Now when this repressed, or let's call it dissociated material— the word 'dissociation' implying a splitting off from the mainstream of consciousness—well, when this type of material is sufficiently strong, or where the subject's personality is disorganized and weak, the result can be schizophrenic psychosis. Now that isn't the same," he cautioned, "as *dual* personality. Schizophrenia means a *shattering* of personality. But where the dissociated material is strong enough to somehow come glued together, to somehow organize in the individual's subconscious—why, then it's been known, at times, to function independently as a separate personality; to take over the bodily functions."

He took a breath. Chris listened intently and he went on. "That's one theory. There are several others, some of them involving the notion of escape into unawareness; escape from some conflict or emotional problem. Getting back to Regan, she hasn't any history of schizophrenia and the EEG didn't show up the brain-wave pattern that normally accompanies it. So I tend to reject schizophrenia. Which leaves us the general field of hysteria."

"I gave last week," Chris murmured bleakly.

The worried psychiatrist smiled thinly. "Hysteria," he continued, "is a form of neurosis in which emotional disturbances are converted into bodily disorders. Now, in certain of its forms, there's dissociation. In psychasthenia, for example, the individual loses consciousness of his actions, but he sees himself act and attributes his actions to someone else. His idea of the second personality is vague, however, and Regan's seems specific. So we come to what Freud used to call the 'conversion' form of hysteria. It grows from unconscious feelings of guilt and the need to be punished. Dissociation is the paramount feature here, even multiple personality. And the syndrome might also include epileptoid-like convulsions; hallucinations; abnormal motor excitement."

"Gee, that does sound a lot like Regan," Chris ventured moodily. "Don't you think? I mean, except for the guilt part. What would she have to feel guilty *about*?"

"Well, a cliché answer," the psychiatrist responded, "might be the divorce. Children often feel *they* are the ones rejected and assume the full responsibility for the departure of one of their parents. In the case of your daughter, there's reason to believe that that *could* be the case. Here I'm thinking of the brooding and the deep depression over the notion of people dying: thanatophobia. In children, you'll find it accompanied by guilt formation that's related to family stress, very often fear of the loss of a parent. It produces rage and intense frustration. In addition, the guilt in this type of hysteria needn't be known to the conscious mind. It could even be the guilt that we call 'free-floating,' a general guilt that relates to nothing in particular," he concluded.

Chris gave her head a shake. "I'm confused," she murmured. "I mean, where does this new personality come in?"

"Well, again, it's a guess," he replied, "just a guess—but assuming that it *is* conversion hysteria stemming from guilt, then the second personality is simply the agent who handles the punishing. If Regan herself were to do it, you see, that would mean she would *recognize* her guilt. But she wants to escape that recognition. Therefore, a second personality."

"And that's what you think she's got?"

"As I said, I don't know," replied the psychiatrist, still evasive. He seemed to be choosing his words as he would moss-covered stones to cross a stream. "It's extremely unusual for a child of Regan's age to be able to pull together and organize the components of a new personality. And certain—well, other things are puzzling. Her performance with the Ouija board, for example, would indicate extreme suggestibility; and yet apparently I never really hypnotized her." He shrugged. "Well, perhaps she resisted. But the really striking thing," he noted, "is the new personality's apparent precocity. It isn't a twelve-year-old at all. It's much, much older. And then there's the language she was speaking. . . ." He stared at the rug in front of the fireplace, thoughtfully tugging at his lower lip. "There's a similar state, of course, but we don't know much about it: a form of somnambulism where the subject suddenly manifests knowledge or skills that he's never learned—and where the intention of the second personality is the destruction of the first. However . . ."

The word trailed away. Abruptly the psychiatrist looked up at Chris. "Well, it's terribly complicated," he told her, "and I've oversimplified outrageously."

"So what's the bottom line?" Chris asked.

"At the moment," he told her, "a blank. She needs an intensive examination by a team of experts, two or three weeks of really concentrated study in a clinical atmosphere; say, the Barringer Clinic in Dayton."

Chris looked away.

"It's a problem?"

"No. No problem," She sighed. "I just lost *Hope*, that's all."

"Didn't get you."

"It's an inside tragedy."

The psychiatrist telephoned the Barringer Clinic from Chris's study. They agreed to take Regan the following day.

The doctors left.

Chris swallowed pain with remembrance of Dennings, with remembrance of death and the worm and the void and unspeakable loneliness and stillness, darkness, underneath the sod, with nothing moving, no, no motion. . . . Briefly, she wept. *Too much . . . too much . . .* Then she put it away and began to pack.

She was standing in her bedroom selecting a camouflaging wig to wear in Dayton when Karl appeared. There was someone to see her, he told her.

"Who?"

"Detective."

"And he wants to see *me*?"

He nodded. Then he handed her a business card. She looked it over blankly. WILLIAM F. KINDERMAN, it announced, LIEUTENANT OF DETECTIVES; and tucked in the lower-left-hand corner like a poor relation: *Homicide Division.* It was printed in an ornate, raised Tudor typeface that might have been selected by a dealer in antiques.

She looked up from the card with a sniffing suspicion. "Has he got something with him that might be a script? Like a big manila envelope or something?"

There was no one in the world, Chris had come to discover, who didn't have a novel or a script or a notion for one or both tucked away in a drawer or a mental sock. She seemed to attract them as priests did drunks.

But Karl shook his head. Chris immediately grew curious and walked down the stairs. Burke? Was it something to do with Burke?

He was sagging in the entry hall, the brim of his limp and crumpled hat clutched tight with short fat fingers freshly manicured. Plump. In his middle fifties. Jowly cheeks that gleamed of soap. Yet rumpled trousers, cuffed and baggy, mocked the sedulous care that he gave his body. A gray tweed coat hung loose and old-fashioned, and his moist brown eyes, which dropped at the corners, seemed to be staring at times gone by. He wheezed asthmatically as he waited.

Chris approached. The detective extended his hand with a weary and somewhat fatherly manner, and spoke in a hoarse, emphysematous whisper. "I'd know that face in any lineup, Miss MacNeil."

"Am I *in* one?" Chris asked him earnestly as she took his hand.

"Oh, my goodness, oh, no," he said, brushing at the notion with his hand as if swatting at a fly. He'd closed his eyes and inclined his head; the other hand rested lightly on his paunch. Chris was expecting a *God forbid!* "No, it's strictly routine," he assured her, "routine. Look, you're busy? Tomorrow. I'll come again tomorrow."

He was turning away as if to leave, but Chris said anxiously, "What is it? Burke? Burke Dennings?"

The detective's drooping, careless ease had somehow tightened the springs of her tension.

"A shame. What a shame," the detective breathed with lowered eyes and a shake of the head.

"Was he *killed?*" Chris asked with a look of shock. "I mean, is that why you're here? He was killed? Is that it?"

"No, no, no, it's routine," he repeated, "routine. You know, a man so important, we just couldn't pass it. We couldn't," he pleaded with a helpless look. "At least one or two questions. Did he fall? Was he pushed?" As he asked, he was listing from side to side with his head and his hand. Then he shrugged and huskily whispered, "Who knows?"

"Was he *robbed?*"

"No, not robbed, Miss MacNeil, never robbed, but then who needs a motive in times like these?" His hands were constantly in motion, like a flabby glove informed by the fingers of a yawning puppeteer. "Why, today, for a murderer, Miss MacNeil, a motive is only an encumbrance; in fact, a deterrent." He shook his head. "These drugs, these drugs," he bemoaned. "These drugs. This LSD."

He looked at Chris as he tapped his chest with the tips of his fingers. "Believe me, I'm a father, and when I see what's going on, it breaks my heart. You've got children?"

"Yes, one."

"A son?"

"A daughter."

"Well . . ."

"Listen, come on in the study," Chris interrupted anxiously, turning about to lead the way. She was losing all patience.

"Miss MacNeil, could I trouble you for something?"

She turned with the dim and weary expectation that he wanted her autograph for his children. It was never for themselves. It was always for their children. "Yeah, sure," she said.

"My stomach." He gestured with a trace of a grimace. "Do you keep any Calso water, maybe? If it's trouble, never mind; I don't want to be trouble."

"No, no trouble at all," she sighed. "Grab a chair in the study." She pointed, then turned and headed for the kitchen. "I think there's a bottle in the fridge."

"No, I'll come to the kitchen," he told her, following. "I hate to be a bother."

"No bother."

"No, really, you're busy, I'll come. You've got children?" he asked as they walked. "No, that's right; yes, a daughter; you told me; that's right. Just the one."

"Just the one."

"And how old?"

"She just turned twelve."

"Then you don't have to worry," he breathed. "No, not yet. Later on, though, watch out." He was shaking his head. Chris noticed that his walk was a modified waddle. "When you see all the sickness day in and day out," he continued. "Unbelievable. Incredible. Crazy. You know, I looked at my wife just a couple of days ago—or weeks ago—I forget. I said,

Mary, the world—the *entire world*—is having a massive nervous breakdown. All. The whole world." He gestured globally.

They had entered the kitchen, where Karl was polishing the interior of the oven. He neither turned nor acknowledged their presence.

"This is really so embarrassing," the detective wheezed hoarsely as Chris was opening the refrigerator door. Yet his gaze was on Karl, brushing swiftly and questioningly over his back and his arms and his neck like a small, dark bird skimming over a lake. "I meet a famous motion-picture star," he continued, "and I ask for some Calso water. Ah, boy."

Chris had found the bottle and now was looking for an opener. "Ice?" she asked.

"No, plain; plain is fine."

She was opening the bottle.

"You know that film you made called *Angel?*" he said. "I saw that film six times."

"If you were looking for the killer," she murmured as she poured out the bubbling Calso, "arrest the producer and the cutter."

"Oh, no, no, it was excellent—really—I loved it!"

"Sit down." She was nodding at the table.

"Oh, thank you." He sat. "No, the film was just lovely," he insisted. "So touching. But just one thing," he ventured, "one little tiny, minuscule point. Oh, thank you."

She'd set down the glass of Calso and sat on the other side of the table, hands clasped before her.

"One minor flaw," he resumed apologetically. "Only minor. And please believe me, I'm only a layman. You know? I'm just audience. What do I know? However, it seemed to me— to a layman—that the musical score was getting in the way of certain scenes. It was too intrusive." He was earnest now; caught up. "It kept on reminding me that this was a movie. You know? Like so many of these fancy camera angles lately.

134

So distracting. Incidentally, the score, Miss MacNeil—did he steal that perhaps from Mendelssohn?"

Chris drummed her fingertips lightly on the table. Strange detective. And why was he constantly glancing to Karl?

"I wouldn't know," she said, "but I'm glad you liked the picture. Better drink that," she told him, nodding to the Calso. "It tends to get flat."

"Yes, of course. I'm so garrulous. You're busy. Forgive me." He lifted the glass as if in toast and drained its contents, his little finger arching demurely away from the others. "Ah, good, that's good," he exhaled, contented, as he put aside the glass, his eye falling lightly on Regan's sculpture of the bird. It was now the centerpiece of the table, its beak floating mockingly and at length above the salt and pepper shakers. "Quaint." He smiled. "Nice." He looked up. "The artist?"

"My daughter," Chris told him.

"Very nice."

"Look, I hate to be—"

"Yes, yes, I know, I'm a nuisance. Well, look, just a question or two and we're done. In fact, only one question and then I'll be going." He was glancing at his wristwatch as if he were anxious to get away to some appointment. "Since poor Mr. Dennings," he labored breathily, "had completed his filming in this area, we wondered if he might have been visiting someone on the night of the accident. Now other than yourself, of course, did he have any friends in this area?"

"Oh, he was *here* that night," Chris told him.

"Oh?" His eyebrows sickled upward. "Near the time of the accident?"

"When did it happen?" she asked him.

"Seven-o-five," he told her.

"Yes, I think so."

"Well, that settles it, then." He nodded, turning in his chair as if preparatory to rising. "He was drunk, he was leaving, he fell down the steps. Yes, that settles it. Definitely.

Listen, though, just for the sake of the record, can you tell me approximately what time he left the house?"

He was pawing at truth like a weary bachelor pinching vegetables at market. How did he ever make lieutenant? Chris wondered. "I don't know," she replied. "I didn't see him."

"I don't understand."

"Well, he came and left while I was out. I was over at a doctor's office in Rosslyn."

"Ah, I see." He nodded. "Of course. But then how do you know he was here?"

"Oh, well, Sharon said—"

"Sharon?" he interrupted.

"Sharon Spencer. She's my secretary. She was here when Burke dropped by. She—"

"He came to see *her*?" he asked.

"No, me."

"Yes, of course. Yes, forgive me for interrupting."

"My daughter was sick and Sharon left him here while she went to pick up some prescriptions. By the time I got home, though, Burke was gone."

"And what time was that, please?"

"Seven-fifteen or so, seven-thirty."

"And what time had you left?"

"Maybe six-fifteenish."

"What time had Miss Spencer left?"

"I don't know."

"And between the time Miss Spencer left and the time you returned, who was here in the house with Mr. Dennings besides your daughter?"

"No one."

"No one? He left her alone?"

She nodded.

"No servants?"

"No, Willie and Karl were—"

"Who are they?"

Chris abruptly felt the earth shift under her feet. The nuzzling interview, she realized, was suddenly steely interrogation. "Well, Karl's right there." She motioned with her head, her glance fixed dully on the servant's back. Still polishing the oven . . . "And Willie's his wife," she resumed. "They're my housekeepers." Polishing . . . "They'd taken the afternoon off and when I got home, they weren't back yet. Willie . . ." Chris paused.

"Willie what?"

"Oh, well, nothing." She shrugged as she tugged her gaze away from the manservant's brawny back. The oven was clean, she had noticed. Why was Karl still polishing?

She reached for a cigarette. Kinderman lit it.

"So then only your daughter would know when Dennings left the house."

"It was really an accident?"

"Oh, of course. It's routine, Miss MacNeil, it's routine. Mr. Dennings wasn't robbed and he had no enemies, none that we know of, that is, in the District."

Chris darted a momentary glance to Karl but then shifted it quickly back to Kinderman. Had he noticed? Apparently not. He was fingering the sculpture.

"It's got a name, this kind of bird; I can't think of it. Something." He noticed Chris staring and looked vaguely embarrassed. "Forgive me, you're busy. Well, a minute and we're done. Now your daughter, she would know when Mr. Dennings left?"

"No, she wouldn't. She was heavily sedated."

"Ah, dear me, a shame, a shame." His droopy eyelids seeped concern. "It's serious?"

"Yes, I'm afraid it is."

"May I ask . . . ?" he probed with a delicate gesture.

"We still don't know."

"Watch out for drafts," he cautioned firmly.

Chris looked blank.

"A draft in the winter when a house is hot is a magic carpet for bacteria. My mother used to say that. Maybe that's folk myth. Maybe." He shrugged. "But a myth, to speak plainly, to me is like a menu in a fancy French restaurant: glamorous, complicated camouflage for a fact you wouldn't otherwise swallow, like maybe lima beans," he said earnestly.

Chris relaxed. The shaggy dog padding fuddled through cornfields had returned.

"That's hers, that's her room"—he was thumbing toward the ceiling—"with that great big window looking out on those steps?"

Chris nodded.

"Keep the window closed and she'll get better."

"Well, it's always closed and it's always shuttered," Chris said as he dipped a pudgy hand in the inside pocket of his jacket.

"She'll get better," he repeated sententiously. "Just remember, 'An ounce of prevention . . .' "

Chris drummed her fingertips on the tabletop again.

"You're busy. Well, we're finished. Just a note for the record—routine—we're all done."

From the pocket of the jacket he'd extracted a crumpled mimeographed program of a high-school production of *Cyrano de Bergerac* and now groped in the pockets of his coat, where he netted a toothmarked yellow stub of a number 2 pencil, whose point had the look of having been sharpened with the blade of a scissors. He pressed the program flat on the table, brushing out the wrinkles. "Now just a name or two," he puffed. "That's Spencer with a c?"

"Yes, c."

"A c," he repeated, writing the name in a margin of the program. "And the housekeepers? John and Willie . . . ?"

"*Karl* and Willie Engstrom."

"Karl. That's right, it's Karl. Karl Engstrom." He scribbled the names in a dark, thick script. "Now the times I remem-

138

ber," he told her huskily, turning the program around in search of white space. "Times I— Oh. Oh, no, wait. I forgot. Yes, the housekeepers. You said they got home at what time?"

"I didn't say. Karl, what time did you get in last night?" Chris called to him.

The Swiss turned around, his face inscrutable. "Exactly nine-thirty, madam."

"Yeah, that's right, you'd forgotten your key. I remember I looked at the clock in the kitchen when you rang the door-bell."

"You saw a good film?" the detective asked Karl. "I never go by reviews," he explained to Chris in a breathy aside. "It's what the *people* think, the *audience*."

"Paul Scofield in *Lear*," Karl informed the detective.

"Ah, I saw that; that's excellent. Excellent. Marvelous."

"Yes, at the Crest," Karl continued. "The six-o'clock show-ing. Then immediately after I take the bus from in front of the theater and—"

"Please, that's not necessary," the detective protested with a gesture. "*Please.*"

"I don't mind."

"If you insist."

"I get off at Wisconsin Avenue and M Street. Nine-twenty, perhaps. And then I walk to the house."

"Look, you didn't have to tell me," the detective told him, "but anyway, thank you, it was very considerate. You liked the film?"

"It was excellent."

"Yes, I thought so too. Exceptional. Well, now . . ." He turned back to Chris and to scribbling on the program. "I've wasted your time, but I have a job." He shrugged. "Well, only a moment and finished. Tragic . . . tragic . . ." he breathed as he jotted down fragments in margins. "Such a talent. And a man who knew people, I'm sure: how to handle them. With so many elements who could make him look good or maybe make him look bad—like the cameraman, the sound man, the composer, whatever. . . . Please correct me if I'm wrong, but it seems to me nowadays a director of importance has also to be almost a Dale Carnegie. Am I wrong?"

"Oh, well, Burke had a temper," Chris sighed.

The detective repositioned the program. "Ah, well, maybe so with the big shots. People his size." Once again he was scribbling. "But the key is the little people, the menials, the people who handle the minor details that if they didn't handle *right* would be *major* details. Don't you think?"

Chris glanced at her fingernails and ruefully shook her head. "When Burke let fly, he never discriminated," she murmured with a weak, wry smile. "No, sir. It was only when he drank, though."

"Finished. We're finished." Kinderman was dotting a final *i*. "Oh, no, wait," he abruptly remembered. "Mrs. Engstrom. They went and came together?" He was gesturing toward Karl.

"No, she went to see a Beatles film," Chris answered just as Karl was turning to reply. "She got in a few minutes after I did."

"Why did I ask that? It wasn't important." He shrugged as he folded up the program and tucked it away in the pocket of his jacket along with the pencil. "Well, that's that. When I'm back in the office, no doubt I'll remember something I *should* have asked. With me, that always happens. Oh, well, I could call you," he puffed, standing up.

Chris rose along with him.

"Well, I'm going out of town for a couple of weeks," she said.

"It can wait," he assured her. "It can wait." He was staring at the sculpture with a smiling fondness. "Cute. So cute," he said. He'd leaned over and picked it up and was rubbing his thumb along its beak.

Chris bent over to pick up a thread on the kitchen floor.

"Have you got a good doctor?" the detective asked her. "I mean for your daughter."

He replaced the figure and began to leave. Glumly Chris followed, winding the thread around her thumb.

"Well, I've sure got enough of them," she murmured. "Anyway, I'm checking her into a clinic that's supposed to be great at doing what you do, only with viruses."

"Let's hope they're a great deal better. It's out of town, this clinic?"

"Yes, it is."

"It's a good one?"

"We'll see."

"Keep her out of the draft."

They had reached the front door of the house. He put a hand on the doorknob. "Well, I would say that it's been a pleasure, but under the circumstances . . ." He bowed his head and shook it. "I'm sorry. Really. I'm terribly sorry."

Chris folded her arms and looked down at the rug. She nodded briefly.

Kinderman opened the door and stepped outside. As he turned to Chris, he was putting on his hat. "Well, good luck with your daughter."

"Thanks." She smiled wanly. "Good luck with the world."

He nodded with a gentle warmth and sadness, then waddled away. Chris watched as he listed toward a waiting squad car parked near the corner in front of a fire hydrant. He flung up a hand to his hat as a shearing wind sprang sharp from the south. The hem of his coat flapped. Chris closed the door.

When he'd entered the passenger side of the squad car, Kinderman turned and looked back at the house. He thought he saw movement at Regan's window, a quick, lithe figure flashing to the side and out of view. He wasn't sure. He'd seen it peripherally as he'd turned. But he noted that the shutters were open. Odd. For a moment he waited. No one appeared. With a puzzled frown, the detective turned and opened the glove compartment, extracting a small brown envelope and a penknife. Unclasping the smallest of the blades of the knife, he held his thumb inside the envelope and surgically scraped paint from Regan's sculpture from under his thumbnail. When he had finished and was sealing the envelope, he nodded to the detective-sergeant behind the wheel. They pulled away.

As they drove down Prospect Street, Kinderman pocketed the envelope. "Take it easy," he cautioned the sergeant, glancing at the traffic building up ahead. "This is business, not pleasure." He rubbed at his eyes with weary fingers. "Ah, what a life," he sighed. "What a life."

Later that evening, while Dr. Klein was injecting Regan with fifty milligrams of Sparine to assure her tranquillity on the journey to Dayton, Lieutenant Kinderman stood brooding in his office, palms pressed flat atop his desk as he pored over fragments of baffling data. The narrow beam of an ancient desk lamp flared on a clutter of scattered reports. There was no other light. He believed that it helped him narrow the focus of concentration.

Kinderman's breathing labored heavy in the darkness as his glance flitted here, now there. Then he took a deep breath and shut his eyes. *Mental Clearance Sale!* he instructed himself, as he did whenever he wished to tidy his brain for a fresh point of view: *Absolutely Everything Must Go!*

When he opened his eyes, he examined the pathologist's report on Dennings:

> . . . tearing of the spinal cord with fractured skull and neck, plus numerous contusions, lacerations and abrasions; stretching of the neck skin; ecchymosis of the neck skin; shearing

of platysma, sternomastoid, splenius, trapezius and various smaller muscles of the neck, with fracture of the spine and of the vertebrae and shearing of both the anterior and posterior spinous ligaments . . .

He looked out a window at the dark of the city. The Capitol dome light glowed. The Congress was working late. He shut his eyes again, recalling his conversation with the District pathologist at eleven-fifty-five on the night of Dennings' death.

"*It could have happened in the fall?*"

"*No, it's very unlikely. The sternomastoids and the trapezius muscles alone are enough to prevent it. Then you've also got the various articulations of the cervical spine to be overcome as well as the ligaments holding the bones together.*"

"*Speaking plainly, however, is it possible?*"

"*Well, of course, he was drunk and these muscles were doubtless somewhat relaxed. Perhaps if the force of the initial impact were sufficiently powerful and—*"

"*Falling maybe twenty or thirty feet before he hit?*"

"*Yes, that, and if immediately after impact his head got stuck in something; in other words, if there were immediate interference with the normal rotation of the head and body as a unit, well maybe—I say just maybe—you could get this result.*"

"*Could another human being have done it?*"

"*Yes, but he'd have to be an exceptionally powerful man.*"

Kinderman had checked Karl Engstrom's story regarding his whereabouts at the time of Dennings' death. The show times matched, as did the schedule that night of a D.C. Transit bus. Moreover, the driver of the bus that Karl had claimed he had boarded by the theater went off duty at Wisconsin and M, where Karl had stated he alighted at approximately twenty minutes after nine. A change of drivers had taken place, and the off-duty driver had logged the time of his arrival at the transfer point: precisely nine-eighteen.

Yet on Kinderman's desk was a record of a felony charge against Engstrom on August 27, 1963, alleging he had stolen a quantity of narcotics over a period of months from the home of a doctor in Beverly Hills where he and Willie were then employed.

> . . . born April 20, 1921, in Zurich, Switzerland. Married to Willie nee Braun September 7, 1941. Daughter, Elvira, born New York City, January 11, 1943, current address unknown. Defendant . . .

The remainder the detective found baffling:

The doctor, whose testimony was *sine qua non* for successful prosecution, abruptly—and without any explanation—dropped the charges.

Why had he done so?

The Engstroms were hired by Chris MacNeil only two months later, which meant that the doctor had given them a favorable reference.

Why would he do so?

Engstrom had certainly pilfered the drugs, and yet a medical examination at the time of the charge had failed to yield the slightest sign that the man was an addict, or even a user.

Why not?

With his eyes still closed, the detective softly recited Lewis Carroll's "Jabberwocky": " ' 'Twas brillig and the slithy toves . . .' " Another of his mind-clearing tricks.

When he'd finished reciting, he opened his eyes and fixed his gaze on the Capitol rotunda, trying to keep his mind a blank. But as usual, he found the task impossible. Sighing, he glanced at the police psychologist's report on the recent desecrations at Holy Trinity: "*. . . statue . . . phallus . . . human excrement . . . Damien Karras,*" he had underscored in red. He breathed in the silence and then reached for a scholarly work on witchcraft, turning to a page he had marked with a paper clip:

Black Mass . . . a form of devil worship, the ritual, in the main, consisting of (1) exhortation (the "sermon") to performance of evil among the community, (2) coition with the demon (reputedly painful, the demon's penis invariably described as "icy cold"), and (3) a variety of desecrations that were largely sexual in nature. For example, communion Hosts of unusual size were prepared (compounded of flour, feces, menstrual blood and pus), which then were slit and used as artificial vaginas with which the priests would ferociously copulate while raving that they were ravishing the Virgin Mother of God or that they were sodomizing Christ. In another instance of such practice, a statue of Christ was inserted deep in a girl's vagina while into her anus was inserted the Host, which the priest then crushed as he shouted blasphemies and sodomized the girl. Life-sized images of Christ and the Virgin Mary also played a frequent role in the ritual. The image of the Virgin, for example—usually painted to give her a dissolute, sluttish appearance—was equipped with breasts which the cultists sucked and also a vagina into which the penis might be inserted. The statues of Christ were equipped with a phallus for fellatio by both the men and the women, and also for insertion into the vagina of the women and the anus of the men. Occasionally, rather than an image, a human figure was bound to a cross and made to function in place of the statue, and upon the discharge of his semen it was collected in a blasphemously consecrated chalice and used in the making of the communion host, which was destined to be consecrated on an altar covered with excrement. This—

Kinderman flipped the pages to an underlined paragraph dealing with ritualistic murder. He read it slowly, nibbling at the pad of an index finger, and when he had finished he frowned at the page and shook his head. He lifted a brooding glance to the lamp. He flicked it out. He left his office and drove to the morgue.

The young attendant at the desk was munching at a ham

and cheese sandwich on rye, and brushed the crumbs from a crossword puzzle as Kinderman approached him.

"Dennings," the detective whispered hoarsely.

The attendant nodded, filling in a five-letter horizontal, then rose with his sandwich and moved down the hall. Kinderman followed him, hat in hand, followed faint scent of caraway seed and mustard to rows of refrigerated lockers, to the dreamless cabinet used for the filing of sightless eyes.

They halted at locker 32. The expressionless attendant slid it out. He bit at his sandwich, and a fragment of mayonnaise-speckled crust fell lightly to the shroud.

For a moment, Kinderman stared down; then, slowly and gently, he pulled back the sheet to expose what he'd seen and yet could not accept.

Burke Dennings' head was turned completely around, facing backward.

five

Cupped in the warm, green hollow of the campus, Damien Karras jogged alone around an oval, loamy track in khaki shorts and a cotton T-shirt drenched with the cling of healing sweat. Up ahead, on a hillock, the lime-white dome of the astronomical observatory pulsed with the beat of his stride; behind him, the medical school fell away with churned-up shards of earth and care.

Since release from his duties, he came here daily, lapping the miles and chasing sleep. He had almost caught it; almost eased the clutch of grief that gripped at his heart like a deep tattoo. It held him gentler now.

Twenty laps . . .

Much gentler.

More! Two more!

Much gentler . . .

Powerful leg muscles blooded and stinging, rippling with a

long and leonine grace, Karras thumped around a turn when he noticed someone sitting on a bench to the side where he'd laid out his towel, sweater and pants: a middle-aged man in a floppy overcoat and pulpy, crushed felt hat. He seemed to be watching him. Was he? Yes . . . head turning as Karras passed.

The priest accelerated, digging at the final lap with pounding strides that jarred the earth, then he slowed to a panting, gulping walk as he passed the bench without a glance, both hands pressed light to his throbbing sides. The heave of his rock-muscled chest and shoulders stretched his T-shirt, distorting the stenciled word PHILOSOPHERS inscribed across the front in once-black letters now faded to a hint by repeated washings.

The man in the overcoat stood up and began to approach him.

"Father Karras?" Lieutenant Kinderman called hoarsely.

The priest turned around and nodded briefly, squinting into sunlight, waiting for Kinderman to reach him, then beckoned him along as once again he began to move. "Do you mind? I'll cramp," he panted.

"Yes, of course," the detective answered, nodding with a wincing lack of enthusiasm as he tucked his hands into his pockets. The walk from the parking lot had tired him.

"Have—have we met?" asked the Jesuit.

"No, Father. No, but they said that you looked like a boxer; some priest at the residence hall; I forget." He was tugging out his wallet. "So bad with names."

"And yours?"

"William Kinderman, Father." He flashed his identification. "Homicide."

"Really?" Karras scanned the badge and identification card with a shining, boyish interest. Flushed and perspiring, his face had an eager look of innocence as he turned to the waddling detective. "What's this about?"

"Hey, you know something, Father?" Kinderman answered,

inspecting the Jesuit's rugged features. "It's true, you *do* look like a boxer. Excuse me; that scar, you know, there by your eye?" He was pointing. "Like Brando, it looks like, in *Waterfront*, just *exactly* Marlon Brando. They gave him a scar"—he was illustrating, pulling at the corner of his eye—"that made his eye look a little bit closed, just a little, made him look a little dreamy all the time, always sad. Well, that's you," he said, pointing. "You're Brando. People tell you that, Father?"

"No, they don't."

"Ever box?"

"Oh, a little."

"You're from here in the District?"

"New York."

"Golden Gloves. Am I right?"

"You just made captain." Karras smiled. "Now what can I do for you?"

"Walk a little slower, please. Emphysema." The detective was gesturing at his throat.

"Oh, I'm sorry." Karras slowed his pace.

"Never mind. Do you smoke?"

"Yes, I do."

"You shouldn't."

"Well, now tell me the problem."

"Of course; I'm digressing. Incidentally, you're busy?" the detective inquired. "I'm not interrupting?"

"Interrupting what?" asked Karras, bemused.

"Well, mental prayer, perhaps."

"You *will* make captain." Karras smiled cryptically.

"Pardon me, I missed something?"

Karras shook his head; but the smile lingered. "I doubt that you ever miss a thing," he remarked. His sidelong glance toward Kinderman was sly and warmly twinkling.

Kinderman halted and mounted a massive and hopeless effort at looking befuddled, but glancing at the Jesuit's crinkling eyes, he lowered his head and chuckled ruefully. "Ah, well.

Of course . . . of course . . . a psychiatrist. Who am I kidding?"
He shrugged. "Look, it's habit with me, Father. Forgive me.
Schmaltz—that's the Kinderman method: pure *schmaltz*.
Well, I'll stop and tell you straight what it's all about."

"The desecrations," Karras said, nodding.

"So I wasted my schmaltz," the detective said quietly.

"Sorry."

"Never mind, Father; that I deserved. Yes, the things in the
church," he confirmed. "Correct. Only maybe something else
besides, something serious."

"Murder?"

"Yes. Kick me again, I enjoy it."

"Well, Homicide Division." The Jesuit shrugged.

"Never mind, never mind, Marlon Brando; never mind.
People tell you for a priest you're a little bit smart-ass?"

"*Mea culpa*," Karras murmured. Though he was smiling, he
felt a regret that perhaps he'd diminished the man's self-
esteem. He hadn't meant to. And now he felt glad of a chance
to express a sincere perplexity. "I don't get it, though," he
added, taking care that he wrinkled his brow. "What's the connection?"

"Look, Father, could we keep this between us? Confidential?
Like a matter of confession, so to speak?"

"Of course." He was eyeing the detective earnestly. "What
is it?"

"You know that director who was doing the film here,
Father? Burke Dennings?"

"Well, I've seen him."

"You've seen him." The detective nodded. "You're also
familiar with how he died?"

"Well, the papers . . ." Karras shrugged again.

"That's just part of it."

"Oh?"

"Only part of it. Part. Just a part. Listen, what do you know
on the subject of witchcraft?"

"What?"

"Listen, patience; I'm leading up to something. Now witch-craft, please—you're familiar?"

"A little."

"From the witching end, not the hunting."

"Oh, I once did a paper on it." Karras smiled. "The psychiatric end."

"Oh, really? Wonderful! Great! That's a bonus. A plus. You could help me a lot, a lot more than I thought. Listen, Father. Now witchcraft . . ."

He reached up and gripped at the Jesuit's arm as they rounded a turn and approached the bench. "Now me, I'm a layman and, plainly speaking, not well educated. Not formally. No. But I read. Look, I know what they say about self-made men, that they're horrible examples of unskilled labor. But me, I'll speak plainly, I'm not ashamed. Not at all, I'm—"Abruptly he arrested the flow, looked down and shook his head. "*Schmaltz*. It's habit. I can't stop the *schmaltz*. Look, forgive me; you're busy."

"Yes, I'm praying."

The Jesuit's soft delivery had been dry and expressionless. Kinderman halted for a moment and eyed him. "You're serious? No."

The detective faced forward again and they walked. "Look, I'll come to the point: the desecrations. They remind you of anything to do with witchcraft?"

"Maybe. Some rituals used in Black Mass."

"A-plus. And now Dennings—you read how he died?"

"In a fall."

"Well, I'll tell you, and—*please*—*confidential!*"

"Of course."

The detective looked suddenly pained as he realized that Karras had no intention of stopping at the bench. "Do you mind?" he asked wistfully.

"What?"

151

"Could we stop? Maybe sit?"

"Oh, sure." They began to move back toward the bench.

"You won't cramp?"

"No, I'm fine now."

"You're sure?"

"I'm fine."

"All right, all right, if you insist."

"You were saying?"

"In a second, please, just one second."

Kinderman settled his aching bulk on the bench with a sigh of content. "Ah, better, that's better," he said as the Jesuit picked up his towel and wiped his perspiring face. "Middle age. What a life."

"Burke Dennings?"

"Burke Dennings, Burke Dennings, Burke Dennings . . ." The detective was nodding down at his shoes. Then he glanced up at Karras. The priest was wiping the back of his neck. "Burke Dennings, good Father, was found at the bottom of that long flight of steps at exactly five minutes after seven with his head turned completely around and backward."

Peppery shouts drifted muffled from the baseball diamond where the varsity team held practice. Karras stopped wiping and held the lieutenant's steady gaze. "It didn't happen in the fall?" he said at last.

"Sure, it's possible." Kinderman shrugged. "But . . ."

"Unlikely," Karras brooded.

"And so what comes to mind in the context of witchcraft?"

The Jesuit sat down slowly, looking pensive. "Well," he said finally, "supposedly demons broke the necks of witches that way. At least, that's the myth."

"A myth?"

"Oh, largely," he said, turning to Kinderman. "Although people did die that way, I suppose: likely members of a coven who either defected or gave away secrets. That's just a guess. But I know it was a trademark of demonic assassins."

Kinderman nodded. "Exactly. Exactly. I remembered the connection from a murder in London. That's *now*. I mean, lately, just four or five years ago, Father. I remembered that I read it in the papers."

"Yes, I read it too, but I think it turned out to be some sort of hoax. Am I wrong?"

"No, that's right, Father, absolutely right. But in this case, at least, you can see some connection, maybe, with that and the things in the church. Maybe somebody crazy, Father, maybe someone with a spite against the Church. Some unconscious rebellion, perhaps . . ."

"Sick priest," murmured Karras. "That it?"

"Listen, you're the psychiatrist, Father; you tell me."

"Well, of course, the desecrations are clearly pathological," Karras said thoughtfully, slipping on his sweater. "And if Dennings was murdered—well, I'd guess that the killer's pathological too."

"And perhaps had some knowledge of witchcraft?"

"Could be."

"Could be," the detective grunted. "So who fits the bill, also lives in the neighborhood, and also has access in the night to the church?"

"Sick priest," Karras said, reaching out moodily beside him to a pair of sun-bleached khaki pants.

"Listen, Father, this is hard for you—please!—I understand. But for priests on the campus here, you're the psychiatrist, Father, so—"

"No, I've had a change of assignment."

"Oh, really? In the middle of the year?"

"That's the Order." Karras shrugged as he pulled on the pants.

"Still, you'd know who was sick at the time and who wasn't, correct? I mean, *this* kind of sickness. You'd *know* that."

"No, not necessarily, Lieutenant. Not at all. It would only

be an accident, in fact, if I did. You see, I'm not a psycho-analyst. All I do is counsel. Anyway," he commented, buttoning his trousers, "I really know of no one who fits the description."

"Ah, yes; doctor's ethics. If you knew, you wouldn't tell."

"No, I probably wouldn't."

"Incidentally—and I mention it only in passing—this ethic is lately considered illegal. Not to bother you with trivia, but lately a psychiatrist in sunny California, no less, was put in jail for not telling the police what he knew about a patient."

"That a threat?"

"Don't talk paranoid. I mention it in passing."

"I could always tell the judge it was a matter of confession," said the Jesuit, grinning wryly as he stood to tuck his shirt in. "Plainly speaking," he added.

The detective glanced up at him, faintly gloomy. "Want to go into business, Father?" he said. Then looked away dismally. " 'Father' . . . what 'Father'?" he asked rhetorically. "You're a Jew; I could tell when I met you."

The Jesuit chuckled.

"Yes, laugh," said Kinderman. "Laugh." But then he smiled, looking impishly pleased with himself. He turned with beaming eyes. "That reminds me. The entrance examination to be a policeman, Father? When I took it, one question went something like: 'What are rabies and what would you do for them?' Know what some dumbhead put down for an answer? *Emis?* 'Rabies,' he said, 'are Jew priests, and I would do anything that I could for them.' Honest!" He'd raised up a hand as in oath.

Karras laughed. "Come on, I'll walk you to your car. Are you parked in the lot?"

The detective looked up at him, reluctant to move. "Then we're finished?"

The priest put a foot on the bench, leaning over, an arm resting heavily on his knee. "Look, I'm really not covering up," he said. "Really. If I knew of a priest like the one you're looking

154

for, the least I would do is to tell you that there was such a man without giving you his name. Then I guess I'd report it to the Provincial. But I don't know of anyone who even comes close."

"Ah, well," the detective sighed. "I never thought it was a priest in the first place. Not really." He nodded toward the parking lot. "Yes, I'm over there."

They started walking.

"What I really suspect," the detective continued, "if I said it out loud you would call me a nut. I don't know. I don't know." He was shaking his head. "All these clubs and these cults where they kill for no reason. It makes you start thinking peculiar things. To keep up with the times, these days, you have to be a little bit crazy."

Karras nodded.

"What's that thing on your shirt?" the detective asked him, motioning his head toward the Jesuit's chest.

"What thing?"

"On the T-shirt," the detective clarified. "The writing. 'Philosophers.'"

"Oh, I taught a few courses one year," said Karras, "at Woodstock Seminary in Maryland. I played on the lower-class baseball team. They were called the Philosophers."

"Ah, and the upper-class team?"

"Theologians."

Kinderman smiled and shook his head. "Theologians three, Philosophers two," he mused.

"Philosophers three, Theologians two."

"Of course."

"Of course."

"Strange things," the detective brooded. "Strange. Listen, Father," he began on a reticent tack. "Listen, *doctor*. . . . Am I crazy, or could there be maybe a witch coven here in the District right now? Right today?"

"Oh, come on," said Karras.

"Then there could."

"Didn't get that."

"Now *I'll* be the doctor," the detective announced to him, punching at the air with an index finger. "You didn't say no, but instead you were smart-ass again. That's defensive, good Father, defensive. You're afraid you'll look gullible, maybe; a superstitious priest in front of Kinderman the mastermind, the rationalist"—he was tapping the finger at his temple—"the genius beside you, here, the walking Age of Reason. Right? Am I right?"

The Jesuit stared at him now with mounting surmise and respect. "Why, that's very astute," he remarked.

"Well, all right, then," Kinderman grunted. "So I'll ask you again: could there maybe be witch covens here in the District?"

"Well, I really wouldn't know," answered Karras thoughtfully, arms folded across his chest. "But in parts of Europe they say Black Mass."

"Today?"

"Today."

"You mean just like the old days, Father? Look, I read about those things, incidentally, with the sex and the statues and who knows whatever. Not meaning to disgust you, by the way, but they did all those things? It's for real?"

"I don't know."

"Your opinion, then, Father Defensive."

The Jesuit chuckled. "All right, then; I think it's for real. Or at least I suspect so. But most of my reasoning's based on pathology. Sure, Black Mass. But anyone doing those things is a very disturbed human being, and disturbed in a very special way. There's a clinical name for that kind of disturbance, in fact; it's called satanism—means people who can't have any sexual pleasure unless it's connected to a blasphemous action. Well, it's not that uncommon, not even today, and Black Mass was just used as the justification."

"Again, please forgive me, but the things with the statues of Jesus and Mary?"

"What about them?"

"They're true?"

"Well, I think this might interest you as a policeman." His scholarly interest aroused and stirring, Karras' manner grew quietly animated. "The records of the Paris police still carry the case of a couple of monks from a nearby monastery—let's see . . ." He scratched his head as he tried to recall. "Yes, the one at Crépy, I believe. Well, whatever." He shrugged. "Close by. At any rate, the monks came into an inn and got rather belligerent about wanting a bed for three. Well, the third they were carrying: a life-size statue of the Blessed Mother."

"Ah, boy, that's shocking," breathed the detective. "Shocking."

"But true. And a fair indication that what you've been reading is based on fact."

"Well, the sex, maybe so, maybe so. I can see. That's a whole other story altogether. Never mind. But the ritual murders now, Father? That's true? Now come on! Using blood from the newborn babies?" The detective was alluding to something else he had read in the book on witchcraft, describing how the unfrocked priest at Black Mass would at times slit the wrist of a newborn infant so that the blood poured into a chalice and later was consecrated and consumed in the form of communion. "That's just like the stories they used to tell about the Jews," the detective continued. "How they stole Christian babies and drank their blood. Look, forgive me, but your people told all those stories."

"If we did, forgive me."

"You're absolved, you're absolved."

Something dark, something sad, passed across the priest's eyes, like the shadow of pain briefly remembered. He quickly fixed his eyes on the path just ahead.

"Well, I really don't know about ritual murder," said Karras. "I don't. But a midwife in Switzerland once confessed to the murder of thirty or forty babies for use at Black Mass. Oh, well, maybe she was tortured," he amended. "Who knows? But she certainly told a convincing story. She said she'd hide a long, thin needle up her sleeve, so that when she was delivering the baby, she'd slip out the needle and stick it through the crown of the baby's head, and then hide the needle again. No marks," he said, glancing at Kinderman. "The baby looked stillborn. You've heard of the prejudice European Catholics used to have against midwives? Well, that's how it started."

"That's frightening."

"This century hasn't got the lock on insanity. Anyway—"

"Wait a minute, wait now, forgive me. These stories—they were told by some people who were tortured, correct? So they're basically not so reliable. They signed the confessions and later, the *machers*, they filled in the blanks. I mean, then there was nothing like habeas corpus, no writs of 'Let My People Go,' so to speak. Am I right? Am I right?"

"Yes, you're right, but then too, many of the confessions were voluntary."

"So who would volunteer such things?"

"Well, possibly people who were mentally disturbed."

"Aha! *Another* reliable source!"

"Well, of course you're quite right, Lieutenant. I'm just playing devil's advocate. But one thing that sometimes we tend to forget is that people psychotic enough to confess to such things might conceivably be psychotic enough to have done them. For example, the myths about werewolves. So, fine, they're ridiculous: no one can turn himself into a wolf. But what if a man were so disturbed that he not only thought that he was a werewolf, but also acted like one?"

"Terrible. What is this—theory now, Father, or fact?"

"Well, there's William Stumpf, for example. Or Peter. I can't remember. Anyway, a German in the sixteenth century who thought he was a werewolf. He murdered perhaps twenty or thirty young children."

"You mean, he confessed it?"

"Well, yes, but I think the confession was valid."

"How so?"

"When they caught him, he was eating the brains of his two young daughters-in-law."

From the practice field, crisp in the thin, clear April sunlight, came echoes of chatter and ball against bat. *"C'mon, Mullins, let's shag it, let's go, get the lead out!"*

They had come to the parking lot, priest and detective. They walked now in silence.

When they came to the squad car, Kinderman absently reached out toward the handle of the door. For a moment he paused, then lifted a moody look to Karras.

"So what am I looking for, Father?" he asked him.

"A madman," said Damien Karras softly. "Perhaps someone on drugs."

The detective thought it over, then silently nodded. He turned to the priest. "Want a ride?" he asked, opening the door of the squad car.

"Oh, thanks, but it's just a short walk."

"Never mind that; enjoy!" Kinderman gestured impatiently, motioning Karras to get into the car. "You can tell all your friends you went riding in a police car."

The Jesuit grinned and slipped into the back.

"Very good, very good," the detective breathed hoarsely, then squirmed in beside him and closed the door. "No walk is short," he commented. "None."

With Karras guiding, they drove toward the modern Jesuit residence hall on Prospect Street, where the priest had taken new quarters. To remain in the cottage, he'd felt, might encourage the men he had counseled to continue to seek his professional help.

"You like movies, Father Karras?"

159

"Very much."

"You saw *Lear?*"

"Can't afford it."

"I saw it. I get passes."

"That's nice."

"I get passes for the very best shows. Mrs. K., she gets tired, though; never likes to go."

"That's too bad."

"It's too bad; yes, I hate to go alone. You know, I love to talk film; to discuss; to critique." He was staring out the window, gaze averted to the side and away from the priest.

Karras nodded silently, looking down at his large and very powerful hands. They were clasped between his legs. A moment passed. Then Kinderman hesitantly turned with a wistful look. "Would you like to see a film with me sometime, Father? It's free. . . . I get passes," he added quickly.

The priest looked at him, grinning. "As Elwood P. Dowd used to say in *Harvey*, Lieutenant: When?"

"Oh, I'll call you, I'll call you!" The detective beamed eagerly.

They'd come to the residence hall and parked. Karras put a hand on the door and clicked it open. "Please do. Look, I'm sorry that I wasn't much help."

"Never mind, you were help." Kinderman waved limply. Karras was climbing out of the car. "In fact, for a Jew who's trying to pass, you're a very nice man."

Karras turned, closed the door and leaned into the window with a faint, warm smile. "Do people ever tell you you look like Paul Newman?"

"Always. And believe me, inside this body, Mr. Newman is struggling to get out. Too crowded. Inside," he said, "is also Clark Gable."

Karras waved with a grin and started away.

"Father, wait!"

Karras turned. The detective was squeezing out of the car.

"Listen, Father, I forgot," he puffed, approaching. "Slipped my mind. You know, that card with the dirty writing on it? The one that was found in the church?"

"You mean the altar card?"

"Whatever. It's still around?"

"Yes, I've got it in my room. I was checking the Latin. You want it?"

"Yes, maybe it shows something. Maybe."

"Just a second, I'll get it."

While Kinderman waited outside by the squad car, the Jesuit went to his ground-floor room facing out on Prospect Street and found the card. He came outside again and gave it to Kinderman.

"Maybe some fingerprints," Kinderman wheezed as he looked it over. Then, "No, wait, you've been handling it," he seemed to realize quickly. "Good thinking. Before you, the Jewish Mr. Moto." He was fumbling at the card's clear plastic sheath. "Ah, no, wait, it comes *out*, it comes *out*, it comes *out*!" Then he glanced up at Karras with incipient dismay. "You've been handling the inside as well, Kirk Douglas?"

Karras grinned ruefully, nodding his head.

"Never mind, maybe still we could find something else. Incidentally, you studied this?"

"Yes, I did."

"Your conclusion?"

Karras shrugged. "Doesn't look like the work of a prankster. At first, I thought maybe a student. But I doubt it. Whoever did *that* thing is pretty deeply disturbed."

"As you said."

"And the Latin . . ." Karras brooded. "It's not just flawless, Lieutenant, it's—well, it's got a definite style that's very individual. It's as if whoever did it's used to *thinking* in Latin."

"Do priests?"

"Oh, come on, now!"

"Just answer the question, please, Father Paranoia."

161

"Well, yes; at a point in their training, they do. At least, Jesuits and some of the other orders. At Woodstock Seminary, certain philosophy courses were taught in Latin."

"How so?"

"For precision of thought. It's like law."

"Ah, I see."

Karras suddenly looked earnest; grave. "Look, Lieutenant, can I tell you who I *really* think did it?"

The detective leaned closer. "No, who?"

"Dominicans. Go pick on them."

Karras smiled, waved good-bye and walked away.

"I lied!" the detective called after him sullenly. "You look like Sal Mineo!"

Kinderman watched as the priest gave another little wave and entered the residence hall, then he turned and got into the squad car. He wheezed, sitting motionless, staring at the floorboard. "He hums, he hums, that man," he murmured. "Just like a tuning fork under the water." For a moment longer he held the look; and then turned and told the driver, "All right, back to headquarters. Hurry. Break laws."

They pulled away.

Karras' new room was simply furnished: a single bed, a comfortable chair, a desk and bookshelves built into the wall. On the desk was an early photo of his mother, and in silent rebuke on the wall by his bed hung a metal crucifix.

The narrow room was world enough for him. He cared little for possessions; only that those he had be clean.

He showered, scrubbing briskly, then slipped on khaki pants and a T-shirt and ambled to dinner in the priests' refectory, where he spotted pink-cheeked Dyer sitting alone at a table in a corner. He moved to join him.

"Hi, Damien," said Dyer. The young priest was wearing a faded Snoopy sweatshirt.

Karras bowed his head as he stood by a chair and murmured

a rapid grace. Then he blessed himself, sat and greeted his friend.

"How's the loafer?" asked Dyer as Karras spread a napkin on his lap.

"Who's a loafer? I'm working."

"One lecture a week?"

"It's the quality that counts," said Karras. "What's dinner?"

"Can't you smell it?"

"Oh, shit, is it dog day?" Knackwurst and sauerkraut.

"It's the quantity that counts," replied Dyer serenely.

Karras shook his head and reached out for the aluminum pitcher of milk.

"I wouldn't do that," murmured Dyer without expression as he buttered a slice of whole wheat bread. "See the bubbles? Saltpeter."

"I need it," said Karras. As he tipped up his glass to fill it with milk, he could hear someone joining them at the table.

"Well, I finally read that book," said the newcomer brightly.

Karras glanced up and felt aching dismay, felt the soft crushing weight, press of lead, press of bone, as he recognized the priest who had come to him recently for counseling, the one who could not make friends.

"Oh, and what did you think of it?" Karras asked. He set down the pitcher as if it were the booklet for a broken novena.

The young priest talked, and half an hour later, Dyer was table-hopping, spiking the refectory with laughter. Karras checked his watch. "Want to pick up a jacket?" he asked the young priest. "We can go across the street and take a look at the sunset."

Soon they were leaning against a railing at the top of the steps down to M Street. End of day. The burnished rays of the setting sun flamed glory at the clouds of the western sky and shattered in rippling, crimson dapples on the darkening waters of the river. Once Karras met God in this sight. Long ago. Like a lover forsaken, he still kept the rendezvous.

"Sure a sight," said the younger man.

"Yes, it is," agreed Karras. "I try to get out here every night."

The campus clock boomed out the hour. It was 7:00 P.M.

At 7:23, Lieutenant Kinderman pondered a spectrographic analysis showing that the paint from Regan's sculpture matched a scraping of paint from the desecrated statue of the Virgin Mary.

And at 8:47, in a slum in the northeast section of the city, an impassive Karl Engstrom emerged from a rat-infested tenement house, walked three blocks south to a bus stop, waited alone for a minute, expressionless, then crumpled, sobbing, against a lamppost.

Lieutenant Kinderman, at the time, was at the movies.

six

On Wednesday, May 11, they were back
in the house. They put Regan to bed, installed a lock on the
shutters and stripped all the mirrors from her bedroom and
bathroom.

"... *fewer and fewer lucid moments, and now there's a total
blacking out of her consciousness during the fits, I'm afraid.
That's new and would seem to eliminate genuine hysteria. In
the meantime, a symptom or two in the area of what we call
parapsychic phenomena have. . . ."*

Dr. Klein came by, and Chris attended with Sharon as he
drilled them in proper procedures for administering Sustagen
feedings to Regan during her periods of coma. He inserted the
nasogastric tubing. "First . . ."

Chris forced herself to watch and yet not see her daughter's
face; to grip at the words that the doctor was saying and push
away others she'd heard at the clinic. They seeped through her

consciousness like fog through the branches of a willow tree.

"Now you stated 'No religion' here, Mrs. MacNeil. Is that right? No religious education at all?"

"Oh, well, maybe just 'God.' You know, general. Why?"

"Well, for one thing, the content of much of her raving—when it isn't that gibberish she's been spouting—is religiously oriented. Now where do you think she might get that?"

"Well, give me a for instance."

"Oh, 'Jesus and Mary, sixty-nine,' for ex—"

Klein had guided the tubing into Regan's stomach. "First you check to see if fluid's gotten into the lung," he instructed, pinching on the tube in order to clamp off the flow of Sustagen. "If it . . ."

". . . syndrome of a type of disorder that you rarely ever see anymore, except among primitive cultures. We call it somnambuliform possession. Quite frankly, we don't know much about it except that it starts with some conflict or guilt that eventually leads to the patient's delusion that his body's been invaded by an alien intelligence; a spirit, if you will. In times gone by, when belief in the devil was fairly strong, the possessing entity was usually a demon. In relatively modern cases, however, it's mostly the spirit of someone dead, often someone the patient has known or seen and is able unconsciously to mimic, like the voice and the mannerisms, even the features of the face, at times. They . . ."

After the gloomy Dr. Klein had left the house, Chris phoned her agent in Beverly Hills and announced to him lifelessly that she wouldn't be directing the segment. Then she called Mrs. Perrin. She was out. Chris hung up the phone with a mounting feeling of desperation. Someone. She would have to have help from . . .

". . . Cases where it's spirits of the dead are more easy to deal with; you don't find the rages in most of those cases, or the hyperactivity and motor excitement. However, in the other

166

main type of somnambuliform possession, the new person-ality's always malevolent, always hostile toward the first. Its primary aim, in fact, is to damage, torture and sometimes even kill it."

A set of restraining straps was delivered to the house and Chris stood watching, wan and spent, while Karl affixed them to Regan's bed and then to her wrists. Then as Chris moved a pillow in an effort to center it under Regan's head, the Swiss straightened up and looked pityingly at the child's ravaged face. "She is going to be well?" he asked. A hint of some emo-tion had tinged his words; they were lightly italicized with concern.

But Chris could not answer. As Karl was addressing her, she'd picked up an object that had been tucked under Regan's pillow. "Who put this crucifix here?" she demanded.

"The syndrome is only the manifestation of some conflict, of some guilt, so we try to get at it, find out what it is. Well, the best procedure in a case like this is hypnotherapy; however, we can't seem to put her under. So then we took a shot at narcosynthesis—that's a treatment that uses narcotics—but, frankly, that looks like another dead end."

"So what's next?"

"Mostly time, I'm afraid, mostly time. We'll just have to keep trying and hope for a change. In the meantime, she's going to have to be hospitalized for a . . ."

Chris found Sharon in the kitchen setting up her typewriter on the table. She had just brought it up from the basement playroom. Willie sliced carrots at the sink for a stew.

"Was it you who put the crucifix under her pillow, Shar?" Chris asked with the strain of tension.

"What do you mean?" asked Sharon, fuddled.

"You didn't?"

"Chris, I don't even know what you're talking about. Look, I told you. I told you on the plane, all I've ever said to Rags is 'God made the world' and maybe things about—"

"Fine, Sharon, fine, I believe you, but—"

"Me, I don't put it," growled Willie defensively.

"*Somebody* put it there, dammit!" Chris erupted, then wheeled on Karl as he entered the kitchen and opened the refrigerator door. "Look, I'll ask you again," she gritted in a tone that verged on shrillness: "Did you put that crucifix under her pillow?"

"No, madam," he answered levelly. He was folding ice cubes into a face towel. "No. No cross."

"*That fucking cross didn't just walk up there, damn you! One of you is lying!*" She was shrieking with a rage that stunned the room. "*Now you tell me who put it there, who—*" Abruptly she slumped to a chair and began to sob into trembling hands. "Oh, I'm sorry, I'm sorry, I don't know what I'm doing!" she wept. "Oh, my God, I don't know what I'm doing!"

Willie and Karl watched silently as Sharon came up beside her and kneaded her neck with a comforting hand. "Hey, okay. It's okay."

Chris wiped at her face with the back of a sleeve. "Yeah, I guess whoever did it"—she sniffled—"was only trying to help."

"*Look, I'm telling you again and you'd better believe it, I'm not about to put her in a goddam asylum!*"

"It's—"

"*I don't care what you call it! I'm not letting her out of my sight!*"

"Well, I'm sorry."

"Yeah, sorry! *Christ! Eighty-eight doctors and all you can tell me with all of your bullshit is . . .*"

Chris smoked a cigarette, tamped it out nervously and went upstairs to look in on Regan. She opened the door. In the gloom of the bedroom, she made out a figure by Regan's bedside, sitting in a straight-backed wooden chair. Karl. What was he doing? she wondered.

As Chris moved closer, he did not look up, but kept his gaze on the child's face. He had his arm outstretched and was touching it. What was in his hand? As Chris reached the bedside, she saw what it was: the improvised ice pack he had fashioned in the kitchen. Karl was cooling Regan's forehead.

Chris was touched, stood watching with surprise, and when Karl did not move or acknowledge her presence, she turned and quietly left the room.

She went to the kitchen, drank black coffee and smoked another cigarette. Then on an impulse she went to the study. Maybe . . . maybe . . .

". . . an outside chance, since possession is loosely related to hysteria insofar as the origin of the syndrome is almost always autosuggestive. Your daughter must have known about possession, believed in possession, and known about some of its symptoms, so that now her unconscious is producing the syndrome. If that can be established, you might take a stab at a form of cure that's autosuggestive. I think of it as shock treatment in these cases, though most other therapists wouldn't agree, I suppose. Oh, well—as I said, it's a very outside chance, and since you're opposed to your daughter being hospitalized, I'll—"

"Name it, for God's sake! What is it?!"

"Have you ever heard of exorcism, Mrs. MacNeil?"

The books in the study were part of the furnishings and Chris was unfamiliar with them. Now she was scanning the titles, searching, searching. . . .

". . . stylized ritual now out of date in which rabbis and priests tried to drive out the spirit. It's only the Catholics who haven't discarded it yet, but they keep it pretty much in the closet as sort of an embarrassment, I think. But to someone who thinks that he's really possessed, I would say that the ritual's rather impressive. It used to work, in fact, although not for the reason they thought, of course; it was purely the force of suggestion. The victim's belief in possession helped cause it, or at least the appearance of the syndrome, and in just the same way his belief in the power of the exorcism can make it disappear. It's—ah, you're frowning. Well, perhaps I should tell you about the Australian aborigines. They're convinced that if some wizard thinks a 'death ray' at them from a distance, why, they're definitely going to die, you see. And the fact is that they do! They just lie down and slowly die! And the only thing that saves them, at times, is a similar form of suggestion: a counteracting 'ray' by another wizard!"

"Are you telling me to take her to a witch doctor?"

"Yes, I suppose that I'm saying just that: as a desperate measure, perhaps to a priest. That's a rather bizarre little piece of advice, I know, even dangerous, in fact, unless we can definitely ascertain whether Regan knew anything at all about possession, and particularly exorcism, before this all came on. Do you think she might have read it?"

"No, I don't."

"Seen a movie about it sometime? Something on television?"

"No."

"Read the gospels, perhaps? The New Testament?"

"Why?"

"There are quite a few accounts of possession in them; of exorcisms by Christ. The descriptions of the symptoms, in fact, are the same as in possession today. If you—"

"Look, it's no good. Never mind, just forget it! That's all I need is to have her father hear that I called in a bunch of . . ."

Chris's index fingernail clicked slowly from binding to binding. Nothing. No Bible. No New Testament. Not a—

Hold it!

Her eyes darted quickly back to a title on the bottom shelf. The volume on witchcraft that Mary Jo Perrin had sent her. Chris plucked it out from the shelf and turned to the table of contents, running her thumbnail down the . . .

There!

The title of a chapter pulsed like a heartthrob: "States of Possession."

Chris closed the book and her eyes at the same time, wondering, wondering. . . .

Maybe . . . just maybe . . .

She opened her eyes and walked slowly to the kitchen. Sharon was typing. Chris held up the book. "Did you read this, Shar?"

Sharon kept typing, never glancing up. "Read what?" she answered.

"This book on witchcraft."

"No."

"Did you put it in the study?"

"No. Never touched it."

"Where's Willie?"

"At the market."

Chris nodded, considering. Then went back upstairs to Regan's bedroom. She showed Karl the book. "Did you put this in the study, Karl? On the bookshelf?"

"No, madam."

"Maybe Willie," Chris murmured as she stared at the book. Soft thrills of surmise rippled through her. Were the doctors at Barringer Clinic right? Was this it? Had Regan plucked her disorder through autosuggestion from the pages of this book? Would she find her symptoms listed here? Something specific that Regan was doing?

Chris sat at the table, opened to the chapter on possession and began to search, to search, to read:

> Immediately derivative of the prevalent belief in demons was the phenomenon known as possession, a state in which many individuals believed that their physical and mental functions had been invaded and were being controlled by either a demon (most common in the period under discussion) or the spirit of someone dead. There is no period of history or quarter of the globe where this phenomenon has

not been reported, and in fairly constant terms, and yet it is still to be adequately explained. Since Traugott Oesterreich's definitive study, first published in 1921, very little has been added to the body of knowledge, the advances of psychiatry notwithstanding.

Not fully explained? Chris frowned. She'd had a different impression from the doctors.

What is known is the following: that various people, at various times, have undergone massive transformations so complete that those around them feel they are dealing with another person. Not only the voice, the mannerisms, facial expressions and characteristic movements are altered, but the subject himself now thinks of himself as totally distinct from the original person and as having a name—whether human or demonic—and separate history of its own. . . .

The symptoms. Where were the symptoms? Chris wondered impatiently.

. . . In the Malay Archipelago, where possession is even today an everyday, common occurrence, the possessing spirit of someone dead often causes the possessed to mimic its gestures, voice and mannerisms so strikingly, that relatives of the deceased will burst into tears. But aside from so-called quasi-possession—those cases that are ultimately reducible to fraud, paranoia and hysteria—the problem has always lain with interpreting the phenomena, the oldest interpretation being the spiritist, an impression that is likely to be strengthened by the fact that the intruding personality may have accomplishments quite foreign to the first. In the demoniacal form of possession, for example, the "demon" may speak in languages unknown to the first personality, or . . .

There! Something! Regan's gibberish! An attempt at a language? She read on quickly.

. . . or manifest various parapsychic phenomena, telekinesis for example: the movement of objects without application of material force.

The rappings? The flinging up and down on the bed?

. . . In cases of possession by the dead, there are manifestations such as Oesterreich's account of a monk who, abruptly, while possessed, became a gifted and brilliant dancer although he had never, before his possession, had occasion to dance so much as a step. So impressive, at times, are these manifestations that Jung, the psychiatrist, after studying a case at first hand, could offer only partial explanation for what he was certain could "not have been fraud" . . .

Worrisome. The tone of this was worrisome.

. . . and William James, the greatest psychologist that America has ever produced, resorted to positing "the plausibility of the spiritualist interpretation of the phenomenon" after closely studying the so-called "Watseka Wonder," a teenaged girl in Watseka, Illinois, who became indistinguishable in personality from a girl named Mary Roff who had died in a state insane asylum twelve years prior to the possession. . . .

Frowning, Chris did not hear the doorbell chime; did not hear Sharon stop typing to rise and go answer it.

The demoniacal form of possession is usually thought to have had its origin in early Christianity; yet in fact both possession and exorcism pre-date the time of Christ. The ancient Egyptians as well as the earliest civilizations of the Tigris and the Euphrates believed that physical and spiritual disorders were caused by invasion of the body by demons. The following, for example, is the formula for exorcism against maladies of children in ancient Egypt: "Go hence, thou who comest in darkness, whose nose is turned backwards, whose face is upside down. Hast thou come to kiss this child? I will not let thee . . ."

"Chris?"

She kept reading, absorbed. "Shar, I'm busy."

"There's a homicide detective wants to see you."

"Oh, Christ, Sharon, tell him to—"

She stopped.

"No, no, hold it." Chris frowned, still staring at the book. "No. Tell him to come in. Let him in."

Sound of walking.

Sound of waiting.

What am I waiting for? Chris wondered. She sat on expectancy that was known yet undefined, like the vivid dream one can never remember.

He came in with Sharon, his hat brim crumpled in his hand, wheezing and listing and deferential. "So sorry. You're busy, you're busy, I'm a bother."

"How's the world?"

"Very bad, very bad. How's your daughter?"

"No change."

"Ah, I'm sorry, I'm terrible sorry." He was hulking by the table now, his eyelids dripping concern. "Look, I wouldn't even bother; your daughter; it's a worry. God knows, when my Ruthie was down with the—no no no no, it was Sheila, my little—"

"Please sit down," Chris cut in.

"Oh, yes, thank you," he exhaled, gratefully settling his bulk in a chair across the table from Sharon, who had now returned to her typing of letters.

"I'm sorry; you were saying?" Chris asked the detective.

"Well, my daughter, she—ah, never mind." He dismissed it. "You're busy. I get started, I'll tell my life story, you could maybe make a film of it. Really! It's incredible! If you only knew *half* of the things used to happen in my crazy family, you know, like my—ah, well, you're— One! I'll tell *one!* Like

174

my mother, every Friday she made us gefilte fish, right? Only all week long, the whole week, no one gets to take a bath on account of my mother has the carp in the bathtub, it's swimming back and forth, back and forth, the whole week, because my mother said this cleaned out the *poison* in its system! You're prepared? Because it . . . Ah, that's enough now; enough." He sighed wearily, motioning his hand in a gesture of dismissal. "But now and then a laugh just to keep us from crying."

Chris watched him expressionlessly, waiting. . . .

"Ah, you're reading." He was glancing at the book on witchcraft. "For a film?" he inquired.

"Just reading."

"It's good?"

"I just started."

"Witchcraft," he murmured, his head angled, reading the title at the top of the pages.

"What's doin'?" Chris asked him.

"Yes, I'm sorry. You're busy. You're busy. I'll finish. As I said, I wouldn't bother you, except . . ."

"Except what?"

He looked suddenly grave and clasped his hands on the table. "Well, Mr. Dennings, Mrs. MacNeil . . ."

"Well . . ."

"*Darn it,*" snapped Sharon with irritation as she ripped out a letter from the platen of the typewriter. She balled it up and tossed it at a wastepaper basket near Kinderman. "Oh, I'm sorry," she apologized as she saw that her outburst had interrupted them.

Chris and Kinderman were staring.

"You're Miss Fenster?" Kinderman asked her.

"Spencer," said Sharon, pulling back her chair in order to rise and retrieve the letter.

"Never mind, never mind," said Kinderman as he reached to the floor near his foot and picked up the crumpled page.

"Thanks," said Sharon.

"Nothing. Excuse me—you're the secretary?"

"Sharon, this is . . ."

"Kinderman," the detective reminded her. "William Kinderman."

"Right. This is Sharon Spencer."

"A pleasure," Kinderman told the blonde, who now folded her arms on the typewriter, eyeing him curiously. "Perhaps you can help," he added. "On the night of Mr. Dennings' demise, you went out to a drugstore and left him alone in the house, correct?"

"Well, no; Regan was here."

"That's my daughter," Chris clarified.

Kinderman continued to question Sharon. "He came to see Mrs. MacNeil?"

"Yes, that's right."

"He expected her shortly?"

"Well, I told him I expected her back pretty soon."

"Very good. And you left at what time? You remember?"

"Let's see. I was watching the news, so I guess—oh, no, wait—yes, that's right. I remember being bothered because the pharmacist said the delivery boy had gone home. I remember I said, 'Oh, come on, now,' or something about its only being six-thirty. Then Burke came along just ten, maybe twenty minutes after that."

"So a median," concluded the detective, "would have put him here at six-forty-five."

"And so what's this all about?" asked Chris, the nebulous tension in her mounting.

"Well, it raises a question, Mrs. MacNeil," wheezed Kinderman, turning his head to gaze at her. "To arrive in the house at say quarter to seven and leave only twenty minutes later . . ."

"Oh, well, that was Burke," said Chris. "Just like him."

"Was it also like Mr. Dennings," asked Kinderman, "to frequent the bars on M Street?"

"No."

"No, I thought not. I made a little check. And was it also not his custom to travel by taxi? He wouldn't call a cab from the house when he left?"

"Yes, he would."

"Then one wonders—not so?—how he came to be walking on the platform at the top of the steps. And one wonders why taxicab companies do not show a record of calls from this house on that night," added Kinderman, "except for the one that picked up your Miss Spencer here at precisely six-forty-seven."

"I don't know," answered Chris, her voice drained of color . . . and waiting . . .

"You knew all along!" gasped Sharon at Kinderman, perplexed.

"Yes, forgive me," the detective told her. "However, the matter has now grown serious."

Chris breathed shallowly, fixing the detective with a steady gaze. "In what way?" she asked. Her voice came thin from her throat.

He leaned over hands still clasped on the table, the page of typescript balled between them. "The report of the pathologist, Mrs. MacNeil, seems to show that the chance that he died accidentally is still very possible. However . . ."

"Are you saying he was murdered?" Chris tensed.

"The position—now I know this is painful—"

"Go ahead."

"The position of Dennings' head and a certain shearing of the muscles of the neck would—"

"Oh, God!" Chris winced.

"Yes, it's painful. I'm sorry; I'm terribly sorry. But you see, this condition—we can skip the details—but it never could happen, you see, unless Mr. Dennings had fallen some distance before he hit the steps; for example, some twenty or thirty feet before he went rolling down to the bottom. So a clear possibility, plainly speaking, is maybe . . . Well, first let me ask you . . ."

He'd turned now to a frowning Sharon. "When you left, he was where, Mr. Dennings? With the child?"

"No, down here in the study. He was fixing a drink."

"Might your daughter remember"—he turned to Chris—"if perhaps Mr. Dennings was in her room that night?"

Has she ever been alone with him?

"Why do you ask?"

"Might your daughter remember?"

"No, I told you before, she was heavily sedated and—"

"Yes, yes, you told me; that's true; I recall it; but perhaps she awakened—not so?—and . . ."

"No chance. And—"

"She was also sedated," he interrupted, "when last we spoke?"

"Oh, well, yes; as a matter of fact she was," Chris recalled. "So what?"

"I thought I saw her at her window that day."

"You're mistaken."

He shrugged. "It could be, it could be; I'm not sure."

"Listen, why are you asking all this?" Chris demanded.

"Well, a clear possibility, as I was saying, is maybe the deceased was so drunk that he stumbled and fell from the window in your daughter's bedroom."

Chris shook her head. "No way. No chance. In the first place, the window was always closed, and in the second place, Burke was *always* drunk, but he never got sloppy, never sloppy at all. That right, Shar?"

"Right."

"Burke used to *direct* when he was smashed. Now how could he stumble and fall out a window?"

"Were you maybe expecting someone else here that night?" he asked her.

"No."

"Have you friends who drop by without calling?"

"Just Burke," Chris answered. "Why?"

The detective lowered his head and shook it, frowning at the crumpled paper in his hands. "Strange . . . so baffling." He exhaled wearily. "Baffling." Then he lifted his glance to Chris. "The deceased comes to visit, stays only twenty minutes without even seeing you, and leaves all alone here a very sick girl. And speaking plainly, Mrs. MacNeil, as you say, it's not likely he would fall from a window. Besides that, a fall wouldn't do to his neck what we found except maybe a chance in a thousand." He nodded with his head at the book on witchcraft. "You've read in that book about ritual murder?"

Some prescience chilling her, Chris shook her head.

"Maybe not in that book," he said. "However—forgive me; I mention this only so maybe you'll think just a little bit harder—poor Mr. Dennings was discovered with his neck wrenched around in the style of ritual murder by so-called demons, Mrs. MacNeil."

Chris went white.

"Some lunatic killed Mr. Dennings," the detective continued, eyeing Chris fixedly. "At first, I never told you to spare you the hurt. And besides, it could technically still be an accident. But me, I don't think so. My hunch. My opinion. I believe he was killed by a powerful man: point one. And the fracturing of his skull—point two—plus the various things I have mentioned, would make it very probable—probable, not certain—the deceased was killed and then afterward pushed from your daughter's window. But no one was here except your daughter. So how could this be? It could be one way: if someone came calling between the time Miss Spencer left and the time you returned. Not so? Maybe so. Now I ask you again, please: who might have come?"

"Judas priest, just a second!" Chris whispered hoarsely, still in shock.

"Yes, I'm sorry. It's painful. And perhaps I'm all wrong—
I'll admit. But you'll think now? Who? Tell me who might
have come?"

Chris had her head down, frowning in thought. Then she
looked up at Kinderman. "No. No, there's no one."

"Maybe you then, Miss Spencer?" he asked her. "Someone
comes here to see you?"

"Oh, no, no one," said Sharon, her eyes very wide.

Chris turned to her. "Does the horseman know where you
work?"

"The horseman?" asked Kinderman.

"Her boyfriend," Chris explained.

The blonde shook her head. "He's never come here. Besides, he was in Boston that night. Some convention."

"He's a salesman?"

"A lawyer."

The detective turned again to Chris. "The servants? They
have visitors?"

"Never. Not at all."

"You expected a package that day? Some delivery?"

"Not that I know of. Why?"

"Mr. Dennings was—not to speak ill of the dead, may he
rest in peace—but as you said, in his cups he was somewhat—
well, call it irascible: capable, doubtless, of provoking an argument; an anger; in this case a rage from perhaps a delivery man
who came by to drop a package. So were you expecting something? Like dry cleaning, maybe? Groceries? Liquor? A package?"

"I really wouldn't know," Chris told him. "Karl handles all
of that."

"Oh, I see."

"Want to ask him?"

The detective sighed and leaned back from the table, stuff-
ing his hands in the pockets of his coat. He stared glumly at

the witchcraft book. "Never mind, never mind; it's remote. You've got a daughter very sick, and—well, never mind." He made a gesture of dismissal and rose from the chair. "Very nice to have met you, Miss Spencer."

"Same here." Sharon nodded remotely.

"Baffling," said Kinderman with a headshake. "Strange." He was focused on some inner thought. Then he looked at Chris as she rose from her chair. "Well, I'm sorry. I've bothered you for nothing. Forgive me."

"Here, I'll walk you to the door," Chris told him, thoughtful.

"Don't bother."

"No bother."

"If you insist. Incidentally," he said as they moved from the kitchen, "just a chance in a million, I know, but your daughter—you could possibly ask her if she saw Mr. Dennings in her room that night?"

Chris walked with folded arms. "Look, he wouldn't have had a reason to be up there in the first place."

"I know that; I realize; that's true; but if certain British doctors never asked, 'What's this fungus?' we wouldn't today have penicillin. Right? Please ask. You'll ask?"

"When she's well enough, yes; I'll ask."

"Couldn't hurt. In the meantime . . ." They'd come to the front door and Kinderman faltered, embarrassed. He put fingertips to mouth in a hesitant gesture. "Look, I really hate to ask you; however . . ."

Chris tensed for some new shock, the prescience tingling again in her bloodstream. "What?"

"For my daughter . . . you could maybe give an autograph?" He'd reddened, and Chris almost laughed with relief; at herself; at despair and the human condition.

"Oh, of course. Where's a pencil?" she said.

"Right here!" he responded instantly, whipping out the stub

of a chewed-up pencil from the pocket of his coat while he dipped his other hand in a pocket of his jacket and slipped out a calling card. "She would love it," he said as he handed them both to Chris.

"What's her name?" Chris asked, pressing the card against the door and poising the pencil stub to write. There followed a weighty hesitation. She heard only wheezing. She glanced around. In Kinderman's eyes she saw some massive, terrible struggle.

"I lied," he said finally, his eyes at once desperate and defiant. "It's for me."

He fixed his gaze on the card and blushed. "Write 'To William—William Kinderman'—it's spelled on the back."

Chris eyed him with a wan and unexpected affection, checked the spelling of his name and wrote, *William F. Kinderman, I love you!* And signed her name. Then she gave him the card, which he tucked in his pocket without reading the inscription.

"You're a very nice lady," he told her sheepishly, gaze averted.

"You're a very nice man."

He seemed to blush harder. "No, I'm not. I'm a bother." He was opening the door. "Never mind what I said here today. It's upsetting. Forget it. Keep your mind on your daughter. Your *daughter*."

Chris nodded, her despondency surging up again as Kinderman stepped outside onto the stoop and donned his hat.

"But you'll ask her?" he reminded as he turned.

"I will," Chris whispered. "I promise. I will."

"Well, good-bye. And take care."

Once more Chris nodded; then added, "You too."

She closed the door softly. Then instantly opened it again as he knocked.

"What a nuisance. I'm a nuisance. I forgot my pencil." He grimaced in apology.

Chris eyed the stub in her hand, smiled faintly and gave it to Kinderman.

"And another thing . . ." He hesitated. "It's pointless, I know—it's a bother, it's dumb—but I know I won't sleep thinking maybe there's a lunatic loose or a doper if every little point I don't cover, whatever. Do you think I could—no, no, it's dumb, it's a —yes; yes, I should. Could I maybe have a word with Mr. Engstrom, do you think? The deliveries . . . the question of deliveries. I really should. . . ."

"Sure, come on in," Chris said wearily.

"No, you're busy. Enough. I can talk to him here. This is fine. Here is fine."

He had leaned against a railing.

"If you insist." Chris smiled thinly. "He's with Regan. I'll send him right down."

"I'm obliged."

Quickly Chris closed the door. A minute later, Karl opened it. He stepped down to the stoop with his hand on the door-knob, holding the door slightly ajar. Standing tall and erect, he looked at Kinderman with eyes that were clear and cool. "Yes?" he asked without expression.

"You have the right to remain silent," Kinderman greeted him, steely gaze locked tight on Karl's. "If you give up the right to remain silent," he intoned rapidly in a flat, deadly cadence, "anything you say can and will be used against you in a court of law. You have the right to speak with an attorney and to have the attorney present during questioning. If you so desire, and cannot afford one, an attorney will be appointed for you without charge prior to questioning. Do you understand each of these rights I've explained to you?"

Birds twittered softly in the branches of the elder tree, and the traffic sounds of M Street came up to them muted like the humming of bees from a distant meadow. Karl's gaze never wavered as he answered, "Yes."

"Do you wish to give up the right to remain silent?"

"Yes."

"Do you wish to give up the right to speak to an attorney and have him present during questioning?"

"Yes."

"Did you previously state that on April twenty-eighth, the night of the death of Mr. Dennings, you attended a film that was showing at the Crest?"

"Yes."

"And what time did you enter the theater?"

"I do not remember."

"You stated previously you attended the six-o'clock showing. Does that help you to remember?"

"Yes. Yes, six o'clock show. I remember."

"And you saw the picture—the *film*—from the beginning?"

"I did."

"And you left at the film's conclusion?"

"I did."

"Not before?"

"No, I see entire film."

"And leaving the theater, you boarded the D.C. Transit bus in front of the theater, debarking at M Street and Wisconsin Avenue at approximately nine-twenty P.M.?"

"Yes."

"And walked home?"

"I walk home."

"And were back in this residence at approximately nine-thirty P.M.?"

"I am back here *exactly* nine-thirty," Karl answered.

"You're sure."

"Yes, I look at my watch. I am positive."

"And you saw the whole film to the very end?"

"Yes, I said that."

"Your answers are being electronically recorded, Mr. Engstrom. I want you to be absolutely positive."

"I am positive."

"You're aware of the altercation between an usher and a drunken patron that happened in the last five minutes of the film?"

"Yes."

"Can you tell me the cause of it?"

"The man, he was drunk and was making disturbance."

"And what did they do with him finally?"

"Out. They throw him out."

"There was no such disturbance. Are you also aware that during the course of the six o'clock showing a technical breakdown lasting approximately fifteen minutes caused an interruption in the showing of the film?"

"I am not."

"You recall that the audience booed?"

"No, nothing. No breakdown."

"You're sure?"

"There was nothing."

"There was, as reflected in the log of the projectionist, showing that the film ended not at eight-forty that night, but at approximately eight-fifty-five, which would mean that the earliest bus from the theater would put you at M Street and Wisconsin not at nine-twenty, but nine-forty-five, and that therefore the earliest you could be at the house was approximately five before ten, not nine-thirty, as testified also by Mrs. MacNeil. Would you care now to comment on this puzzling discrepancy?"

Not for a moment had Karl lost his poise and he held it now as he answered, "No."

The detective stared at him mutely for a moment, then sighed and looked down as he turned off the monitor control that was tucked in the lining of his coat. He held his gaze down for a moment, then looked up at Karl. "Mr. Engstrom . . ." he began in a tone that was weary with understanding. "A serious crime may have been committed. You are under suspicion. Mr. Dennings abused you, I have learned from other sources. And apparently you've lied about your whereabouts at the time of his demise. Now it sometimes happens—we're human; why not?—that a man who is married is sometimes someplace where he says that he is not. You will notice I arranged we are talking in private? Away from the others? Away from your wife? I'm not now recording. It's off. You can trust me. If it happens you were out with a woman not your wife on that night, you can tell me, I'll have it checked out, you'll be out of this trouble and your wife, she won't know. Now then tell me, where were you at the time Dennings died?"

For a moment something flickered in the depths of Karl's eyes; and then was smothered.

"At movies!" he insisted through narrowed lips.

The detective eyed him steadily, silent and unmoving, no sound but his wheezing as the seconds ticked heavily, heavily. . . .

"You are going to arrest me?" Karl asked the silence at last in a voice that subtly wavered.

The detective made no answer but continued to eye him, unblinking, and when Karl seemed again about to speak, the detective abruptly pushed away from the railing, moving toward the squad car with hands in his pockets. He walked unhurriedly, viewing his surroundings to the left and the right like an interested visitor to the city.

From the stoop, Karl watched, his features stolid and impassive as Kinderman opened the door of the squad car, reached inside to a box of Kleenex fixed to the dashboard, extracted a tissue and blew his nose while staring idly across the river as if considering where to have lunch. Then he entered the car without glancing back.

As the car pulled away and rounded the corner of Thirty-fifth, Karl looked at the hand that was not on the doorknob and saw it was trembling.

When she heard the front door being closed, Chris was brooding at the bar in the study, pouring out a vodka over ice. Footsteps. Karl going up the stairs. She picked up her vodka and moved slowly back toward the kitchen, stirring her drink with an index finger; picking her way with absent eyes. Something . . . something was horribly wrong. Like light from a room leaking under the door, a glow of dread seeped into the darkened hall of her mind. What lay behind the door? What was it?

Don't look!

She entered the kitchen, sat at the table and sipped at her drink.

"I believe he was killed by a powerful man . . ."

She dropped her glance to the book on witchcraft.

Something . . .

Footsteps. Sharon returning from Regan's bedroom. Entering. Sitting at the table by the typewriter. Cranking fresh stationery into the roller.

Something . . .

"Pretty creepy," Sharon murmured, fingertips resting on the keyboard and eyes on her steno notes to the side.

No answer. Uneasiness hung in the room. Chris sipped absently at her drink.

Sharon probed at the silence in a strained, low voice. "They've got an awful lot of hippie joints down around M Street and Wisconsin. Pot-heads. Occultists. The police call them 'hellhounds.'" She paused as if waiting for comment, her eyes still fixed upon the notes; then continued: "I wonder if Burke might have—"

"Oh, *Christ*, Shar! Forget about it, will you!" Chris erupted. "I've got all I can think about with Rags! Do you mind?" She had her eyes shut. She clenched the book.

Sharon returned instantly to the keys of the typewriter, clicking off words at a furious tempo for a minute, then ab-

187

ruptly bolted up from her chair and out of the kitchen. "I'm going for a walk!" she said icily.

"Stay the hell away from M Street!" Chris rumbled at her moodily, her gaze on the book over folded arms.

"I will!"

"And N!"

Chris heard the front door being opened, then closed. She sighed. Felt a pang of regret. But the flurry had siphoned off tension. Not all. Still the glow in the hall. Very faint.

Shut it out!

Chris took a deep breath and tried to focus on the book. She found her place; grew impatient; started hastily flipping through pages, skimming, searching for descriptions of Regan's symptoms. " . . . demonic possession . . . syndrome . . . case of an eight-year-old girl . . . abnormal . . . four strong men to restrain him from . . . "

Turning a page, Chris stared—and froze.

Sounds. Willie coming in with groceries.

"Willie? . . . Willie?" Chris asked tonelessly.

"Yes, madam," Willie answered, setting down her bags. Without looking up, Chris held up the book. "Was it you put this book in the study, Willie?"

Willie glanced at the book and nodded, then turned around and began to slip items from the bags.

"Willie, where did you find it?"

"Up in bedroom," Willie answered, putting bacon in the meat compartment of the refrigerator.

"*Which* bedroom, Willie?"

"Miss Regan. I find it under bed when I am cleaning."

"*When* did you find it?" Chris asked, her gaze still locked to the pages of the book.

"After all go to hospital, madam; when I vacuum in Regan bedroom."

"You're sure?"

"I am sure, madam. Yes. I am sure."

Chris did not move, did not blink, did not breathe as the headlong image of an open window in Regan's bedroom the night of Dennings' accident rushed at her memory, talons extended, like a bird of prey who knew her name; as she recognized a sight that was numbingly familiar; as she stared at the facing page of the book.

A narrow strip had been surgically shaved from the length of its edge.

Chris jerked her head up at the sounds of commotion in Regan's bedroom.

Rappings, rapid, with a nightmarish resonance; massive, like a sledgehammer pounding in a tomb!

Regan screaming in anguish; in terror; imploring!

Karl! Karl bellowing angrily at Regan!

Chris bolted from the kitchen.

God almighty, what's happening?

Frenzied, Chris raced for the stairs, toward the bedroom, heard a blow, someone reeling, someone crashing like a boulder to the floor with her daughter crying, *"No! Oh, no, don't! Oh, no, please!"* and Karl bellowing— No! No, not Karl! Someone else! A thundering bass that was threatening, raging!

Chris plunged down the hall and burst into the bedroom, gasped, stood rooted in paralyzing shock as the rappings boomed massively, shivering through walls; as Karl lay unconscious on the floor near the bureau; as Regan, her legs propped up and spread wide on a bed that was violently bouncing and shaking, clutched the bone-white crucifix in raw-knuckled hands, the bone-white crucifix poised at her vagina, the bone-white crucifix she stared at with terror, eyes bulging in a face that was bloodied from the nose, the nasogastric tubing ripped out.

"Oh, please! Oh, no, *please!*" she was shrieking as her hands brought the crucifix closer; as she seemed to be straining to push it away.

"You'll do as I *tell* you, filth! You'll *do* it!"

The threatening bellow, the words, came from *Regan*, her voice coarse and guttural, bristling with venom, while in an instantaneous flash her expression and features were hideously transmuted into those of the feral, demonic personality that had appeared in the course of hypnosis. And now faces and voices, as Chris watched stunned, interchanged with rapidity:

"*No!*"

"*You'll do it!*"

"*Please!*"

"*You will*, you bitch, or I'll kill you!"

"*Please!*"

"Yes, you're going to let Jesus *fuck* you, *fuck* you, f—"

Regan now, eyes wide and staring, flinching from the rush of some hideous finality, mouth agape shrieking at the dread of some ending. Then abruptly the demonic face once more possessed her, now filled her, the room choking suddenly with a stench in the nostrils, with an icy cold that seeped from the walls as the rappings ended and Regan's piercing cry of terror turned to a guttural, yelping laugh of malevolent spite and rage triumphant while she thrust down the crucifix into her vagina and began to masturbate ferociously, roaring in that deep, coarse, deafening voice, "Now you're *mine*, now you're *mine*, you stinking cow! You bitch! Let Jesus *fuck* you, *fuck* you!"

Chris stood rooted to the ground in horror, frozen, her hands pressing tight against her cheeks as again the demonic, loud laugh cackled joyously, as Regan's vagina gushed blood onto sheets with her hymen, the tissues ripped. Abruptly, with a shriek clawing raw from her throat, Chris rushed at the bed, grasped blindly at the crucifix, was still screaming as Regan flared up at her in fury, features contorted infernally, reached out a hand, clutching Chris's hair, and yanked her head down, pressing her face hard against her vagina, smearing it with blood while she frantically undulated her pelvis.

"Aahhh, little pig mother!" Regan crooned with a guttural, rasping, throaty eroticism. "*Lick* me, *lick* me, *lick* me! Aahhhhh!" Then the hand that was holding Chris's head down jerked it upward while the other arm smashed her a blow across the chest that sent Chris reeling across the room and crashing to a wall with stunning force while Regan laughed with bellowing spite.

Chris crumpled to the floor in a daze of horror, in a swirling of images, sounds in the room, as her vision spun madly, blurring, unfocused, her ears ringing loud with chaotic distortions as she tried to raise herself, was too weak, faltered, then looked toward the still-blurred bed, toward Regan with her back to her, thrusting the crucifix gently and sensually into her vagina, then out, then in, with that deep, bass voice crooning, "Ahh, there's my sow, yes, my sweet honey piglet, my piglet, my—"

The words were cut off as Chris started crawling painfully toward the bed with her face smeared with blood, with her eyes still unfocused, limbs aching, past Karl. Then she cringed, shrinking back in incredulous terror as she thought she saw hazily, in a swimming fog, her daughter's head turning slowly around on a motionless torso, rotating monstrously, inexorably, until at last it seemed facing backward.

"Do you know what she *did*, your cunting daughter?" giggled an elfin, familiar voice.

Chris blinked at the mad-staring, grinning face, at the cracked, parched lips and foxlike eyes.

She screamed until she fainted.

III: The Abyss

They said, "What sign can you give us to see, so that we may believe you?"

John 6: 30–31

. . . A [Vietnam] brigade commander once ran a contest to rack up his unit's 10,000th kill; the prize was a week of luxury in the colonel's own quarters. . . .

Newsweek, 1969

You do not believe although you have seen. . . .

John 6: 36–37

one

She was standing on the Key Bridge walk-
way, arms atop the parapet, fidgeting, waiting, while home-
ward-bound traffic stuttered thickly behind her, while drivers
with everyday cares honked horns and bumpers nudged bumpers with scraping indifference. She had reached Mary Jo; told
her lies.

*"Regan's fine. By the way, I've been thinking of another
little dinner party. What was the name of that Jesuit psychiatrist again? I thought maybe I'd include him in the . . . "*

Laughter floating up from below her: a blue-jeaned young
couple in a rented canoe. With a quick, nervous gesture, she
flicked ash from her cigarette and glanced up the walkway of
the bridge toward the District. Someone hurrying toward her:
khaki pants and blue sweater; not a priest; not him. She looked
down at the river again, at her helplessness swirling in the

wake of the bright-red canoe. She could make out the name on its side: *Caprice*.

Footsteps. The man in the sweater coming closer, slowing down as he reached her. Peripherally, she saw him rest a forearm on the top of the parapet and quickly she averted her head toward Virginia.

"Keep movin', creep," she rumbled at him huskily, flipping her cigarette into the river, "or, I swear to Christ, I'll yell for a cop!"

"Miss MacNeil? I'm Father Karras."

She started, reddened, jerked swiftly around. The chipped, rugged face. "Oh, my God! Oh, I'm— *Jesus!*"

She was tugging at her sunglasses, flustered, and immediately pushing them back as the sad, dark eyes probed hers.

"I should have told you that I wouldn't be in uniform. Sorry."

His voice was cradling, stripping her of burden, as his powerful hands clasped gently together. They were large and yet sensitive: veined Michelangelos. Chris felt her gaze somehow drawn to them instantly.

"I thought it would be much less conspicuous," he continued. "You seemed so concerned about keeping this quiet."

"Guess I should have been concerned about not making such an ass of myself," she retorted, quickly fumbling through her purse. "I just thought you were—"

"Human?" he interjected with a smile.

"I knew *that* when I saw you one day on the campus," she said, as she searched now in the pockets of her suit. "That's why I called. You seemed human." She looked up and saw him staring at her hands. "Got a cigarette, Father?"

He reached into the pocket of his shirt. "Can you go a non-filter?"

"Right now I'd smoke rope."

He tapped out a Camel from the packet. "On my allowance, I frequently do."

"Vow of poverty," she murmured as she slipped out the cigarette, smiling tightly.

"A vow of poverty has uses," he commented, reaching in his pocket for matches.

"Like what?"

"Makes rope taste better." Again, a half smile as he watched her hand holding the cigarette. It trembled. He saw the cigarette wavering in quick, erratic jumps, and without pausing, he took it from her fingers and put it up to his mouth. He lit it, his hands cupped around the match. He puffed. Gave the cigarette back to Chris, his eyes on the cars passing over the bridge. "Lots easier. Breeze from the traffic," he told her.

"Thanks, Father."

Chris looked at him appraisingly, with gratitude, even with hope. She knew what he'd done. She watched as he lit up a Camel for himself. He forgot to cup his hands. As he exhaled, they each leaned an elbow on the parapet.

"Where are you from, Father Karras? Originally."

"New York."

"Me too. Wouldn't ever go back, though. Would you?"

Karras fought down the rise in his throat. "No, I wouldn't." He forced a smile. "But I don't have to make those decisions."

"God, I'm dumb. You're a priest. You have to go where they send you."

"That's right."

"How'd a shrink ever get to be a priest?" she asked.

He was anxious to know what the urgent problem was that she'd mentioned when she telephoned. She was feeling her way, he sensed—toward what? He must not prod. It would come . . . it would come.

"It's the other way around," he corrected her gently. "The Society—"

"Who?"

"The Society of Jesus. Jesuit is short for that."

197

"Oh, I see."

"The Society sent me through medical school and through psychiatric training."

"Where?"

"Oh, well, Harvard; Johns Hopkins; Bellevue."

He was suddenly aware that he wanted to impress her. Why? he wondered; and immediately saw the answer in the slums of his boyhood; in the balconies of theaters on the Lower East Side. Little Dimmy with a movie star.

"Not bad," she said appraisingly, nodding her head.

"We don't take vows of mental poverty."

She sensed an irritation; shrugged; turned front, facing out to the river. "Look, it's just that I don't know you, and . . . " She dragged on the cigarette, long and deep, and then exhaled, crushing out the butt on the parapet. "You're a friend of Father Dyer's, that right?"

"Yes, I am."

"Pretty close?"

"Pretty close."

"Did he talk about the party?"

"At your house?"

"At my house."

"Yes, he said you seemed human."

She missed it; or ignored it. "Did he talk about my daughter?"

"No, I didn't know you had one."

"She's twelve. He didn't mention her?"

"No."

"He didn't tell you what she did?"

"He never mentioned her."

"Priests keep a pretty tight mouth, then; that right?"

"That depends," answered Karras.

"On what?"

"On the priest."

At the fringe of his awareness drifted a warning about women with neurotic attractions to priests who desired, unconsciously and under the guise of some other problem, to seduce the unattainable.

"Look, I mean like confession. You're not allowed to talk about it, right?"

"Yes, that's right."

"And outside of confession?" she asked him. "I mean, what if some . . ." Her hands were now agitated; fluttering. "I'm curious. I . . . No. No, I'd really like to know. I mean, what if a person, let's say, was a criminal, like maybe a murderer or something, you know? If he came to you for help, would you have to turn him in?"

Was she seeking instruction? Was she clearing off doubts in the way of conversion? There were people, Karras knew, who approached salvation as if it were an unreliable bridge overhanging an abyss. "If he came to me for spiritual help, I'd say, no," he replied.

"You wouldn't."

"No. No, I wouldn't. But I'd try to persuade him to turn himself in."

"And how do you go about getting an exorcism?"

"Beg pardon?"

"If a person's possessed by some kind of demon, how do you go about getting an exorcism?"

"Well, first you'd have to put him in a time machine and get him back to the sixteenth century."

She was puzzled. "What do you mean by that? Didn't get you."

"Well, it just doesn't happen anymore, Miss MacNeil."

"Since when?"

"Since we learned about mental illness; about paranoia; split personality; all those things that they taught me at Harvard."

"You kidding?"

Her voice wavered helpless, confused, and Karras regretted his flipness. Where had it come from? he wondered. It had leaped to his tongue unbidden.

"Many educated Catholics, Miss MacNeil," he told her in a gentler tone, "don't believe in the devil anymore, and as far as possession is concerned, since the day I joined the Jesuits I've never met a priest who's ever in his life performed an exorcism. Not one."

"Are you really a priest," she demanded with a bitter, disappointed sharpness, "or from Central Casting? I mean, what about all of those stories in the Bible about Christ driving out all those demons?"

Again, he was answering crisply, unthinking: "Look, if Christ had said those people who were supposedly possessed had schizophrenia, which I imagine they did, they would probably have crucified him three years earlier."

"Oh, really?" Chris put a shaking hand to her sunglasses, deepening her voice in an effort at control. "Well, it happens, Father Karras, that someone very close to me is probably possessed. She needs an exorcism. Will you do it?"

To Karras, it suddenly seemed unreal: Key Bridge; across the river, the Hot Shoppe; traffic; Chris MacNeil, the movie star. As he stared at her, groping for an answer, she slipped off the glasses and Karras felt momentary, wincing shock at the redness, at the desperate pleading in those haggard eyes. The woman was serious, he realized.

"Father Karras, it's my daughter," she told him huskily, "my *daughter!*"

"Then all the more reason," he at last said gently, "to forget about exorcism and—"

"*Why?* God, I don't understand!" she burst out in a voice that was cracking and distraught.

He took her wrist in a comforting hand. "In the first place," he told her in soothing tones, "it could make things worse."

"But *how?*"

"The ritual of exorcism is dangerously suggestive. It could plant the notion of possession, you see, where it didn't exist before, or if it did, it could tend to fortify it. And secondly, Miss MacNeil, before the Church approves an exorcism, it conducts an investigation to see if it's warranted. That takes time. In the meantime, your—"

"Couldn't you do the exorcism yourself?" she pleaded, her lower lip starting to tremble. Her eyes were filling up with tears.

"Look every priest has the power to exorcise, but he has to have Church approval, and frankly, it's rarely ever given, so—"

"Can't you even look at her?"

"Well, as a psychiatrist, yes, I could, but—"

"She needs a *priest!*" Chris suddenly cried out, her features contorted with anger and fear. "I've taken her to every goddam, fucking doctor, psychiatrist in the world and they sent me to *you;* now you send me to *them!*"

"But your—"

"Jesus Christ, won't somebody *help me?*" The heart-stopping shriek bolted raw above the river. Startled birds shot up screeching from its banks. "Oh, my God, someone help me!" Chris moaned as she crumpled to Karras' chest with convulsive sobs. "Please help me! Help me! Please! Please, help! . . ."

The Jesuit looked down at her, lifted up comforting hands to her head as the riders in traffic-locked automobiles glanced out windows to watch them with passing disinterest.

"It's all right," Karras whispered as he patted her shoulder. He wanted only to calm her; to humor; stem hysteria. " . . . *my daughter*"? It was *she* who needed psychiatric help. "It's all right. I'll go see her," he told her. "I'll see her."

He approached the house with her in silence, with a lingering sense of unreality, with thoughts of the next day's lecture at the Georgetown Medical School. He had yet to prepare his notes.

They climbed the front stoop. Karras glanced down the street at the Jesuit residence hall and realized he would now miss dinner. It was ten before six. He looked at Chris as she slipped the key in the lock. She hesitated, turned to him. "Father . . . do you think you should wear your priest clothes?"

The voice: how childlike it was; how naïve. "Too dangerous," he told her.

She nodded and started opening the door, and it was then that Karras felt it: a chill, tugging warning. It scraped through his bloodstream like particles of ice.

"Father Karras?"

He looked up. Chris had entered. She was holding the door.

For a hesitant moment he stood unmoving; then abruptly he went forward, stepping into the house with an odd sense of ending.

Karras heard commotion. Upstairs. A deep, booming voice was thundering obscenities, threatening in anger, in hate, in frustration.

Karras glanced at Chris. She was staring at him mutely. Then she moved on ahead. He followed her upstairs and along the hall to Regan's bedroom, where Karl leaned against the wall just opposite her door, his head sagging low over folded arms. As the servant looked slowly up at Chris, Karras saw bafflement and fright in his eyes. The voice from the bedroom, this close, was so loud that it almost seemed amplified electronically. "It wants no straps, still," Karl told Chris in an awed, cracking voice.

"I'll be back in a second, Father," Chris told the priest dully.

Karras watched her walk down the hall and into her own bedroom; then he glanced at Karl. The Swiss was looking at him fixedly.

"You are priest?" Karl asked.

Karras nodded, then looked quickly back to the door of Regan's room. The raging voice had been displaced by the long, strident lowing of some animal that might have been a steer.

Something prodding at his hand. He looked down. "That's her," Chris was saying, "that's Regan." She was giving him a photograph. He took it. Young girl. Very pretty. Sweet smile.

"That was taken four months ago," Chris said numbly. She took back the photo and motioned with her head at the bedroom door. "Now you go and take a look at her now." She leaned against the wall beside Karl. "I'll wait here."

"Who's in there with her?" Karras asked her.

"No one."

He held her steady gaze and then turned with a frown to the bedroom door. As he grasped the doorknob, the sounds from within ceased abruptly. In the ticking silence, Karras hesitated, then entered the room slowly, almost flinching backward at the pungent stench of moldering excrement that hit him in the face like a palpable blast.

Quickly reining back his revulsion, he closed the door. Then his eyes locked, stunned, on the thing that was Regan, on the creature that was lying on its back in the bed, head propped against a pillow while eyes bulging wide in their hollow sockets shone with mad cunning and burning intelligence, with interest and with spite as they fixed upon his, as they watched him intently, seething in a face shaped into a skeletal, hideous mask of mind-bending malevolence. Karras shifted his gaze to the tangled, thickly matted hair; to the wasted arms and legs; the distended stomach jutting up so grotesquely; then back to the eyes: they were watching him . . . pinning him . . . shifting now to follow as he moved to a desk and chair near the window.

"Hello, Regan," said the priest in a warm, friendly tone. He picked up the chair and took it over by the bed.

"I'm a friend of your mother's. She tells me that you haven't been feeling too well." He sat down. "Do you think you'd like to tell me what's wrong? I'd like to help you."

The eyes gleamed fiercely, unblinking, and a yellowish saliva dribbled down from a corner of her mouth to her chin. Then her lips stretched taut into a feral grin, into bow-mouthed mockery.

"Well, well, well," gloated Regan sardonically, and hairs prickled on the back of Karras' neck, for the voice was an impossibly deep bass thick with menace and power. "So it's you . . . they sent you! Well, we've nothing to fear from you at all."

"Yes, that's right. I'm your friend. I'd like to help," said Karras.

"You might loosen these straps, then," Regan croaked. She had tugged up her wrists so that now Karras noticed that they were bound with a double set of restraining straps.

"Are they uncomfortable for you?" he asked her.

"Extremely. They're a nuisance. An *infernal* nuisance." The eyes glinted slyly with secret amusement.

Karras saw the scratch marks on her face; the cuts on her lips where apparently she'd bitten them. "I'm afraid you might hurt yourself, Regan."

"I'm not Regan," she rumbled, still with the hideous grin that now seemed to Karras to be her permanent expression. How incongruous the braces on her teeth looked, he reflected.

"Oh, I see. Well, then, maybe we should introduce ourselves. I'm Damien Karras," said the priest. "Who are you?"

"I'm the devil."

"Ah, good, very good." Karras nodded approvingly. "Now we can talk."

"A little chat?"

"If you like."

"Very good for the soul. However, you will find that I cannot talk freely while bound with these straps. I'm accustomed to gesturing." Regan drooled. "As you know, I've spent much of my time in Rome, dear Karras. Now kindly undo the straps!"

What precocity of language and thought, mused Karras. He

leaned forward in his chair with professional interest. "You say you're the devil?" he asked.

"I assure you."

"Then why don't you just make the straps disappear?"

"That's much too vulgar a display of power, Karras. Too crude. After all, I'm a prince!" A chuckle. "I much prefer persuasion, Karras; togetherness; community involvement. Moreover, if I loosen the straps myself, my friend, I deny you the opportunity of performing a charitable act."

"But a charitable act," said Karras, "is a virtue and that's what the devil would want to prevent; so in fact I'd be *helping* you now if I *didn't* undo the straps. Unless, of course"—he shrugged—"you're really not the devil. And in that case, perhaps I *would* undo the straps."

"How very foxy of you, Karras. If only dear Herod were here to enjoy this."

"Which Herod?" asked Karras with narrowed eyes. Was she punning on Christ's calling Herod "that fox"? "There were two. Are you talking about the King of Judea?"

"The tetrarch of Galilee!" she blasted him with anger and scorching contempt; then abruptly she was grinning again, cajoling in that sinister voice: "There, you see how these damnable straps have upset me? Undo them. Undo them and I'll tell you the future."

"Very tempting."

"My forte."

"But then how do I know that you can read the future?"

"I'm the devil."

"Yes, you say so, but you won't give me proof."

"You have no faith."

Karras stiffened. "In what?"

"In *me*, dear Karras; in *me!*" Something mocking and malicious danced hidden in those eyes. "All these proofs, all these signs in the sky!"

"Well, now, something very simple might do," offered

Karras. "For example: the devil knows everything, correct?"

"No, *almost* everything, Karras—almost. You see? They keep saying that I'm proud. I am not. Now, then, what are you up to, fox?" The yellowed, bloodshot eyes gleamed craftily.

"I thought we might test the extent of your knowledge."

"Ah, yes! The largest lake in South America," japed Regan, eyes bulging with glee, "is Lake Titicaca in Peru! Will that do it?"

"No, I'll have to ask something only the devil would know. For example, where is Regan? Do you know?"

"She is here."

"Where is 'here'?"

"In the pig."

"Let me see her."

"Why?"

"Why, to prove that you're telling me the truth."

"Do you want to fuck her? Loose the straps and I will let you go at it!"

"Let me see her."

"Very succulent cunt," leered Regan, her furred and lolling tongue licking spittle across cracked lips. "But a poor conversationalist, my friend. I strongly advise you to stay with me."

"Well, it's obvious you don't know where she is"—Karras shrugged—"so apparently you aren't the devil."

"I *am!*" Regan bellowed with a sudden jerk forward, her face contorting with rage. Karras shivered as the massive, terrifying voice boomed crackling off the walls of the room. "I am!"

"Well, then, let me see Regan," said Karras. "That would prove it."

"I will show you! I will read your mind!" it seethed furiously. "Think of a number between one and ten!"

"No, that wouldn't prove a thing. I would have to see Regan."

Abruptly it chuckled, leaning back against the headboard.

"No, nothing would prove anything at all to you, Karras. How splendid. How splendid indeed! In the meantime, we shall try to keep you properly beguiled. After all, now, we would not wish to lose you."

"Who is 'we'?" Karras probed with alert, quick interest.

"We are quite a little group in the piglet," it said, nodding. "Ah, yes, quite a stunning little multitude. Later I may see about discreet introductions. In the meantime, I am suffering from a maddening itch that I cannot reach. Would you loosen one strap for a moment, Karras?"

"No; just tell me where it itches and I'll scratch it."

"Ah, sly, very sly!"

"Show me Regan and perhaps I'll undo one strap," offered Karras. "If—"

Abruptly he flinched in shock as he found himself staring into eyes filled with terror, at a mouth gaping wide in a soundless shriek for help.

But then quickly the Regan identity vanished in a blurringly rapid remolding of features. "Won't you take off these straps?" asked a wheedling voice in a clipped British accent.

In a flash, the demonic personality returned. "Couldjya help an old altar boy, Faddah?" it croaked, and then threw back its head in laughter.

Karras sat stunned, felt the glacial hands at the back of his neck again, more palpable now, more firm. The Regan-thing broke off its laughter and fixed him with taunting eyes.

"Incidentally, your mother is here with us, Karras. Do you wish to leave a message? I will see that she gets it." Then Karras was suddenly dodging a projectile stream of vomit, leaping out of his chair. It caught a portion of his sweater and one of his hands.

His face now colorless, the priest looked down at the bed. Regan cackled with glee. His hand dripped vomit onto the rug. "If that's true," the priest said numbly, "then you must know my mother's first name. What is it?"

The Regan-thing hissed at him, mad eyes gleaming, head gently undulating like a cobra's.

"What is it?"

Regan lowed like a steer in an angry bellow that pierced the shutters and shivered through the glass of the large bay window. The eyes rolled upward into their sockets.

For a time Karras watched as the bellowing continued; then he looked at his hand and walked out of the room.

Chris pushed herself quickly away from the wall, glancing with distress at the Jesuit's sweater. "What happened? Did she vomit?"

"Got a towel?" he asked her.

"There's a bathroom right there!" she said hurriedly, pointing at a hallway door. "Karl, take a look at her!" she instructed, and followed the priest to the bathroom.

"I'm so sorry!" she exclaimed in agitation, whipping a towel off the bar. The Jesuit moved to the washbasin.

"Have you got her on tranquilizers?" he asked.

Chris turned on the water taps. "Yes, Librium. Here, take off that sweater and then you can wash."

"What dosage?" he asked her, tugging at the sweater with his clean left hand.

"Here, I'll help you." She pulled at the sweater from the bottom. "Well, today she's had four hundred milligrams, Father."

"Four *hundred?*"

She had the sweater pulled up to his chest. "Yeah, that's how we got her into those straps. It took all of us together to—"

"You gave your daughter four hundred milligrams *at once?*"

"C'mon, get your arms up, Father." He raised them and she tugged delicately. "She's so strong you can't believe it."

She pulled back the shower curtain, tossing the sweater into the tub. "I'll have Willie get it cleaned for you, Father. I'm sorry."

"Never mind. It doesn't matter." He unbuttoned the right sleeve of his starched white shirt and rolled it up, exposing a matting of fine brown hairs on a bulging, thickly muscled forearm.

"I'm sorry," Chris repeated quietly, slowly sitting down on the edge of the tub.

"Is she taking any nourishment at all?" asked Karras. He held his hand beneath the hot-water tap to rinse away the vomit.

She clutched and unclutched the towel. It was pink, the name *Regan* embroidered in blue. "No, Father. Just Sustagen when she's been sleeping. But she ripped out the tubing."

"Ripped it out?"

"Today."

Disturbed, Karras soaped and rinsed his hands, and after a pause said gravely, "She ought to be in a hospital."

"I just can't do that," answered Chris in a toneless voice.

"Why not?"

"I just can't!" she repeated with quavering anxiety. "I can't have anyone else involved! She's . . ." Chris dropped her head. Inhaled. Exhaled. "She's done something, Father. I can't take the risk of someone else finding out. Not a doctor . . . not a nurse . . ." She looked up. "Not anyone."

Frowning, he turned off the taps. ". . . *What if a person, let's say, was a criminal* . . ." He lowered his head, staring down at the basin. "Who's giving her the Sustagen? the Librium? her medicines?"

"We are. Her doctor showed us how."

"You need prescriptions."

"Well, you can do some of that, can't you, Father?"

Karras turned to her, hands upraised above the basin like a surgeon after washup. For a moment he met her haunted gaze, felt some terrible secret in them, some dread. He nodded at the towel in her hands. She stared blankly. "Towel, please," he said softly.

"Oh, I'm sorry!" Very quickly, she fumbled it out to him, still watching him with a tight expectancy. The Jesuit dried his hands. "Well, Father, what's it look like?" Chris finally asked him. "Do you think she's possessed?"

"Do you?"

"I don't know. I thought you were the expert."

"How much do you know about possession?"

"Just a little that I've read. Some things that the doctors told me."

"What doctors?"

"At Barringer Clinic."

He folded the towel and carefully draped it over the bar. "Are you Catholic?"

"No."

"Your daughter?"

"No."

"What religion?"

"None, but I—"

"Why did you come to me, then? Who advised it?"

"I came because I'm desperate!" she blurted excitedly. "No one advised me!"

He stood with his back to her, fringes of the towel still lightly in his grip. "You said earlier psychiatrists advised you to come to me."

"Oh, I don't know *what* I was saying! I've been practically out of my head!"

"Look, I couldn't care less about your motive," he answered with a carefully tempered intensity. "All I care about is doing what's best for your daughter. But I'll tell you right now that if you're looking for an exorcism as an autosuggestive shock cure, you're much better off calling Central Casting, Miss MacNeil, because the Church won't buy it and you'll have wasted precious time." Karras clutched at the towel rack to steady his trembling hands. *What's wrong? What's happened?*

"Incidentally, it's *Mrs.* MacNeil," he heard Chris telling him drily.

He lowered his head and gentled his tone. "Look, whether it's a demon or a mental disorder, I'll do everything I possibly can to help. But I've got to have the truth. It's important for Regan. At the moment, I'm groping in a state of ignorance, which is nothing supernatural for me or abnormal, it's just my usual condition. Now why don't we both get out of this bathroom and go downstairs where we can talk." He had turned back to her with a faint, warm smile of reassurance and reached out his hand to help her up. "I could use a cup of coffee."

"I could use a drink."

While Karl and Sharon looked after Regan, they sat in the study, Chris on the sofa, Karras in a chair beside the fireplace, and Chris related the history of Regan's illness, though she carefully withheld any mention of phenomena related to Dennings.

The priest listened, saying very little: an occasional question; a nod; a frown.

Chris admitted that at first she'd considered exorcism as shock treatment. "Now I don't know," she said, shaking her head. Freckled, clasped fingers twitched in her lap. "I just don't know." She lifted a look to the pensive priest. "What do you think, Father?"

"Compulsive behavior produced by guilt, perhaps, put together with split personality."

"Father, I've *had* all that garbage! Now how can you say that after all you've just seen!"

"If you've seen as many patients in psychiatric wards as I have, you can say it very easily," he assured her. "Come on, now. Possession by demons, all right: let's assume it's a fact of life, that it happens. But your daughter doesn't say she's a demon; she insists she's the *devil himself*, and that's the same thing as saying you're Napoleon Bonaparte! You see?"

"Then explain all those rappings and things."

"I haven't heard them."

"Well, they heard them at Barringer, Father, so it wasn't just here in the house."

"Well, perhaps, but we'd hardly need a devil to explain them."

"So explain them," she demanded.

"Psychokinesis."

"What?"

"Well, you have heard of poltergeist phenomena, haven't you?"

"Ghosts throwing dishes and things?"

Karras nodded. "It's not that uncommon, and usually happens around an emotionally disturbed adolescent. Apparently, extreme inner tension of the mind can sometimes trigger some unknown energy that seems to move objects around at a distance. There's nothing supernatural about it. Like Regan's abnormal strength. Again, in pathology it's common. Call it mind over matter, if you will."

"I call it weird."

"Well, in any case, it happens outside of possession."

"Boy, isn't this beautiful," she said wearily. "Here I am an atheist and here you are a priest and—"

"The best explanation for any phenomenon," Karras overrode her, "is always the simplest one available that accommodates all the facts."

"Well, maybe I'm dumb," she retorted, "but telling me an unknown gizmo in somebody's head throws dishes at a ceiling tells me nothing at all! So what *is* it? Can you tell me for pete's sake what it *is?*"

"No, we don't under—"

"What the hell's split personality, Father? You *say* it; I *hear* it. What *is* it? Am I really that stupid? Will you tell me what it is in a way I can finally get it through my head?" In the red-veined eyes was a plea of despairing confusion.

"Look, there's no one in the world who pretends to understand it," the priest told her gently. "All we know is that it happens, and anything beyond the phenomenon itself is only the purest speculation. But think of it this way, if you like: the human brain contains, say, seventeen billion cells."

Chris leaned forward, frowning intently.

"Now looking at these brain cells," continued Karras, "we see that they handle approximately a hundred million messages per second; that's the number of sensations bombarding your body. They not only integrate all of these messages, but they do it efficiently, they do it without ever stumbling or getting in each other's way. Now how could they do that without some form of communication? Well, it seems as if they couldn't. So apparently each of these cells has a consciousness, maybe, of its own. Now imagine that the human body is a massive ocean liner, all right? and that all of your brain cells are the crew. Now one of these cells is up on the bridge. He's the captain. But he never knows *precisely* what the rest of the crew below decks is doing. All he knows is that the ship keeps running smoothly, that the job's getting done. Now the captain is you, it's your *waking* consciousness. And what happens in dual personality—maybe—is that one of those crew cells down below decks comes up on the bridge and takes over command. In other words, mutiny. Now—does that help you understand it?"

She was staring in unblinking incredulity. "Father, that's so far out of sight that I think it's almost easier to believe in the *devil!*"

"Well—"

"Look, I don't know about all these theories and stuff," she interrupted in a low, intense voice. "But I'll tell you something, Father; you show me Regan's identical twin: same face, same voice, same smell, same everything down to the way she dots her *i*'s, and still I'd know in a second that it wasn't really her! I'd know it! I'd know it in my *gut* and I'm telling you I *know that thing upstairs is not my daughter! I know it! I know!"*

She leaned back, drained. "Now you tell me what to do," she challenged. "Go ahead: you tell me that you know for a *fact* there's nothing wrong with my daughter except in her head; that you know for a *fact* that she doesn't need an exorcism; that you *know* it wouldn't do her any good. Go ahead! You tell me! You tell me what to do!"

For long, troubled seconds, the priest was still. Then he answered softly, "Well, there's little in this world that I know for a fact."

He brooded, sunk back in his chair. Then he spoke again. "Does Regan have a low-pitched voice?" he asked. "Normally?"

"No. In fact, I'd say it's very light."

"Would you consider her precocious?"

"Not at all."

"Do you know her IQ?"

"About average."

"And her reading habits?"

"Nancy Drew and comic books, mostly."

"And her style of speech, right now: how much different would you say it is from normal?"

"Completely. She's never used *half* of those words."

"No, I don't mean the *content* of her speech; I mean the *style*."

"Style?"

"The way she puts words together."

"Gee, I'm really not sure I know what you mean."

"Would you have any letters she's written? Compositions? A recording of her voice would be—"

"Yes, there's a tape of her talking to her father," she interrupted. "She was making it to send to him as a letter but she never got it finished. You want it?"

"Yes, I do, and I'll also need her medical records, especially the file from Barringer."

"Look, Father, I've been that route and I—"

"Yes, yes, I know, but I'll have to see the records for myself."

"So you're still against an exorcism."

"I'm only against the chance of doing your daughter more harm than good."

"But you're talking now strictly as a psychiatrist, right?"

"No, I'm talking now also as a priest. If I go to the Chancery Office, or wherever it is I have to go, to get their permission to perform an exorcism, the first thing I'd have to have is a pretty substantial indication that your daughter's condition isn't a purely psychiatric problem. After that, I'd need evidence that the Church would accept as signs of possession."

"Like what?"

"I don't know. I'll have to go and look it up."

"Are you kidding? I thought you were supposed to be an expert."

"You probably know more about demonic possession right now than most priests. In the meantime, when can you get me the Barringer records?"

"I'll charter a plane if I have to!"

"And that tape?"

She stood up. "I'll go see if I can find it."

"And just one other thing," he added. She paused beside his chair. "That book that you mentioned with the section on possession: do you think you can remember now if Regan ever read it *prior* to the onset of the illness?"

She concentrated, fingernails scraping at teeth. "Gee, I seem to remember her reading something the day before the shi—before the trouble really started," she amended, "but I really just can't be sure. But she did it sometime, I think. I mean, I'm sure. *Pretty* sure."

"I'd like to see it. May I have it?"

"It's yours. It's overdue at your library. I'll get it." She was moving from the study. "That tape's in the basement, I think. I'll look. Be right back in a second."

Karras nodded absently, staring at a pattern in the rug, and then after many minutes he got up, walked slowly to the entry hall and stood motionless in the darkness, stood without expression, in another dimension, staring into nothing with his hands in his pockets as he listened to the grunting of a pig from upstairs, to the yelping of a jackal, to hiccups, to hissing.

"Oh, you're there! I went looking in the study."

Karras turned to see Chris flicking on the light.

"Are you leaving?" She came forward with the book and the tape.

"I'm afraid I've got a lecture to prepare for tomorrow."

"Oh? Where?"

"At the med school." He accepted the book and the tape from her hands. "I'll try to get by here sometime tomorrow afternoon or evening. In the meantime, if anything urgent develops, you be sure that you call me, no matter what time. I'll leave word at the switchboard to let your ring through." She nodded. The Jesuit opened the door. "Now how are you fixed for medication?" he asked.

"Okay," she said. "It's all on refillable prescription."

"You won't call your doctor in again?"

The actress closed her eyes and very slightly shook her head.

"You know, I'm not a GP," he cautioned.

"I can't," she whispered. "I can't."

He could feel her anxiety pounding like waves on an unknown beach. "Well, now, sooner or later, I'm going to have to tell one of my superiors what I'm up to, especially if I'm going to be coming by here at various unusual hours of the night."

"Do you have to?" She frowned at him worriedly.

"Well, otherwise, it might look a little bit odd, don't you think?"

She looked down. "Yeah, I see what you mean," she murmured.

"Do you mind? I'll tell him only what I have to. Don't worry," he assured her. "It won't get around."

She lifted a helpless, tormented face to the strong, sad eyes; saw strength; saw pain.

"Okay," she said weakly.

She trusted the pain.

He nodded. "We'll be talking."

He started outside, but then hung in the doorway for a moment, thinking, a hand to his lips. "Did your daughter know a priest was coming over?"

"No. No, nobody knew but me."

"Did you know that my mother had died just recently?"

"Yes. I'm very sorry."

"Is Regan aware of it?"

"Why?"

"Is she aware of it?"

"No, not at all."

He nodded.

"Why'd you ask?" Chris repeated, her brows slightly puckered with curiosity.

"Not important." He shrugged. "I just wondered." He examined her features with a faint look of worry. "Are you getting any sleep?"

"Oh, a little."

"Get pills, then. Are you taking any Librium?"

"Yes."

"How much?" he asked.

"Ten milligrams, twice a day."

"Try twenty, twice a day. In the meantime, try to keep away from your daughter. The more you're exposed to her present behavior, the greater the chance of some permanent damage being done to your feelings about her. Stay clear. And slow down. You'll be no help to Regan, you know, with a nervous breakdown."

She nodded despondently, eyes lowered.

"Now please go to bed," he said gently. "Will you please go to bed right now?"

"Yeah, okay," she said softly. "Okay. I promise." She looked at him with the trace of a smile. "Good night, Father. Thanks. Thanks a lot."

He studied her for a moment without expression; then quickly moved away.

Chris watched from the doorway. As he crossed the street, it occurred to her that he'd probably missed his dinner. Then briefly she worried that he might be cold. He was rolling his shirt sleeve down.

At the corner of Prospect and P, he dropped the book and stooped quickly to retrieve it, then rounded the corner and vanished from sight. As she watched him disappear, Chris abruptly was aware of a feeling of lightness. She didn't see Kinderman sitting alone in the unmarked car.

She closed the door.

Half an hour later, Damien Karras hurried back to his room in the Jesuit residence hall with a number of books and periodicals taken from the shelves of the Georgetown library. Hastily he dumped them on top of his desk and then rummaged through drawers for a package of cigarettes. Finding a half-empty pack of stale Camels, he lit one, puffed deep and held the smoke in his lungs while he thought about Regan.

Hysteria. He knew that it had to be hysteria. He exhaled the smoke, hooked his thumbs in his belt and looked down at the books. He had Oesterreich's *Possession*; Huxley's *The Devils of Loudun*; *Parapraxis in the Haizman Case of Freud*; Mc-Casland's *Demon Possession and Exorcism in Early Christianity in the Light of Modern Views of Mental Illness*; and extracts from psychiatric journals of Freud's "A Neurosis of

Demoniacal Possession in the 17th Century," and "The Demonology of Modern Psychiatry."

"Couldjya help an old altar boy, Faddah?"

The Jesuit felt at his brow, and then looked at his fingers, rubbing a sticky sweat between them. Then he noticed that his door was open. He crossed the room and closed it, and then went to a shelf for his red-bound copy of *The Roman Ritual*, a compendium of rites and prayers. Clamping the cigarette between his lips, he squinted through smoke as he turned to the "General Rules" for exorcists, looking for the signs of demonic possession. He scanned and then started to read more slowly:

> . . . The exorcist should not believe too readily that a person is possessed by an evil spirit; but he ought to ascertain the signs by which a person possessed can be distinguished from one who is suffering from some illness, especially one of a psychological nature. Signs of possession may be the following: ability to speak with some facility in a strange language or to understand it when spoken by another; the faculty of divulging future and hidden events; display of powers which are beyond the subject's age and natural condition; and various other conditions which, when taken together as a whole, build up the evidence.

For a time Karras pondered, then he leaned against the bookshelf and read the remainder of the instructions. When he had finished, he found himself glancing back up at instruction number 8:

> Some reveal a crime which has been committed and the perpetrators thereof—

He looked up at the door as he heard a knock. "Damien?"
"Come in."

It was Dyer. "Hey, Chris MacNeil was trying to reach you. She ever get hold of you?"

"When? You mean, tonight?"

"No, this afternoon."

"Oh, yes; yes, I spoke to her."

"Good," said Dyer. "Just wanted to be sure you got the message."

The diminutive priest was prowling the room now, picking at objects like an elf in a thrift shop.

"What do you need, Joe?" Karras asked him.

"Got any lemon drops?"

"What?"

"I've looked all through the hall for some lemon drops. Nobody's got any. Boy, I really crave one," Dyer brooded, still prowling. "I once spent a year hearing children's confessions, and I wound up a lemon-drop junkie. I got hooked. The little bastards keep *breathing* it on you along with all that pot. Between the two, it's addictive, I think." He lifted the lid of a pipe-tobacco humidor where Karras had stored some pistachio nuts. "What are these—dead Mexican jumping beans?"

Karras turned to his bookshelves, looking for a title. "Listen, Joe, I've got a—"

"Isn't that Chris really nice?" interrupted Dyer, flopping on the bed. He stretched full length with his hands clasped comfortably behind his head. "Nice lady. Have you met her?"

"We've talked," answered Karras, plucking out a green-bound volume called *Satan*, a collection of articles and Catholic position papers by various French theologians. He carried it back with him toward the desk. "Look, I've really got to—"

"Plain. Down-to-earth. Unaffected," continued Dyer. "She can help us with my plan for when we both quit the priesthood."

"Who's quitting the priesthood?"

"Faggots. In droves. Basic black has gone out. Now I—"

"Joe, I've got a lecture to prepare for tomorrow," said Karras as he set down the books on his desk.

"Yeah, okay. Now my plan is we go to Chris MacNeil—

got the picture?—with this notion that I've got for a screen-play based on the life of Saint Ignatius Loyola. The title is *Brave Jesuits Marching*, and—"

"Would you get your ass out of here, Joe?" prodded Karras, tamping out his cigarette butt in an ashtray.

"Is this boring?"

"I've got work to do."

"Who the hell's stopping you?"

"Come on, now, I mean it." Karras had started to unbutton his shirt. "I'm going to jump in the shower and then I've got to work."

"Didn't see you at dinner, by the way," said Dyer, rising reluctantly from the bed. "Where'd you eat?"

"I didn't."

"That's foolish. Why diet when you only wear frocks?" He had come to the desk and was sniffing at a cigarette. "Stale."

"Is there a tape recorder here in the hall?"

"There isn't even a lemon drop here in the hall. Use the language lab."

"Who's got a key? Father President?"

"No. Father Janitor. You need it tonight?"

"Yes, I do," said Karras, as he draped his shirt on the back of the desk chair. "Where do I find him?"

"Want me to get it for you?"

"Could you do that? I'm really in a bind."

"No sweat, Great Beatific Jesuit Witch Doctor. Coming." Dyer opened the door and walked out.

Karras showered and then dressed in a T-shirt and trousers. Sitting down to his desk, he discovered a carton of Camel non-filters, and beside it a key that was labeled LANGUAGE LAB and another tagged REFECTORY REFRIGERATOR. Appended to the latter was a note: *Better you than the rats.* Karras smiled at the signature: *The Lemon Drop Kid.* He put the note aside, then unfastened his wristwatch and placed it in front of him

221

on the desk. The time was 10:58 P.M. He began to read. Freud. McCasland. *Satan.* Oesterreich's exhaustive study. And at a little after 4 A.M., he had finished. Was rubbing at his face. At his eyes. They were smarting. He glanced at the ashtray. Ashes and the twisted butts of cigarettes. Smoke hanging thick in the air. He stood up and walked wearily to a window. Slid it open. He gulped at the coolness of the moist morning air and stood there thinking. Regan had the physical syndrome of possession. That much he knew. About that he had no doubt. For in case after case, irrespective of geography or period of history, the symptoms of possession were substantially constant. Some Regan had not evidenced as yet: stigmata; the desire for repugnant foods; the insensitivity to pain; the frequently loud and irrepressible hiccuping. But the others she had manifested clearly: the involuntary motor excitement; foul breath; furred tongue; the wasting away of the frame; the distended stomach; the irritations of the skin and mucous membrane. And most significantly present were the basic symptoms of the hard core of cases which Oesterreich had characterized as "genuine" possession: the striking change in the voice and in the features, plus the manifestation of a new personality.

Karras looked up and stared darkly down the street. Through the branches of trees he could see the house and the large bay window of Regan's bedroom. When possession was voluntary, as with mediums, the new personality was often benign. *Like Tia,* brooded Karras. Spirit of a woman who'd possessed a man. A sculptor. Briefly. An hour at a time. Until a friend of the sculptor fell desperately in love. With Tia. Pleaded with the sculptor to permit her to permanently remain in possession of his body. *But in Regan, there's no Tia,* Karras reflected grimly. The invading personality was vicious. Malevolent. Typical of cases of demonic possession where the new personality sought the destruction of the body of its host. And frequently achieved it.

Moodily the Jesuit walked back to his desk, where he picked up a package of cigarettes; lit one. *So okay. She's got the syndrome of demonic possession. Now how do you cure it?*

He fanned out the match. *That depends on what caused it.* He sat on the edge of his desk. Considered. The nuns at the convent of Lille. Possessed. In early-seventeenth-century France. They'd confessed to their exorcists that while helpless in the state of possession, they had regularly attended Satanic orgies; had regularly varied their erotic fare: Mondays and Tuesdays, heterosexual copulation; Thursdays, sodomy, fellatio and cunnilingus, with homosexual partners; Saturday, bestiality with domestic animals and dragons. *And dragons!* . . . The Jesuit shook his head. As with Lille, he thought the causes of many possessions were a mixture of fraud and mythomania. Still others, however, seemed caused by mental illness: paranoia; schizophrenia; neurasthenia; psychasthenia; and this was the reason, he knew, that the Church had for years recommended that the exorcist work with a psychiatrist or a neurologist present. Yet not all possessions had causes so clear. Many had led Oesterreich to characterize possession as a separate disorder all its own; to dismiss the explanatory "split personality" label of psychiatry as no more than an equally occult substitution for the concepts of "demon" and "spirit of the dead."

Karras rubbed a finger in the crease beside his nose. The indications from Barringer, Chris had told him, were that Regan's disorder might be caused by suggestion; by something that was somehow related to hysteria. And Karras thought it likely. He believed the majority of the cases he had studied had been caused by precisely these two factors. *Sure. For one thing, it mostly hits women. For another, all those outbreaks of possession epidemics. And then those exorcists* . . . Karras frowned. They often themselves became the victims of possession. He thought of Loudun. France. The Ursuline Convent of nuns. Of four of the exorcists sent there to deal with an epidemic of

possession, three—Fathers Lucas, Lactance and Tranquille—
not only became possessed, but died soon after, apparently of
shock. And the fourth, Père Surin, who was thirty-three years
old at the time of his possession, became insane for the subsequent twenty-five years of his life.

He nodded to himself. If Regan's disorder was hysterical;
if the onset of possession was the product of suggestion, then
the source of the suggestion could only be the chapter in the
book on witchcraft. *The chapter on possession. Did she read
it?*

He pored over its pages. Were there striking similarities
between any of its details and Regan's behavior? *That might
prove it. It might.*

He found some correlations:

. . . The case of an eight-year-old girl who was described in
the chapter as "bellowing like a bull in a thunderous, deep
bass voice." (*Regan's lowing like a steer.*)

. . . The case of Helene Smith, who'd been treated by the
great psychologist Flournoy; his description of her changing her
voice and her features with "lightning rapidity" into those of
a variety of personalities. (*She did that with me. The personality who spoke with a British accent. Quick change. Instantaneous.*)

. . . A case in South Africa, reported firsthand by the noted
ethnologist Junod; his description of a woman who'd vanished
from her dwelling one night being found on the following
morning "tied to the top" of a very tall tree by "fine lianas,"
and then afterward "gliding down the tree, head down, while
hissing and rapidly flicking her tongue in and out like a
snake. She then hung suspended, for a time, and proceeded
to speak in a language that no one had ever heard." (*Regan
gliding like a snake when she was following Sharon. The gibberish. An attempt at an "unknown language."*)

. . . The case of Joseph and Thiebaut Burner, aged eight and
ten; description of them "lying on their backs and suddenly

whirling like tops with the utmost rapidity." (*Sounds pretty close to her whirling like a dervish.*)

There were other similarities; still other reasons for suspecting suggestion: mention of abnormal strength; of obscenity of speech; and accounts of possession from the gospels, which perhaps were the basis, thought Karras, of the curiously religious content of Regan's ravings at Barringer Clinic. Moreover, in the chapter there was mention of the onset of possession in stages: ". . . The first, *infestation,* consists of an attack through the victim's surroundings; noises—odors—the displacement of objects; and the second, *obsession,* consists in a personal attack on the subject designed to instill terror through the kind of injury that one man might inflict on another through blows and kicks." The rappings. The flingings. The attacks by Captain Howdy.

Maybe . . . maybe she read it. But Karras wasn't convinced. *Not at all . . . not at all.* And Chris. She had seemed so uncertain about it.

He walked to the window again. *What's the answer, then? Genuine possession? A demon?* He looked down and shook his head. *No way. No way. Paranormal happenings? Sure. Why not?* Too many competent observers had reported them. Doctors. Psychiatrists. Men like Junod. *But the problem is how do you interpret the phenomena?* He thought back to Oesterreich. Reference to a shaman of the Altai. Siberia. Voluntarily possessed and examined in a clinic while performing an apparently paranormal action: levitation. Just prior, his pulse rate had spurted to one hundred, then, afterward, leaped to an amazing two hundred. Marked changes in temperature as well. In respiration. *So his paranormal action was tied to physiology. It was caused by some bodily energy or force.* But as proof of possession the Church wanted clear and exterior phenomena that suggested . . .

He'd forgotten the wording. Looked it up. Traced a finger down the page of a book on his desk. Found it: ". . . verifiable exterior phenomena which suggest the idea that they are due to the extraordinary intervention of an intelligent cause other than man." Was that the case with the shaman? Karras asked himself. No. *And is that the case with Regan?*

He turned to a passage he had underlined in pencil: *"The exorcist will simply be careful that none of the patient's manifestations are left unaccounted for. . . ."*

He nodded. *Okay, then. Let's see.* Pacing, he ran through the manifestations of Regan's disorder along with their possible explanations. He ticked them off mentally, one by one:

The startling change in Regan's features.

Partly her illness. Partly undernourishment. Mostly, he concluded, it was due to physiognomy being an expression of psychic constitution. *Whatever the hell that means!* he added wryly.

The startling change in Regan's voice.

He had yet to hear the *original* voice. And even if that had been light, as reported by her mother, constant shrieking would thicken the vocal cords, with a consequent deepening of the voice. The only problem here, he reflected, was the massive volume of that voice, for even with a thickening of the cords this would seem to be physiologically impossible. And yet, he considered, in states of anxiety or pathology, displays of paranormal strength in excess of muscular potential were known to be a commonplace. Might not vocal cords and voice box be subject to the same mysterious effect?

Regan's suddenly extended vocabulary and knowledge.

Cryptomnesia: buried recollections of words and data she had once been exposed to, even in infancy, perhaps. In somnambulists—and frequently in people at the point of death—the buried data often came to the surface with almost photographic fidelity.

Regan's recognition of him as a priest.

Good guess. If she *had* read the chapter on possession, she might have expected a visit by a priest. And according to Jung, the unconscious awareness and sensitivity of hysterical patients could at moments be fifty times greater than normal, which accounted for seemingly authentic "thought-reading" via table-tapping by mediums, for what the medium's unconscious was actually "reading" were the tremors and vibrations created in the table by the hands of the person whose thoughts were supposedly being read. The tremors formed a pattern of letters or numbers. Thus, Regan might conceivably have "read" his identity merely from his manner; from the look of his hands; from the scent of sacramental wine.

Regan's knowledge of the death of his mother.

Good guess. He was forty-six.

"Couldjya help an old altar boy, Faddah?"

Textbooks in use in Catholic seminaries accepted telepathy as both a reality and a natural phenomenon.

Regan's precocity of intellect.

In the course of personally observing a case of multiple personality involving alleged occult phenomena, the psychiatrist Jung had concluded that in states of hysterical somnambulism not only were unconscious perceptions of the senses heightened, but also the functioning of the intellect, for the new personalities in the case in question seemed clearly more intelligent than the first. And yet, puzzled Karras, did merely reporting the phenomenon *explain* it?

Abruptly he stopped pacing and hovered by his desk, for it suddenly dawned upon him that Regan's pun on Herod was even more complicated than at first it had appeared: when the Pharisees told Christ of Herod's threats, he remembered, Christ had answered them: "Go and tell that fox that I cast out devils. . . ."

He glanced at the tape of Regan's voice for a moment, then sat wearily at the desk. He lit another cigarette . . . exhaled . . . thought again of the Burner boys; of the case of the eight-year-old girl who had manifested symptoms of full-blown possession. What book had *this* girl read that had enabled her unconscious mind to simulate the symptoms to such perfection? And how did the unconscious of victims in China communicate the symptoms to the various unconscious minds of people possessed in Siberia, in Germany, in Africa, so that the symptoms were always the same?

"Incidentally, your mother is here with us, Karras. . . ."

He stared unseeing as smoke from his cigarette rose like whispered curls of memory. The priest leaned back, looking down at the bottom left-hand drawer of the desk. For a time, he kept staring. Then slowly he leaned down, pulled open the drawer and extracted a faded language exercise book. Adult education. His mother's. He set it on the desk and thumbed the pages with a tender care. Letters of the alphabet, over and over. Then simple exercises:

LESSON VI

MY COMPLETE ADDRESS

Between the pages, an attempt at a letter:

Dear Dimmy,
I have been waiting

Then another beginning. Incomplete. He looked away. Saw her eyes at the window . . . waiting. . . .

" '*Domine, non sum dignus. . . .*' "

The eyes became Regan's . . . eyes shrieking . . . eyes waiting. . . .

" '*Speak but the word. . . .*' "

He glanced at the tape of Regan's voice.

He left the room. Took the tape to the language lab. Found a tape recorder. Sat down. He threaded the tape to an empty

228

reel. Clamped on earphones. Turned on the switch. Then leaned forward and listened. Exhausted. Intense.

For a time, only tape hiss. Squeaking of the mechanism. Suddenly, a thumping sound of activation. Noises. "Hello . . ." Then a whining feedback. Chris MacNeil, tone hushed, in the background: "Not so close to the microphone, honey. Hold it back." "Like this?" "No, more." "Like this?" "Yeah, okay. Go ahead now, just talk." Giggling. The microphone bumping a table. Then the sweet, clear voice of Regan MacNeil:

"Hello, Daddy? This is me. Ummm . . ." Giggling; then a whispered aside: "I can't tell what to say!" "Oh, just tell him how you are, honey. Tell about all of the things you've been doing." More giggling, then: "Umm, Daddy . . . Well, ya see . . . I mean, I hope you can *hear* me okay, and, umm— well, now, let's see. Umm, well, first we're—No, wait, now. . . . See, first we're in Washington, Daddy, ya know? I mean, that's where the President lives, and this house—ya know, Daddy?—it's—No, wait, now; I better start over. See, Daddy, there's . . ."

Karras heard the rest only dimly, from afar, through the roaring of blood in his ears, like the ocean, as up through his chest and his face swelled an overwhelming intuition: *The thing that I saw in that room wasn't Regan!*

He returned to the Jesuit residence hall. Found a cubicle. Said Mass before the rush. As he lifted the Host in consecration, it trembled in his fingers with a hope he dared not hope, that he fought with every particled fiber of his will. " 'For this is My Body . . .' " he whispered tremulously. .

No, bread! This is nothing but bread!

He dared not love again and lose. That loss was too great, that pain too keen. He bowed his head and swallowed the Host like lost illusion. For a moment it stuck in the dryness of his throat.

After Mass, he skipped breakfast. Made notes for his lecture. Met his class at the Georgetown University Medical School. Threaded hoarsely through the ill-prepared talk: "... and in considering the symptoms of manic mood disorders, you will ..." "Daddy, this is me ... this is me. ..."

But who was "me"?

Karras dismissed the class early and returned to his room, where immediately he hunched over his desk, palms of his hands pressed flat, and intently reexamined the Church's position on the paranormal signs of demonic possession. *Was I being too hard-nosed?* he wondered. He scrutinized the high points in *Satan*: "telepathy ... natural phenomenon ... movement of objects from a distance now suspect . . . from the body there may emanate some fluid . . . our forefathers . . . science . . . nowadays we must be more cautious. The paranormal evidence notwithstanding, however . . ." He slowed the pace of his reading. ". . . all conversations held with the patient must be carefully analyzed, for if they present the same system of association of ideas·and of logicogrammatical habits that he exhibits in his normal state, the possession must then be held suspect."

Karras breathed deeply, exhausted. Then exhaled. Dropped his head. *No way. Doesn't cut it.* He glanced to the plate on the facing page. A demon. His gaze flicked down idly to the caption: "Pazuzu." Karras shut his eyes. Something wrong. *Tranquille* . . . He envisioned the exorcist's death: the final agonies . . . the bellowing . . . the hissing . . . the vomiting . . . the hurlings to the ground from his bed by his "demons," who were furious because soon he would be dead and beyond their torment. *And Lucas!* Lucas. Kneeling by the bedside. Praying. But the moment Tranquille was dead, Lucas instantly assumed the identity of his demons, began viciously kicking at the still-warm corpse, at the shattered, clawed body reeking of excrement and vomit, while six strong men were attempting to restrain him, would not stop until the corpse had been carried from the room. Karras saw it. Saw it clearly.

Could it be? Could it possibly, conceivably be? Could the only hope for Regan be the ritual of exorcism? Must he open up that locker of aches?

He could not shake it. Could not leave it untested. He must know. How to know? He opened his eyes. ". . . conversations with the patient must be carefully . . ." Yes. Yes, why not? If discovery that speech patterns of Regan and the "demon" were the same ruled out possession even *with* paranormal occurrences, then certainly . . . *Sure . . . strong difference in the patterns should mean that there probably is possession!*

He paced. *What else? What else? Something quick. She— Wait a minute.* He paused, staring down, hands clasped behind his back. *That chapter . . . that chapter in the book on witchcraft.* Had it mentioned . . . ? Yes, it had: that demons invariably reacted with fury when confronted with the consecrated Host . . . with relics . . . with— *Holy water! Right! That's it! I'll go up there and sprinkle her with tap water! But tell her it's holy water! Sure! If she reacts the way demons are supposed to react, then I'll know she's not possessed . . . that the symptoms are suggestive . . . that she got them from the book! But if she doesn't react it would mean . . .*

Genuine possession?

Maybe . . .

Feverish, he rummaged for a holy-water vial.

Willie admitted him to the house. In the entry, he glanced toward Regan's bedroom. Shouts. Obscenities. And yet not in the deep, coarse voice of the demon. Raspy. Lighter. A broad British . . . Yes! . . . The manifestation that had fleetingly appeared when he'd last seen Regan.

Karras glanced down at the waiting Willie. She was staring puzzled at the Roman collar. At the priestly robes. "Where's Mrs. MacNeil, please?" Karras asked her.

Willie motioned upstairs.

"Thank you."

He moved to the staircase. Climbed. Saw Chris in the hall. She was sitting in a chair near Regan's bedroom, head lowered, her arms folded on her chest. As the Jesuit approached her, Chris heard the swishing of his robes. She glanced up and quickly stood. "Hello, Father."

There were bluish sacs beneath her eyes. Karras frowned. "Did you sleep?"

"Oh, a little."

He was shaking his head in admonishment.

"Well, I couldn't," she sighed at him, motioning her head at Regan's door. "She's been doing that all night."

"Any vomiting?"

"No." She took hold of his sleeve as if to lead him away. "C'mon, let's go downstairs where we can—"

"No, I'd like to see her," he gently interrupted. He resisted the tugging insistence of her lead.

"Right now?"

Something wrong, reflected Karras. She looked tense. Afraid. "Why not now?" he inquired.

She glanced furtively at the door of Regan's bedroom. From within shrieked the hoarse mad voice: "Damned Naa-zi! Naa-zi cunt!"

Chris looked away; then reluctantly nodded. "Go ahead. Go on in."

"You've got a tape recorder?"

Her eyes searched his with quick movements. Little flicks.

"Could you have it brought up to the room with a blank reel of tape, please?"

She frowned with suspicion. "What for?" Then alarm. "You mean, you want to tape . . .?"

"Yes, it's im—"

"Father, I can't have you . . .!"

"I need to make comparisons of patterns of speech," he cut in firmly. "Now please! You're just going to have to trust me!"

They turned to the door as an excoriating stream of obscenities apparently drove Karl out of Regan's bedroom. His face ashen and grim, he was carrying soiled diapers and bedding.

"Get 'em on, Karl?" Chris asked him as the servant closed the bedroom door behind him.

Karl glanced quickly at Karras, then at Chris. "They are on," he said tersely, and went quickly down the hallway toward the staircase.

Chris watched him. She turned back to Karras.

"Okay," she said weakly. "Okay. I'll have it sent up." And abruptly she was walking down the hall.

For a moment Karras watched her. Puzzled. What was wrong? Then he noticed the sudden silence in the bedroom. It was brief. Now the yelping of diabolic laughter. He moved forward. Felt the water vial in his pocket. He opened the door and stepped into the bedroom.

The stench was more powerful than the evening before. He closed the door. Stared. That horror. That thing on the bed.

As he approached, it was watching with mocking eyes. Full of cunning. Full of hate. Full of power.

"Hello, Karras."

The priest heard the sound of diarrhetic voiding into plastic pants.

He spoke calmly from the foot of the bed. "Hello, devil. And how are you feeling?"

"At the moment, very happy to see you. Glad." The tongue lolled out of the mouth while the eyes appraised Karras with insolence. "Flying your colors, I see. Very good." Another rumbling. "You don't mind a bit of stink, do you, Karras?"

"Not at all."

"You're a liar!"

"Does that bother you?"

"Mildly."

"But the devil *likes* liars."

233

"Only good ones, dear Karras, only good ones," it chuckled. "Moreover, who said I'm the devil?"

"Didn't you?"

"Oh, I might have. I might. I'm not well. You believed me?"

"Of course."

"My apologies."

"Are you saying that you *aren't* the devil?"

"Just a poor struggling demon. A devil. A subtle distinction, but one not entirely lost upon Our Father who is in Hell. Incidentally, you won't mention my slip of the tongue to him, Karras, now will you? Eh? When you see him?"

"See him? Is he here?" asked the priest.

"In the pig? Not at all. Just a poor little family of wandering souls, my friend. You don't blame us for being here, do you? After all, we have no place to go. No home."

"And how long are you planning to stay?"

The head jerked up from the pillow, contorted in rage as it roared, "Until the piglet *dies!*" And then as suddenly, Regan settled back into a thick-lipped, drooling grin. "Incidentally, what an excellent day for an exorcism, Karras."

The book! She must have read that in the book!

The sardonic eyes were staring piercingly. "Do begin it soon. Very soon."

Inconsistent. Something off here. "You would like that?"

"Intensely."

"But wouldn't that drive you out of Regan?"

The demon put its head back, cackling maniacally, then broke off. "It would bring us together."

"You and Regan?"

"You and *us*, my good friend," croaked the demon. "You and *us*." And from deep in that throat, muffled laughter.

Karras stared. At the back of his neck, he felt hands. Icy cold. Lightly touching. And then gone. Caused by fear, he concluded. Fear.

Fear of what?

"Yes, you'll join our little family, Karras. You see, the trouble with signs in the sky, my dear morsel, is that once having seen them, one has no excuse. Have you noticed how few miracles one hears about lately? Not our fault, Karras. Don't blame us. We try!"

Karras jerked around his head at a loud, sudden banging. A bureau drawer had popped open, sliding out its entire length. He felt a quick-rising thrill as he watched it abruptly bang shut. *There it is!* And then as suddenly, the emotion dropped away like a rotted chunk of bark from a tree: *Psychokinesis.* Karras heard chuckling. He glanced back to Regan.

"How pleasant to chat with you, Karras," said the demon, grinning. "I feel free. Like a wanton. I spread my great wings. In fact, even my telling you this will serve only to increase your damnation, my doctor, my dear and inglorious physician."

"You did that? You made the dresser drawer move just now?"

The demon wasn't listening. It had glanced toward the door, toward the sound of someone rapidly approaching down the hall, and now its features turned to those of the other personality. "Damned butchering bastard!" it shrieked in the hoarse, British-accented voice. "Cunting Hun!"

Through the door came Karl, moving swiftly with the tape recorder, setting it down by the bed, eyes averted, and then quickly retreating from the room.

"*Out,* Himmler! Out of my sight! Go and visit your club-footed daughter! Bring her *sauerkraut!* Sauerkraut and *heroin,* Thorndike! She will *love* it! She will—"

Gone. Karl was gone. And now abruptly the thing within Regan was cordial, watching Karras as the priest quickly set up the tape recorder; looked for an outlet; plugged it in; threaded tape.

"Oh, yes, hullo hullo hullo. What's up?" it said happily "Are we going to record something, Padre? How fun! Oh, I *do* love to playact, you know! Oh, immensely!"

"I'm Damien Karras," said the priest as he worked. "And who are you?"

"Are you asking for my credits now, ducks? Damned cheeky of you, wouldn't you say?" It giggled. "I was Puck in the junior class play." It glanced around. "Where's a drink, incidentally? I'm parched."

The priest placed the microphone gently on the nightstand. "If you'll tell me your name, I'll try to find one."

"Yes, of course," it responded with a cackle of amusement. "And then drink it yourself, I suppose."

As he pushed the RECORD button, Karras answered, "Tell me your name."

"Fucking plunderer!" it rasped.

And then promptly disappeared and was replaced by the demon. "And what are we doing now, Karras? Recording our little discussion?"

Karras straightened. Stared. Then he pulled up a chair beside the bed and sat down. "Do you mind?" he responded.

"Not at all," croaked the demon. "I have always rather liked infernal engines."

Abruptly a strong, new stench assailed Karras. It was an odor like . . .

"Sauerkraut, Karras. Have you noticed?"

It does *smell like sauerkraut,* the Jesuit marveled. It seemed to be emanating from the bed. From Regan's body. Then it was gone, replaced by the putrid stench of before. Karras frowned. *Did I imagine it? Autosuggestion?* He thought of the holy water. *Now? No, save it. Get more of the speech pattern.* "To whom was I speaking before?" he asked.

"Merely one of the family, Karras."

"A demon?"

"You give too much credit."

"How so?"

"The word 'demon' means 'wise one.' He is stupid."

The Jesuit grew taut. "In what language does 'demon' mean 'wise one'?"

"In Greek."

"You speak Greek?"

"Very fluently."

One of the signs! Karras thought with excitement. *Speaking in an unknown tongue!* It was more than he'd hoped for. *"Pos egnokas hoti presbyteros eimi?"* he quickly inquired in classical Greek.

"I am not in the mood, Karras."

"Oh. Then you cannot—"

"I am *not in the mood!*"

Disappointment. Karras brooded. "You made the dresser drawer come sliding out?" he inquired.

"Most assuredly."

"Very impressive." Karras nodded. "You're certainly a very, very powerful demon."

"I am."

"I was wondering if you'd do it again."

"Yes, in time."

"Do it now, please—I would really like to see it."

"In time."

"Why not now?"

"We must give you some reason for doubt," it croaked. "Some. Just enough to assure the final outcome." It put back its head in a chuckle of malice. "How novel to attack through the truth! Ah, what joy!"

Icy hands lightly touching at his neck. Karras stared. Why the fear again? Fear? *Was it fear?*

"No, not fear," said the demon. It was grinning. "That was me."

Hands gone now. Karras frowned. Felt new wonder. Chipped it down. *Telepathic. Or is she? Find out. Find out now.* "Can you tell me what I'm thinking right now?"

"Your thoughts are too dull to entertain."

"Then you *can't* read my mind."

"You may have it as you wish . . . as you wish."

Try the holy water? Now? He heard the squeaking of the

tape-recorder mechanism. *No. Just keep digging. Get more of a sampling of the speech.* "You're a fascinating person," said Karras.

Regan sneered.

"Oh, no, really," said Karras. "I'd like to know more about your background. You've never told me who you are, for example."

"A devil," rumbled the demon.

"Yes, I know, but *which* devil? What's your name?"

"Ah, now what is in a name, Karras? Never mind my name. Call me Howdy, if you find it more comfortable."

"Oh, yes. Captain Howdy." Karras nodded. "Regan's friend."

"Her very *close* friend."

"Oh, really?"

"Indeed."

"But then why do you torment her?"

"Because I am her friend. The piglet likes it!"

"She likes it?"

"She adores it!"

"But why?"

"Ask her!"

"Would you allow her to answer?"

"No."

"Well, then what would be the point in my asking?"

"None!" The demon's eyes glinted spite.

"Who's the person I was speaking to earlier?" asked Karras.

"You've asked that."

"I know, but you never gave an answer."

"Just another good friend of the sweet, honey piglet, dear Karras."

"May I speak to him?"

"No. He is busy with your mother. She is sucking his cock to the *bristles*, Karras! to the *root!*" It chuckled softly, and then added, "Marvelous tongue, your mother. Good mouth."

It was gleaming at him mockingly, and Karras felt a rage

sweeping through him, a tremor of hatred that the priest quickly realized with a start was directed not at Regan, but at the demon. *The demon! What the hell is the matter with you, Karras?* The Jesuit gripped calm by its edges, breathed deep and then stood up and slipped the vial of water from the pocket of his shirt. He uncorked it.

The demon looked wary. "What is that?"

"Don't you know?" asked Karras, his thumb half covering the mouth of the vial as he started to sprinkle its contents on Regan. "It's holy water, devil."

Immediately the demon was cringing, writhing, bellowing in terror and in pain: "It burns! It burns! Ahh, stop it! Cease, priest bastard! Cease!"

Expressionless, Karras stopped sprinkling. *Hysteria. Suggestion. She did read the book.* He glanced at the tape recorder. *Why bother?*

He noticed the silence. Looked at Regan. Knit his brows. *What's this? What's going on?* The demonic personality had vanished and in its place were other features, which were similar. Yet different. And the eyes had rolled upward into their sockets, exposing the whites. Now murmuring. Slowly. A feverish gibberish. Karras came around to the side of the bed. Leaned over to listen. *What is it? Nothing.* And yet . . . *It's got cadence. Like a language.* Could it be? He felt the fluttering of wings in his stomach; gripped them hard; held them still. *Come on, don't be an idiot!* And yet . . .

He glanced to the volume monitor on the tape recorder. Not flashing. He turned up the amplification knob and then listened, intent, ear low to Regan's lips. The gibberish ceased and was replaced by breathing, raspy and deep.

Karras straightened. "Who are you?" he asked.

"Nowonmai," the entity answered. Groaning whisper. In pain. Whites of eyes. Lids fluttering. "Nowonmai." The cracked, breathy voice, like the soul of its owner, seemed cloistered in a dark, curtained space beyond time.

"Is that your name?" Karras frowned.

The lips moved. Fevered syllables. Slow. Unintelligible. Then shortly it ceased.

"Are you able to understand me?"

Silence. Only breathing. Deep. Oddly muffled. The eerie sound of sleep in an oxygen tent.

The Jesuit waited. Hoped for more.

Nothing came.

He rewound the tape, packed the tape recorder into its case, picked it up and took the reel of tape. He gave Regan a last look. Loose ends. Irresolute, he left the room and went downstairs.

He found Chris in the kitchen. She was sitting somberly over coffee at the table with Sharon. As they saw him approach, they looked up at him with a questioning, anxious expectancy. Chris said quietly to Sharon, "Better go check on Regan. Okay?"

Sharon took a final sip of coffee, nodded wanly at Karras and left. He sat down wearily at the table.

"So what's doin'?" Chris asked him, searching his eyes.

About to answer, Karras waited as Karl entered quietly from the pantry and went over to the sink to scrub pots.

Chris followed his gaze. "It's okay," she said softly. "Go ahead. What's the drill?"

"There were two personalities I hadn't seen before. Well, no, one I guess I'd seen for just a moment, the one that sounds British. Is that anyone you know?"

"Is that important?" Chris asked.

He saw again the special tension in her face. "It's important."

She looked down and nodded. "Yeah, it's someone I knew."

"Who?"

She looked up. "Burke Dennings."

"The director?"

"Yes."

"The director who—"

"Yes," she cut in.

The Jesuit considered her answer for a moment in silence. He saw her index finger twitching.

"Would you like some coffee or something, Father?"

He shook his head. "Thanks, no." He leaned forward, elbows on the table. "Was Regan acquainted with him?"

"Yes."

"And—"

A clattering. Startled, Chris flinched, turned and saw that Karl had dropped a roasting pan to the floor and was stooping to retrieve it. As he lifted it, he dropped it again.

"God almighty, Karl!"

"Sorry, madam."

"Go on, Karl, get out of here! Go see a movie or something! We can't all stay cooped in this house!" She turned back to Karras, picking up a cigarette packet and slamming it down on the table when Karl protested, "No, I look—"

"Karl, now, I mean it!" Chris snapped at him nervously, raising her voice but not turning her head. "Get out! Just get out of this house for a while! We've *all* got to start getting out! Now just *go!*"

"Yes, you go!" echoed Willie as she entered and snatched away the pan from Karl's grasp. She pushed him irritably toward the pantry.

Karl eyed Karras and Chris briefly and then left.

"Sorry, Father," Chris murmured in apology. She reached for a cigarette. "He's had to take an awful lot lately."

"You were right," said Karras gently. He picked up the matches. "You should *all* make an effort to get out of the house." He lit her cigarette. "You too."

"So what did Burke say?" Chris asked.

"Just obscenities," Karras said, shrugging.

"That's all?"

He caught the faint pulse of fear in her tone. "Pretty much," he responded. Then he lowered his voice. "Incidentally, does Karl have a daughter?"

"A daughter? No, not that I know of. Or if he does, he's never mentioned it."

"You're sure?"

Willie was scouring at the sink. Chris turned to her. "You don't have a daughter, do you, Willie?"

"She die, madam, long, long before."

"Oh, I'm sorry."

Chris turned back to Karras. "That's the first I ever heard of her," she whispered. "Why'd you ask? How'd you know?"

"Regan. She mentioned it," said Karras.

Chris stared.

"Has she ever shown signs of having ESP?" he asked. "I mean, prior to this time."

"Well . . ." Chris hesitated. "Well, I don't know. I'm not sure. I mean, there have been lots of times when she seems to be thinking the same things that I'm thinking, but doesn't that happen with people who are close?"

Karras nodded. Thought. "Now this other personality that I mentioned," he began. "That's the one that emerged in hypnosis once?"

"Talks gibberish?"

"Yes. Who is it?"

"I don't know."

"It's not familiar at all?"

"Not at all."

"Have you sent for the medical records?"

"They'll be here this afternoon. They're being flown down. They'll be coming straight to you." She sipped coffee. "That's the only way I could get them loose, and even at that I had to raise hell."

"Yes, I thought there might be trouble."

"There was. But they're coming." She took another sip. "Now what about the exorcism, Father?"

He looked down, then sighed. "Well, I'm not very hopeful I can sell it to the Bishop."

"What do you mean, 'not very hopeful'?" She set down the coffee cup, frowning anxiously.

He dipped into his pocket and extracted the vial, holding it out to show Chris. "See this?"

She nodded.

"I told her it was holy water," Karras explained. "And when I started to sprinkle her with it, she reacted very violently."

"So?"

"It's not holy water. It's ordinary tap water."

"So maybe some demons just don't know the difference."

"You really believe there's a demon inside her?"

"I believe that there's something inside of Regan that's trying to kill her, Father Karras, and whether it knows piss from water doesn't seem to have very much to do with it all, don't you think? I mean, sorry, but you asked my opinion!" She tamped out her cigarette. "What's the difference between holy water and tap water anyway?"

"Holy water's blessed."

"*Mazel tov*, Father; I'm happy for it! So what are you telling me, meantime—no exorcism?"

"Look, I've only just begun to dig into this," Karras said heatedly. "But the Church has criteria that have to be met, and they have to be met for a very good reason: keeping clear of the superstitious garbage that people keep pinning on her year after year! I give you 'levitating priests,' for example, and statues of the Blessed Mother that supposedly cry on Good Fridays and feast days. Now I think I can live without contributing to that!"

"Would you like a little Librium, Father?"

"I'm sorry, but you asked my opinion."

"I got it."

He was reaching for the cigarettes.

"Me too," Chris said huskily.

He extended the pack. She took one. He popped one in his mouth and lit both. They exhaled with audible sighs and slumped around the table.

"I'm sorry," he told her softly.

"Those nonfilter cigarettes'll kill ya."

He toyed with the cigarette packet, crinkling cellophane. "Here are the signs that the Church might accept. One is speaking in a language that the subject has never known before. Never studied. I'm working on that one. With the tapes. We'll see. Then there's clairvoyance, although nowadays telepathy or ESP might nullify that one."

"You *believe* in that stuff?" She frowned skeptically.

He looked at her. She was serious, he decided. He continued. "And the last one is powers beyond her ability and age. That's a catchall. Anything occult."

"Well, now, what about those poundings in the wall?"

"By itself, it means nothing."

"And the way she was flying up and down off the bed?"

"Not enough."

"Well, then, what about those things on her skin?"

"What things?"

"I didn't tell you?"

"Tell me what?"

"Oh, it happened at the clinic," Chris explained. "There were—well . . ." She traced a finger on her chest. "You know, like writing? Just letters. They'd show up on her chest, then disappear. Just like that."

Karras frowned. "You said 'letters.' Not words?"

"No, no words. Just an *M* once or twice. Then an *L.*"

"And you *saw* this?" he asked her.

"Well, no. But they told me."

"Who told you?"

"The doctors at the clinic. Look, you'll see it in the records. It's for real."

"Yes, I'm sure. But again, that's a natural phenomenon."

"Where? Transylvania?" Chris said, incredulous.

Karras shook his head. "No, I've come across cases of that in the journals. There was one, I remember, where a prison psychiatrist reported that a patient of his—an inmate—could go into a self-induced state of trance and make the signs of the zodiac appear on his skin." He made a gesture at his chest. "Made the skin raise up."

"Boy, miracles sure don't come easy with you, do they?"

"There was once an experiment," he explained to her gently, "in which the subject was hypnotized, put into trance; and then surgical incisions were made in each arm. He was told that his left arm was going to bleed, but that the right arm would not. Well, the left arm bled and the right arm didn't. The power of the mind controlled the blood flow. We don't know how, of course; but it happens. So in cases of stigmata—like the one with that prisoner I mentioned, or with Regan—the unconscious mind is controlling the differential of blood flow to the skin, sending more to the parts that it wants raised up. And so then you have drawings, or letters, or whatever. Mysterious, but hardly supernatural."

"You're a real tough case, Father Karras, do you know that?"

Karras touched a thumbnail to his teeth. "Look, maybe this will help you to understand," he said finally. "The Church—not me—the Church—once published a statement, a warning to exorcists. I read it last night. And what it said was that most of the people who are thought to be possessed or whom *others* believe to be possessed—and now I'm quoting—'are far more in need of a doctor than of an exorcist.' " He looked up into Chris's eyes. "Can you guess when that warning was issued?"

"No, when?"

"The year fifteen eighty-three."

Chris stared in surprise; thought. "Yeah, that sure was one hell of a year," she muttered. She heard the priest rising from his chair. "Let me wait and check the records from the clinic," he was saying.

Chris nodded.

"In the meantime," he continued, "I'll edit the tapes and then take them to the Institute of Languages and Linguistics. It could be this gibberish is some kind of a language. I doubt it. But maybe. And comparing the patterns of speech ... Well, then you'll know. If they're the same, you'll know for sure she's not possessed."

"And what then?" she asked anxiously.

The priest probed her eyes. They were turbulent. *Worried that her daughter is not possessed!* He thought of Dennings. Something wrong. Very wrong. "I hate to ask, but could I borrow your car for a while?"

She looked bleakly at the floor. "You could borrow my life for a while," she murmured. "Just get it back by Thursday. You never know; I might need it."

With an ache, Karras stared at the bowed, defenseless head. He yearned to take her hand and say that all would be well. But how?

"Wait, I'll get you the keys," she said.

He watched her drift away like a hopeless prayer.

When she'd given him the keys, Karras walked back to his room at the residence hall. He left the tape recorder there and collected the tape of Regan's voice. Then he went back across the street to Chris's parked car.

Climbing in, he heard Karl calling out from the doorway of the house: "Father Karras!" Karras looked. Karl was rushing down the stoop, quickly throwing on a jacket. He was waving. "Father Karras! One moment!"

Karras leaned over and cranked down the window on the passenger side. Karl leaned his head in. "You are going which way, Father Karras?"

"Du Pont Circle."

"Ah, yes, good! You could drop me, please, Father? You would mind?"

"Glad to do it. Jump in."

Karl nodded. "I appreciate it, Father!"

Karras started up the engine. "Do you good to get out."

"Yes, I go to see a film. A good film."

Karras put the car in gear and pulled away.

For a time they drove in silence. Karras was preoccupied, searching for answers. *Possession. Impossible. The holy water.* Still . . .

"Karl, you knew Mr. Dennings pretty well, wouldn't you say?"

Karl stared through the windshield; then nodded stiffly. "Yes. I know him."

"When Regan . . . when she appears to be Dennings, do you get the impression that she really *is?*"

Long pause. And then a flat and expressionless "Yes."

Karras nodded, feeling haunted.

There was no more conversation until they reached Du Pont Circle, where they came to a traffic signal and stopped. "I get off here, Father Karras," Karl said, opening the door. "I can catch here the bus." He climbed out, then leaned his head in the window. "Father, thank you very much. I appreciate. Thank you."

He stood back on the safety island and waited for the light to change. He smiled and waved as the priest drove away. He watched the car until at last it disappeared around the bend at the mouth of Massachusetts Avenue. Then he ran for a bus. Boarded. Took a transfer. Changed buses. Rode in silence until finally he debarked at a northeast tenement section of the city, where he walked to a crumbling apartment building and entered.

Karl paused at the bottom of the gloomy staircase, smelling acrid aromas from efficiency kitchens. From somewhere the sound of a baby crying. He lowered his head. A roach scuttled quickly from a baseboard and across a stair in jagging darts. He clutched at the banister and seemed on the verge of turning back, but then shook his head and began to climb. Each groaning footfall creaked like a rebuke.

On the second floor, he walked to a door in a murky wing, and for a moment he stood there, a hand on the door frame. He glanced at the wall: peeling paint; *Nicky and Ellen* in penciled scrawl and below it, a date and a heart whose core was cracking plaster. Karl pushed the buzzer and waited, head down. From within the apartment, a squeaking of bedsprings. Irritable muttering. Then someone approaching: a sound that was irregular: the dragging clump of an orthopedic shoe. Abruptly the door jerked partly open, the chain of a safety latch rattling to its limit as a woman in a slip scowled out through the aperture, a cigarette dangling from the corner of her mouth.

"Oh, it's you," she said huskily. She took off the chain.

Karl met the eyes that were shifting hardness, that were haggard wells of pain and blame; glimpsed briefly the dissolute bending of the lips and the ravaged face of a youth and a beauty buried alive in a thousand motel rooms, in a thousand awakenings from restless sleep with a stifled cry at remembered grace.

"C'mon, tell 'im ta fuck off!" A coarse male voice from within the apartment. Slurred. The boyfriend.

The girl turned her head and snapped quickly, "Oh, shut up, jerk, it's Pop!"

The girl turned to Karl. "He's drunk, Pop. Ya better not come in."

Karl nodded.

The girl's hollow eyes shifted down to his hand as it reached to a back trouser pocket for a wallet. "How's Mama?" she asked him, dragging on her cigarette, eyes on the hands that were dipping in the wallet, hands counting out tens.

248

"She is fine." He nodded tersely. "Your mother is fine."

As he handed her the money, she began to cough rackingly. She threw up a hand to her mouth. "Fuckin' cigarettes!" she choked out.

Karl stared at the puncture scabs on her arm.

"Thanks, Pop."

He felt the money being slipped from his fingers.

"Jesus, hurry it up!" growled the boyfriend from within.

"Listen, Pop, we better cut this kinda short. Okay? Ya know how he gets."

"Elvira . . . !" Karl had suddenly reached through the door and grasped her wrist. "There is clinic in New York now!" he whispered at her pleadingly.

She was grimacing, trying to break free from his grip. "Oh, come on!"

"I will send you! They help you! You don't go to jail! It is—"

"Jesus, come on, Pop!" she screeched, breaking free from his clutch.

"No, no, please! It is—"

She slammed the door in his face.

In the shadowy hall, in the carpeted tomb of his expectations, Karl stared mutely for a moment at the door, and then lowered his head into quiet grief. From within the apartment came muffled conversation. Then a cynical, ringing woman's laugh. It was followed by coughing.

Karl turned away, and felt a sudden stab of shock as he found the way blocked by Lieutenant Kinderman.

"Perhaps we could talk now, Mr. Engstrom," he wheezed. Hands in the pockets of his coat. Eyes sad. "Perhaps we could now have a talk. . . ."

two

Karras threaded tape to an empty reel in the office of the rotund, silver-haired director of the Institute of Languages and Linguistics. Having carefully edited sections of his tapes onto separate reels, he was about to play the first. He started the tape recorder and stepped back from the table. They listened to the fevered voice croaking its gibberish. Then he turned to the director. "What *is* that, Frank? Is it a language?"

The director was sitting on the edge of his desk. By the time the tape ended, he was frowning in puzzlement. "Pretty weird. Where'd you get that?"

Karras stopped the tape. "Oh, it's something that I've had for a number of years from when I worked on a case of dual personality. I'm doing a paper on it."

"I see."

"Well, what about it?"

The director pulled off his glasses and chewed at the tortoise frame. "No, it isn't any language that *I've* ever heard. However . . ." He frowned. And then looked up at Karras. "Want to play it again?"

Karras quickly rewound the tape and played it over. "Now what do you think?" he asked.

"Well, it does have the cadence of speech."

Karras felt a quickening of hope. Fought it down. "Yes, that's what I thought," he agreed.

"But I certainly don't recognize it, Father. Is it ancient or modern? Or do you know?"

"No, I don't."

"Well, why not leave it with me, Father? I'll check it with some of the boys."

"Could you make up a copy of it, Frank? I'd like to keep the original myself."

"Oh, yes, surely."

"In the meantime, I've got something else. Got the time?"

"Yes, of course. Go ahead. What's the problem?"

"Well, what if I gave you fragments of ordinary speech by what are apparently two different people. Could you tell by semantic analysis whether just *one* person might have been capable of both modes of speech?"

"Oh, I think so."

"How?"

"Well, a 'type-token' ratio, I suppose, is as good a way as any. In samples of a thousand words or more, you could just check the frequency of occurrence of the various parts of speech."

"And would you call that conclusive?"

"Oh, yes. Well, pretty much. You see, that sort of test would discount any change in the basic vocabulary. It's not words but expression of the words: the style. We call it 'index of diversity.' Very baffling to the layman, which, of course, is what we want." The director smiled wryly. Then he nodded at the tapes in Karras' hands. "You've got two different people on those, is that it?"

"No. The voice and the words came out of the mouth of just one person, Frank. As I said, it was a case of dual personality. The words and the voices seem totally different to me but both are from the mouth of just one person. Look, I need a big favor from you. . . ."

"You'd like me to test them out? I'd be glad to. I'll give it to one of the instructors."

"No, Frank, that's the really big part of the favor: I'd like you to do it yourself and as *fast* as you can do it. It's terribly important."

The director read the urgency in his eyes. He nodded. "Okay. Okay. I'll get on it."

The director made copies of both the tapes, and Karras returned to the Jesuit residence hall with the originals. He found a message slip in his room. The records from the clinic had arrived.

He hurried to Reception and signed for the package. Back in his room, he began to read immediately; and was soon convinced that his trip to the Institute had been wasted.

". . . indications of guilt obsession with ensuing hysterical-somnambulistic . . ."

Room for doubt. Always room. Interpretation. *But Regan's stigmata* . . . Karras buried his weary face in his hands. The skin stigmata that Chris had described had indeed been reported in Regan's file. But it also had been noted that Regan had hyperreactive skin and could herself have produced the mysterious letters merely by tracing them on her flesh with a finger a short time prior to their appearance. Dermatographia.

She did it herself, brooded Karras. He was certain. For as soon as Regan's hands had been immobilized by restraining straps, the records noted, the mysterious phenomena had ceased and were never repeated.

Fraud. Conscious or unconscious. Still fraud.

He lifted his head and eyed the phone. Frank. Call him off? He picked up the receiver. There was no answer and he left word for him to call. Then, exhausted, he stood up and walked slowly to the bathroom. He splashed cold water on his face. *"The exorcist will simply be careful that none of the patient's manifestations are left. . . ."* He looked up at himself in the mirror. Had he missed something? What? *The sauerkraut odor.* He turned and slipped a towel off the rack and wiped his face. *Autosuggestion,* he remembered. And the mentally ill, in certain instances, seemed able unconsciously to direct their bodies to emit a variety of odors.

Karras wiped his hands. The poundings . . . the opening and closing of the drawer. Psychokinesis? Really? *"You believe in that stuff?"* He paused as he set back the towel; grew aware that he wasn't thinking clearly. *Too tired.* Yet he dared not give Regan up to guess; to opinion; to the savage betrayals of the mind.

He left the hall and went to the campus library. He searched through the *Guide to Periodical Literature: Po . . . Pol . . . Polte . . .* He found what he was looking for and sat down with a scientific journal to read an article on poltergeist-phenomena investigations by the German psychiatrist Dr. Hans Bender.

No doubt about it, he concluded when he finished: psychokinetic phenomena existed; had been thoroughly documented; filmed; observed in psychiatric clinics. And in none of the cases reported in the article was there any connection to demonic possession. Rather, the hypothesis was mind-directed energy unconsciously produced and usually—and significantly, Karras saw—by adolescents in stages of "extremely high inner tension, frustration and rage."

Karras rubbed his tired eyes. He still felt remiss. He ran

back through the symptoms, touching each like a boy going back to touch slats on a white picket fence. Which one had he missed? he wondered. Which?

The answer, he concluded wearily, was None.

He returned the journal to the desk.

He walked back to the MacNeil house. Willie admitted him and led him to the study. The door was closed. Willie knocked. "Father Karras," she announced.

"Come in."

Karras entered and closed the door behind him. Chris was standing with her back to him, brow in her hand, an elbow on the bar. "Hello, Father."

Her voice was a husky and despairing whisper. Concerned, he went over to her. "You okay?" he asked softly.

"Yeah, I'm fine."

Her voice held tension. He frowned. Her hand was obscuring her face. The hand trembled. "What's doin'?" she asked him.

"Well, I've looked at the records from the clinic." He waited. She made no response. He continued. "I believe . . ." He paused. "Well, my honest opinion right now is that Regan can best be helped by intensive psychiatric care."

She shook her head very slowly back and forth.

"Where's her father?" he asked her.

"In Europe," she whispered.

"Have you told him what's happening?"

She had thought about telling him so many times. Had been tempted. The crisis could bring them back together. But Howard and priests . . . For Regan's sake, she'd decided he mustn't be told.

"No," she answered softly.

"Well, I think it would help if he were here."

"Listen, nothing's going to help except something out of *sight!*" Chris suddenly erupted, lifting a tear-stained face to the priest. "Something *way* out of *sight.*"

"I believe you should send for him."

"Why?"

"It would—"

"I've asked you to drive a demon *out*, goddammit, not ask another one *in!*" she cried at Karras in sudden hysteria. Her features were contorted in anguish. "What happened to the *exorcism* all of a sudden?"

"Now—"

"What in the hell do I want with *Howard?*"

"We can talk about it—"

"Talk about it *now*, goddammit! What the hell good is *Howard* right now? What's the *good?*"

"There's a strong probability that Regan's disorder is rooted in a guilt over—"

"Guilt over *what?*" she cried, eyes wild.

"It could—"

"Over the divorce? All that psychiatric bullshit?"

"Now—"

"She's guilty because she *killed Burke Dennings!*" Chris shrieked at him, hands crushing hard against her temples. "She *killed* him! She killed him and they'll put her away; they're going to put her away! Oh, my God, oh, my . . ."

Karras caught her up as she crumpled, sobbing, and guided her toward the sofa. "It's all right," he kept telling her softly, "it's all right. . . ."

"No, they'll put . . . her away," she was sobbing. "They'll put . . . put . . . ohhhhhhh! Oh, my God! Oh, my God!"

"It's all right. . . ."

He eased her down and stretched her out on the sofa. He sat down on the edge and took her hand in both of his. Thoughts of Kinderman. Dennings. Her sobbing. Unreality. "All right . . . it's all right . . . take it easy . . . it's all right. . . ."

Soon the crying subsided and he helped her sit up. He brought her water and a box of tissues he'd found on a shelf behind the bar. Then he sat down beside her.

"Oh, I'm glad," she said, sniffling and blowing her nose. "God, I'm glad I got it out."

Karras was in turmoil, his own shock of realization increasing, the calmer she grew. Quiet sniffles now. Intermittent catches in the throat. And now the weight was on his back again, heavy and oppressive. He inwardly stiffened. *No more! Say no more!* "Do you want to tell me more?" he asked her gently.

Chris nodded. Exhaled. She wiped at an eye and spoke haltingly, in spasms, of Kinderman; of the book; of her certainty that Dennings had been up in Regan's bedroom; of Regan's great strength; of the Dennings personality that Chris thought she had seen with the head turned around and facing backward.

She finished. Now she waited for Karras' reaction. For a time he did not speak as he thought it all over. Then at last he said softly, "You don't *know* that she did it."

"But the head turned around," said Chris.

"You'd hit your own head pretty hard against the wall," Karras answered. "You were also in shock. You imagined it."

"She told me that she did it," Chris intoned without expression.

A pause. "And did she tell you how?" Karras asked her.

Chris shook her head. He turned and looked at her. "No," she said. "No."

"Then it doesn't mean a thing," Karras told her. "No, it wouldn't mean a thing unless she gave you details that no one else could conceivably know but the killer."

She was shaking her head in doubt. "I don't know," she answered. "I don't know if I'm doing what's right. I think she did it and she could kill someone else. I don't know. . . ." She paused. "Father, what should I do?" she asked him hopelessly.

The weight was now set in concrete; in drying, it had shaped itself to his back.

He rested an elbow on his knee and closed his eyes. "Well, you've told someone now," he said quietly. "You've done what you should. Now forget it. Just put it away and leave it all up to me."

He felt her gaze on him and looked at her. "Are you feeling any better now?"

She nodded.

"Will you do me a favor?" he asked her.

"What?"

"Go out and see a movie."

She wiped at an eye with the back of her hand and smiled. "I hate 'em."

"Then go visit a friend."

She put her hands in her lap and looked at him warmly. "Got a friend right here," she said at last.

He smiled. "Get some rest," he advised her.

"I will."

He had another thought. "You think Dennings brought the book upstairs? Or was it there?"

"I think it was already there," Chris answered.

He considered this. Then he stood up. "Well, okay. You need the car?"

"No, you keep it."

"All right, then. I'll be back to you later."

"Ciao, Father."

"Ciao."

He walked out in the street brimming turmoil. Churning. Regan. Dennings. *Impossible! No!* Yet there was Chris's near conviction, her reaction, her hysteria. *And that's just what it is: hysterical imagining. And yet* . . . He chased certainties like leaves in a knifing wind.

As he passed by the long flight of steps near the house, he heard a sound from below, by the river. He stopped and looked down toward the C&O Canal. A harmonica. Someone playing "Red River Valley," since boyhood Karras' favorite song. He listened until traffic noise drowned it out, until his drifting reminiscence was shattered by a world that was now and in torment, that was shrieking for help, dripping blood on exhaust fumes. He thrust his hands into his pockets. Thought feverishly. Of Chris. Of Regan. Of Lucas aiming kicks at Tranquille. He must do something. What? Could he hope to outguess the clinicians at Barringer? ". . . *go to Central Casting!*" Yes; yes, he knew that was the answer; the hope. He remembered the case of Achille. Possessed. Like Regan, he had called himself a devil; like Regan, his disorder had been rooted in guilt: remorse over marital infidelity. The psychologist Janet had effected a cure by hypnotically suggesting the presence of the wife, who appeared to Achille's hallucinated eyes and solemnly forgave him. Karras nodded. Suggestion could work for Regan. But not through hypnosis. They had tried that at Barringer. No. The counteracting suggestion for Regan, he believed, was the ritual of exorcism. She knew what it was; knew its effect. *Her reaction to the holy water. Got that from the book.* And in the book, there were descriptions of successful exorcisms. *It could work! It could! It could work!* But how to get permission from the Chancery Office? How to build up a case without mention of Dennings? Karras could not lie to the Bishop. Would not falsify the facts. *But you can let the facts speak for themselves!*

What facts?

He ran a hand across his brow. Needed sleep. Could not sleep. He felt his temples pound in headache. "*Hello, Daddy?*"

What facts?

The tapes at the Institute. What would Frank find? Was there anything he *could* find? No. But who knew? Regan hadn't known holy water from tap water. *Sure. But if supposedly she's able to read my mind, why is it she didn't know the difference between them?* He put a hand to his forehead. The headache. Confusion. *Jesus, Karras, wake up! Someone's dying! Wake up!*

Back in his room, he called the Institute. No Frank. He put down the telephone. Holy water. Tap water. Something. He opened up the *Ritual* to "Instructions to Exorcists": ". . . evil spirits . . . deceptive answers . . . so it might appear that the afflicted one is in no way possessed. . . ." Karras pondered. Was that it? *What the hell are you talking about?* What "*evil spirit*"?

He slammed shut the book and saw the medical records. He reread them, scanning quickly for anything that might help with the Bishop.

Hold it. No history of hysteria. That's something. But weak. Something else. Some discrepancy. What was it? He dredged desperately through memories of his studies. And then he recalled it. Not much. But something.

He picked up the phone and called Chris. She sounded groggy.

"Hi, Father."

"Were you sleeping? I'm sorry."

"It's okay."

"Chris, where's this Doctor . . ." Karras ran a finger down the records. "Doctor Klein?"

"In Rosslyn."

"In the medical building?"

"Yes."

"Please call him and tell him Doctor Karras will be by and that I'd like to take a look at Regan's EEG. Tell him *Doctor* Karras, Chris. Have you got that?"

"Got it."

"I'll talk to you later."

When he'd hung up the phone, Karras snapped off his collar and got out of his clerical robe and black trousers, changing quickly into khaki pants and a sweatshirt. Over these he wore his priest's black raincoat, buttoning it up to the collar. He looked in a mirror and frowned. *Priests and policemen*, he thought, as he quickly unbuttoned the raincoat: their clothing had identifying smells one couldn't hide. Karras slipped off his shoes and got into the only pair he owned that were not black, his scuffed white tennis shoes.

In Chris's car, he drove quickly toward Rosslyn. As he waited on M Street for the light to cross the bridge, he glanced right through the window and saw something disturbing: Karl getting out of a black sedan on Thirty-fifth Street in front of the Dixie Liquor Store. The driver of the car was Lieutenant Kinderman.

The light changed. Karras gunned the car and shot forward, turning onto the bridge, then looked back through the mirror. Had they seen him? He didn't think so. But what were they doing together? Pure chance? Had it something to do with Regan? with Regan and . . . ?

Forget it! One thing at a time!

He parked at the medical building and went upstairs to Dr. Klein's suite of offices. The doctor was busy, but a nurse handed Karras the EEG and very soon he was standing in a cubicle, studying it, the long narrow band of paper slipping slowly through his fingers.

Klein hurried in, his glance brushing in puzzlement over Karras' dress. "Doctor Karras?"

"Yes. How do you do?"

They shook hands.

"I'm Klein. How's the girl?"

"Progressing."

"Glad to hear it." Karras looked back to the graph and Klein scanned it with him, tracing his finger over patterns of waves. "There, you see? it's very regular. No fluctuations whatsoever."

"Yes, I see." Karras frowned. "Very curious."

"Curious?"

"Presuming that we're dealing with hysteria."

"Don't get it."

"I suppose it isn't very well known," murmured Karras, pulling paper through his hands in a steady flow, "but a Belgian—Iteka—discovered that hysterics seemed to cause some rather odd fluctuations in the graph, a very minuscule but always identical pattern. I've been looking for it here and I don't find it."

Klein grunted noncommittally. "How about that."

Karras glanced at him. "She was certainly disordered when you ran this graph; is that right?"

"Yes, she was. Yes, I'd say so. She was."

"Well, then, isn't it curious that she tested so perfectly? Even subjects in a normal state of mind can influence their brain waves at least within the normal range, and Regan was disturbed at the time. It would seem there would be some fluctuations. If—"

"Doctor, Mrs. Simmons is getting impatient," a nurse interrupted, cracking open the door.

"Yes, I'm coming," sighed Klein. As the nurse hurried off, he took a step toward the hallway then turned with his hand on the door edge. "Speaking of hysteria," he commented dryly. "Sorry. Got to run."

He closed the door behind him. Karras heard his footsteps heading down the hall; heard the opening of a door; heard, "Well, now, how are we feeling today, Mrs. . . ."

Closing of the door. Karras went back to his study of the graph, finished, then folded it up and banded it. He returned it to the nurse in Reception. *Something.* It was something he could use with the Bishop as an argument that Regan was not a hysteric and therefore conceivably was possessed. And yet the EEG had posed still another mystery: why no fluctuations? why none at all?

He drove back toward Chris's house, but at a stop sign at the corner of Prospect and Thirty-fifth he froze behind the wheel: parked between Karras and the Jesuit residence hall was Kinderman. He was sitting alone behind the wheel with his elbow out the window, looking straight ahead.

Karras took a right before Kinderman could see him in Chris's Jaguar. Quickly he found a space, parked and locked the car. Then he walked around the corner as if heading for the residence hall. *Is he watching the house?* he worried. The specter of Dennings rose up again to haunt him. Was it possible that Kinderman thought Regan had . . . ?

Easy. Slow down. Take it easy.

He walked up beside the car and leaned his head through the window on the passenger side. "Hello, Lieutenant."

The detective turned quickly and looked surprised. Then beamed. "Father Karras."

Off key, thought Karras. He noticed that his hands were feeling dampish and cold. *Play it light! Don't let him know that you're worried! Play it light!* "Don't you know you'll get a ticket? Weekdays, no parking between four and six."

"Never mind that," wheezed Kinderman. "I'm talking to a priest. Every cop in this neighborhood is Catholic or passing."

"How've you been?"

"Speaking plainly, Father Karras, only so-so. Yourself?"

"Can't complain. Did you ever solve that case?"

"Which case?"

"The director."

"Oh, that one." He made a gesture of dismissal. "Don't ask. Listen, what are you doing tonight? Are you busy? I've got passes for the Crest. It's *Othello.*"

"Who's starring?"

"Molly Picon, Desdemona, and Othello, Leo Fuchs. You're happy? This is freebies, Father Marlon Particular! This is William F. Shakespeare! Doesn't matter who's starring, who's not! Now, you're coming?"

"I'm afraid I'll have to pass. I'm pretty snowed under."

"I can see. You look terrible, you'll pardon my noticing. You're keeping late hours?"

"I always look terrible."

"Only now more than usual. Come on! Get away for one night! We'll enjoy!"

Karras decided to test; to touch a nerve. "Are you sure that's what's playing?" he asked. His eyes were probing steadily into Kinderman's. "I could have sworn there was a Chris Mac-Neil film at the Crest."

The detective missed a beat, and then said quickly, "No, I'm certain. *Othello.* It's *Othello.*"

"What brings you to the neighborhood, incidentally?"

"You! I came only to invite you to the film!"

"Yes, it's easier to drive than to pick up a phone," said Karras softly.

The detective's eyebrows lifted in unconvincing innocence. "Your telephone was *busy!*" he whispered hoarsely, poising an upraised palm in midair.

The Jesuit stared at him, expressionless.

"What's wrong?" asked Kinderman after a moment.

Gravely Karras reached a hand inside the car and lifted Kinderman's eyelid. He examined the eye. "I don't know. You look terrible. You could be coming down with a case of mythomania."

"I don't know what that means," answered Kinderman as Karras withdrew his hand. "Is it serious?"

"Not fatal."

"What is it? The suspense is now driving me crazy!"

"Look it up," said Karras.

"Listen, don't be so snotty. You should render unto Caesar just a little, now and then. I'm the law. I could have you deported, you know that?"

"What for?"

"A psychiatrist shouldn't make people worry. Plus also the *goyim*, plainly speaking, would love it. You're a nuisance to them altogether anyway, Father. No, frankly, you embarrass them. They would love to get rid of you. Who needs it? a priest who wears sweatshirts and sneakers!"

Smiling faintly, Karras nodded. "Got to go. Take care." He tapped a hand on the window frame, twice, in farewell, and then turned and walked slowly toward the entry of the residence.

"See an analyst!" the detective called after him hoarsely. Then his warm look gave way to worry. He glanced through his windshield up at the house, then started the engine and drove up the street. Passing Karras, he honked his horn and waved.

Karras waved back, watching Kinderman round the corner of Thirty-sixth. Then he stood motionless for a while on the sidewalk, rubbing gently at his brow with a trembling hand. Could she really have done it? Could Regan have murdered Burke Dennings so horribly? With feverish eyes, he looked up at Regan's window. *What in God's name is in that house?* And how much longer before Kinderman demanded to see Regan? had a chance to see the Dennings personality? to hear it? How much longer before Regan would be institutionalized?

Or die?

He had to build the case for the Chancery.

He walked quickly across the street at an angle to Chris's house. He rang the doorbell.

Willie let him in.

"Missiz taking little nap now," she said.

Karras nodded. "Good. Very good." He walked by her and upstairs to Regan's bedroom. He was seeking a knowledge he must clutch by the heart.

He entered and saw Karl in a chair by the window, his arms folded, watching Regan. He was silent and present as a dense, dark wood.

Karras walked up beside the bed and looked down. The whites of the eyes like milky fog. The murmurings. Spells from some other world. Karras glanced at Karl. Then slowly he leaned over and began to unfasten one of Regan's restraining straps.

"Father, *no!*"

Karl rushed to the bedside and vigorously yanked back the priest's arm. "Very bad, Father! Strong! It is strong! Leave on straps!"

In the eyes there was a fear that Karras recognized as genuine, and now he knew that Regan's strength was not theory; it was a fact. She could have done it. Could have twisted Dennings' neck around. *My God, Karras! Hurry! Find some evidence! Think! Hurry before . . . !*

"*Ich möchte Sie etwas fragen, Engstrom!*"

With a stab of discovery and hot-surging hope, Karras jerked around his head and looked down at the bed. The demon grinned mockingly at Karl. "*Tanzt Ihre Tochter gern?*"

German! It had asked if Karl's daughter liked to dance! His heart pounding, Karras turned and saw that the servant's cheeks had flushed crimson, that he trembled, that his eyes glared with fury. "Karl, you'd better step outside," Karras advised him.

The Swiss shook his head, his hands squeezed into white-knuckled fists. "No, I stay!"

"You will go, please," the Jesuit said firmly. His gaze held Karl's implacably.

After a moment of dogged resistance, Karl gave way and hurried from the room.

The laughter had stopped. Karras turned back. The demon was watching him. It looked pleased. "So you're back," it croaked. "I'm surprised. I would think that embarrassment over the holy water might have discouraged you from ever returning. But then I forget that a priest has no shame."

Karras breathed shallowly and forced himself to rein his expectations, to think clearly. He knew that the language test in possession required intelligent conversation as proof that whatever was said was not traceable to buried linguistic recollections. *Easy! Slow down! Remember that girl?* A teen-age servant. Possessed. In delirium, she'd babbled a language that finally was recognized to be Syriac. Karras forced himself to think of the excitement it had caused, of how finally it was learned that the girl had at one time been employed in a boardinghouse where one of the lodgers was a student of theology. On the eve of examinations, he would pace in his room and walk up and down stairs while reciting his Syriac lessons aloud. And the girl had overheard them. *Take it easy. Don't get burned.*

"*Sprechen Sie deutsch?*" asked Karras warily.

"More games?"

"*Sprechen Sie deutsch?*" he repeated, his pulse still throbbing with that distant hope.

"*Natürlich,*" the demon leered at him. "*Mirabile dictu,* wouldn't you agree?"

The Jesuit's heart leaped up. Not only German, but Latin! And in context!

"*Quod nomen mihi est?*" he asked quickly.   What is my name?

"Karras."

And now the priest rushed on with excitement.

"*Ubi sum?*"   Where am I?

"*In cubiculo.*"   In a room.

"*Et ubi est cubiculum?*"   And where is the room?

"*In domo.*"   In a house.

"*Ubi est Burke Dennings?*"   Where is Burke Dennings?

"*Mortuus.*"   He is dead.

"*Quomodo mortuus est?*"   How did he die?

"*Inventus est capite reverso.*"   He was found with his head turned around.

"*Quis occidit eum?*"   Who killed him?

"Regan."

266

"*Quomodo ea occidit illum? Dic mihi exacte!*" How did she kill him? Tell me in detail!

"Ah, well, that's sufficient excitement for the moment," the demon said, grinning. "Sufficient. Sufficient altogether. Though of course it will occur to you, I suppose, that while you were asking your questions in Latin, you were mentally formulating *answers* in Latin." It laughed. "All unconscious, of course. Yes, whatever would we do without unconsciousness? Do you see what I'm driving at, Karras? I cannot speak Latin at all. I read your mind. I merely plucked the responses from your head!"

Karras felt an instant dismay as his certainty crumbled, felt tantalized and frustrated by the nagging doubt now planted in his brain.

The demon chuckled. "Yes, I knew that would occur to you, Karras," it croaked at him. "That is why I'm fond of you. That is why I cherish *all* reasonable men." Its head tilted back in a spate of laughter.

The Jesuit's mind raced rapidly, desperately, formulating questions to which there was no single answer, but rather many. *But maybe I'd think of them all!* he realized. *Okay! Then ask a question that you don't know the answer to!* He could check the answer later to see if it was correct.

He waited for the laughter to ebb before he spoke:

"*Quam profundus est imus Oceanus Indicus?*" What is the depth of the Indian Ocean at its deepest point?

The demon's eyes glittered. "*La plume de ma tante,*" it rasped.

"*Responde Latine.*"

"*Bon jour! Bonne nuit!*"

"*Quam—*"

Karras broke off as the eyes rolled upward into their sockets and the gibberish entity appeared.

Impatient and frustrated, Karras demanded, "Let me speak to the demon again!"

No answer. Only the breathing from another shore.

"*Quis es tu?*" he snapped hoarsely. Voice frayed.

Still the breathing.

"Let me speak to Burke Dennings!"

A hiccup. Breathing. A hiccup. Breathing.

"Let me speak to Burke Dennings!"

The hiccuping, regular and wrenching, continued. Karras shook his head. Then he walked to a chair and sat on its edge. Hunched over. Tense. Tormented. And waiting . . .

Time passed. Karras drowsed. Then jerked his head up. *Stay awake!* With blinking, heavy lids, he looked over at Regan. No hiccuping. Silent.

Sleeping?

He walked over to the bed and looked down. Eyes closed. Heavy breathing. He reached down and felt her pulse, then stooped and carefully examined her lips. They were parched. He straightened up and waited. Then at last he left the room.

He went down to the kitchen in search of Sharon, and found her at the table eating soup and a sandwich. "Can I fix you something to eat, Father Karras?" she asked him. "You must be hungry."

"Thanks, no, I'm not," he answered. Sitting down, he reached over and picked up a pencil and pad by Sharon's typewriter. "She's been hiccuping," he told her. "Have you had any Compazine prescribed?"

"Yes, we've got some."

He was writing on the pad. "Then tonight give her half of a twenty-five-milligram suppository."

"Right."

"She's beginning to dehydrate," he continued, "so I'm switching her to intravenous feedings. First thing in the morning, call a medical-supply house and have them deliver these right away." He slid the pad across the table to Sharon. "In the meantime, she's sleeping, so you could start her on a Sustagen feeding."

"Okay." Sharon nodded. "I will." Spooning soup, she turned the pad around and looked at the list.

Karras watched her. Then he frowned in concentration. "You're her tutor."

"Yes, that's right."

"Have you taught her any Latin?"

She was puzzled. "No, I haven't."

"Any German?"

"Only French."

"What level? *La plume de ma tante?*"

"Pretty much."

"But no German or Latin."

"Huh-uh, no."

"But the Engstroms, don't they sometimes speak German?"

"Oh, sure."

"Around Regan?"

She shrugged. "I suppose." She stood up and took her plates to the sink. "As a matter of fact, I'm pretty sure."

"Have you ever studied Latin?" Karras asked her.

"No, I haven't."

"But you'd recognize the general sound."

"Oh, I'm sure." She rinsed the soup bowl and put it in the rack.

"Has she ever spoken Latin in your presence?"

"Regan?"

"Since her illness."

"No, never."

"Any language at all?" probed Karras.

She turned off the faucet, thoughtful. "Well, I might have imagined it, I guess, but . . ."

"What?"

"Well, I think . . ." She frowned. "Well, I could have sworn I heard her talking in Russian."

Karras stared. "Do you speak it?" he asked her, throat dry.

She shrugged. "Oh, well, so-so." She began to fold the dish-cloth. "I just studied it in college, that's all."

Karras sagged. *She did* pick *the Latin* from *my brain.* Staring bleakly, he lowered his brow to his hand, into doubt, into torments of knowledge and reason: *Telepathy more common in states of great tension: speaking always in a language known to someone in the room: " . . . thinks the same things I'm thinking . . .": "Bon jour . . .": "La plume de ma tante . . .": "Bonne nuit . . ."* With thoughts such as these, he slowly watched blood turning back into wine.

What to do? *Get some sleep. Then come back and try again . . . try again . . . try again.*

He stood up and looked blearily at Sharon. She was leaning with her back against the sink, arms folded, watching him thoughtfully. "I'm going over to the residence," he told her. "As soon as Regan's awake, I'd like a call."

"Yes, I'll call you."

"And the Compazine," he reminded her. "You won't forget?"

She shook her head. "No, I'll take care of it right away," she said.

He nodded. With hands in hip pockets, he looked down, trying to think of what he might have forgotten to tell Sharon. Always something to be done. Always something overlooked when even everything was done.

"Father, what's going on?" he heard her ask gravely. "What is it? What's really going on with Rags?"

He lifted up eyes that were haunted and seared. "I really don't know," he said emptily.

He turned and walked out of the kitchen.

As he passed through the entry hall, Karras heard footsteps coming up rapidly behind him.

"Father Karras!"

He turned. Saw Karl with his sweater.

"Very sorry," said the servant as he handed it over. "I was thinking to finish much before. But I forget."

The vomit stains were gone and it had a sweet smell. "That was thoughtful of you, Karl," the priest said gently. "Thank you."

"Thank you, Father Karras."

There was a tremor in his voice and his eyes were full.

"Thank you for your helping Miss Regan," Karl finished. Then he averted his head, self-conscious, and swiftly left the entry.

Karras watched, remembering him in Kinderman's car. More mystery. Confusion. Wearily he opened the door. It was night. Despairing, he stepped out of darkness into darkness.

He crossed to the residence, groping toward sleep, but as he entered his room he looked down and saw a message slip pink on the floor. He picked it up. From Frank. The tapes. Home number. "Please call...."

He picked up the telephone and requested the number. Waited. His hands shook with desperate hope.

"Hello?" A young boy. Piping voice.

"May I speak to your father, please."

"Yes. Just a minute." Phone clattering. Then quickly picked up. Still the boy. "Who *is* this?"

"Father Karras."

"Father Karits?"

His heart thumping, Karras spoke evenly. "Karras. Father Karras . . ."

Down went the phone again.

Karras pressed digging fingers against his brow.

Phone noise.

"Father Karras?"

"Yes, hello, Frank. I've been trying to reach you."

"Oh, I'm sorry. I've been working on your tapes at the house."

"Are you finished?"

"Yes, I am. By the way, this is pretty weird stuff."

"I know." Karras tried to flatten the tension in his voice. "What's the story, Frank? What have you found?"

"Well, this 'type-token' ratio, first . . ."

"Yes?"

"Well, I didn't have enough of a sampling to be absolutely accurate, you understand, but I'd say it's pretty close, or at least as close as you can get with these things. Well, at any rate, the two different voices on the tapes, I would say, are probably separate personalities."

"Probably?"

"Well, I wouldn't want to swear to it in court. In fact, I'd have to say the variance is really pretty minimal."

"Minimal . . ." Karras repeated dully. *Well, that's the ball game.* "And what about the gibberish?" he asked without hope. "Is it any kind of language?"

Frank chuckled.

"What's funny?" asked the Jesuit moodily.

"Was this really some sneaky psychological testing, Father?"

"I don't know what you mean, Frank."

"Well, I guess you got your tapes mixed around or something. It's—"

"Frank, is it a language or not?" cut in Karras.

"Oh, I'd say it was a language, all right."

Karras stiffened. "Are you kidding?"

"No, I'm not."

"What's the language?" he asked, unbelieving.

"English."

For a moment, Karras was mute, and when he spoke there was an edge to his voice. "Frank, we seem to have a very poor connection; or would you like to let me in on the joke?"

"Got your tape recorder there?" asked Frank.

It was sitting on his desk. "Yes, I do."

"Has it got a reverse-play position?"

"Why?"

"Has it got one?"

"Just a second." Irritable, Karras set down the phone and took the top off the tape recorder to check it. "Yes, it's got one. Frank, what's this all about?"

"Put your tape on the machine and play it backward."

"What?"

"You've got gremlins." Frank laughed. "Look, play it and I'll talk to you tomorrow. Good night, Father."

"Night, Frank."

"Have fun."

Karras hung up. He looked baffled. He hunted up the gibberish tape and threaded it onto the recorder. First he ran it forward, listening. Shook his head. No mistake. It was gibberish.

He let it run through to the end and then played it in reverse. He heard his voice speaking backward. Then Regan—or someone—in *English!*

. . . *Marin marin karras be us let us* . . .

English. Senseless; but English! *How on earth could she do that?* he marveled.

He listened to it all, then rewound and played the tape through again. And again. And then realized that the order of speech was inverted.

He stopped the tape and rewound it. With a pencil and paper, he sat down at the desk and began to play the tape from the beginning while transcribing the words, working laboriously and long with almost constant stops and starts of the tape recorder. When finally it was done, he made another transcription on a second sheet of paper, reversing the order of the words. Then he leaned back and read it:

. . . danger. Not yet. [indecipherable] will die. Little time. Now the [indecipherable]. Let her die. No, no, sweet! it is sweet in the body! I feel! There is [indecipherable]. Better [indecipherable] than the void. I fear the priest. Give us time.

Fear the priest! He is [indecipherable]. No, not this one: the [indecipherable], the one who [indecipherable]. He is ill. Ah, the blood, feel the blood, how it [sings?].

Here, Karras asked, "Who are you?" with the answer:

I am no one. I am no one.

Then Karras: "Is that your name?" and then:

I have no name. I am no one. Many. Let us be. Let us warm in the body. Do not [indecipherable] from the body into void, into [indecipherable]. Leave us. Leave us. Let us be. Karras. [Marin? Marin?] . . .

Again and again he read it over, haunted by its tone, by the feeling that more than one person was speaking, until finally repetition itself dulled the words into commonness. He set down the tablet on which he'd transcribed them and rubbed at his face, at his eyes, at his thoughts. Not an unknown language. And writing backward with facility was hardly paranormal or even unusual. But *speaking* backward: adjusting and altering the phonetics so that playing them backward would make them intelligible; wasn't such performance beyond the reach of even a hyperstimulated intellect? The accelerated unconscious referred to by Jung? No. Something . . .

He remembered. He went to his shelves for a book: Jung's *Psychology and Pathology of So-called Occult Phenomena*. Something similar here, he thought. What?

He found it: an account of an experiment with automatic writing in which the unconscious of the subject seemed able to answer his questions and anagrams.

Anagrams!

He propped the book open on the desk, leaned over and read an account of a portion of the experiment:

What is man? *Tefi hasl esble lies.*
Is that an anagram? *Yes.*
How many words does it contain? *Five.*
What is the first word? *See*
What is the second word? *Eeeee.*
See? Shall I interpret it myself? *Try to!*

The subject found this solution: "*The life is less able.*" He was astonished at this intellectual pronouncement, which seemed to him to prove the existence of an intelligence independent of his own. He therefore went on to ask:

Who are you? *Clelia.*
Are you a woman? *Yes.*
Have you lived on earth? *No.*
Will you come to life? *Yes.*
When? *In six years.*
Why are you conversing with me? *E if Clelia el.*

The subject interpreted this answer as an anagram for "I Clelia feel."

Am I the one who answers the questions? *Yes.*
Is Clelia there? *No.*
Who is there, then? *Nobody.*
Does Clelia exist at all? *No.*
Then with whom was I speaking yesterday? *With nobody.*

Karras stopped reading. Shook his head. Here was no paranormal performance: only the limitless abilities of the mind.

He reached for a cigarette, sat down and lit it. "*I am no one. Many.*" Eerie. Where did it come from, he wondered, this content of her speech?

"*With nobody.*"

From the same place Clelia had come from? Emergent personalities?

"*Marin . . . Marin . . .*" "*Ah, the blood . . .*" "*He is ill. . . .*"

Haunted, he glanced at his copy of *Satan* and moodily leafed to the opening inscription: "Let not the dragon be my leader. . . ."

He exhaled smoke and closed his eyes. He coughed. His throat felt raw and inflamed. He crushed out the cigarette, eyes watering from smoke. Exhausted. His bones felt like iron pipe. He got up and put out a "Do Not Disturb" sign on the door, then he flicked out the room light, shuttered his window blinds, kicked off his shoes and collapsed on the bed. Fragments. Regan. Dennings. Kinderman. What to do? He must help. How? Try the Bishop with what little he had? He did not think so. He could never convincingly argue the case.

He thought of undressing, getting under the covers. Too tired. This burden. He wanted to be free.

"*. . . Let us be!*"

Let me be, he responded to the fragment. He drifted into motionless, dark granite sleep.

The ringing of a telephone awakened him. Groggy, he fumbled toward the light switch. What time was it? A few minutes after three. He reached blindly for the telephone. Answered. Sharon. Would he come to the house right away? He would come. He hung up the telephone, feeling trapped again, smothered and enmeshed.

He went into the bathroom and splashed cold water on his face, dried off and then started from the room, but at the door, he turned around and came back for his sweater. He pulled it over his head and then went out into the street.

The air was thin and still in the darkness. Some cats at a garbage can scurried in fright as he crossed toward the house.

Sharon met him at the door. She was wearing a sweater and

was draped in a blanket. She looked frightened. Bewildered. "Sorry, Father," she whispered as he entered the house, "but I thought you ought to see this."

"What?"

"You'll see. Let's be quiet, now. I don't want to wake up Chris. She shouldn't see this." She beckoned.

He followed her, tiptoeing quietly up the stairs to Regan's bedroom. Entering, the Jesuit felt chilled to the bone. The room was icy. He frowned in bewilderment at Sharon, and she nodded at him solemnly. "Yes. Yes, the heat's on," she whispered. Then she turned and stared at Regan, at the whites of her eyes glowing eerily in lamplight. She seemed to be in coma. Heavy breathing. Motionless. The nasogastric tube was in place, the Sustagen seeping slowly into her body.

Sharon moved quietly toward the bedside and Karras followed, still staggered by the cold. When they stood by the bed, he saw beads of perspiration on Regan's forehead; glanced down and saw her hands gripped firmly in the restraining straps.

Sharon. She was bending, gently pulling the top of Regan's pajamas wide apart, and an overwhelming pity hit Karras at the sight of the wasted chest, the protruding ribs where one might count the remaining weeks or days of her life.

He felt Sharon's haunted eyes upon him. "I don't know if it's stopped," she whispered. "But watch: just keep looking at her chest."

She turned and looked down, and the Jesuit, puzzled, followed her gaze. Silence. The breathing. Watching. The cold. Then the Jesuit's brows knitted tightly as he saw something happening to the skin: a faint redness, but in sharp definition, like handwriting. He peered down closer.

"There, it's coming," whispered Sharon.

Abruptly the gooseflesh on Karras' arms was not from the icy cold in the room; was from what he was seeing on Regan's chest; was from bas-relief script rising up in clear letters of blood-red skin. Two words:

help me

"That's her handwriting," whispered Sharon.

At 9:00 that morning, Damien Karras came to the president of Georgetown University and asked for permission to seek an exorcism. He received it, and immediately afterward went to the Bishop of the diocese, who listened with grave attention to all that Karras had to say.

"You're convinced that it's genuine?" the Bishop asked finally.

"I've made a prudent judgment that it meets the conditions set forth in the *Ritual*," answered Karras evasively. He still did not dare believe. Not his mind but his heart had tugged him to this moment; pity and the hope for a cure through suggestion.

"You would want to do the exorcism yourself?" asked the Bishop.

He felt a moment of elation; saw the door swinging open to fields, to escape from the crushing weight of caring and that meeting each twilight with the ghost of his faith. "Yes, of course," answered Karras.

"How's your health?"

"All right."

"Have you ever been involved with this sort of thing before?"

"No, I haven't."

"Well, we'll see. It might be best to have a man with experience. There aren't too many, of course, but perhaps someone back from the foreign missions. Let me see who's around. In the meantime, I'll call you as soon as we know."

When Karras had left him, the Bishop called the president of Georgetown University, and they talked about him for the second time that day.

"Well, he does know the background," said the president at a point in their conversation. "I doubt there's any danger in just having him assist. There should be a psychiatrist present, anyway."

"And what about the exorcist? Any ideas? I'm blank."

"Well, now, Lankester Merrin's around."

"Merrin? I had a notion he was over in Iraq. I think I read he was working on a dig around Nineveh."

"Yes, down below Mosul. That's right. But he finished and came back around three or four months ago, Mike. He's at Woodstock."

"Teaching?"

"No, working on another book."

"God help us! Don't you think he's too old, though? How's his health?"

"Well, it must be all right or he wouldn't still be running around digging up tombs, don't you think?"

"Yes, I suppose so."

"And besides, he's had experience, Mike."

"I didn't know that."

"Well, at least that's the word."

"When was that?"

"Oh, maybe ten or twelve years ago, I think, in Africa. Supposedly the exorcism lasted for months. I heard it damn near killed him."

"Well, in that case, I doubt that he'd want to do another one."

"We do what we're told here, Mike. All the rebels are over with you seculars."

"Thanks for reminding me."

"Well, what do you think?"

"Look, I'll leave it up to you and the Provincial."

Early that silently waiting evening, a young scholastic preparing for the priesthood wandered the grounds of Woodstock Seminary in Maryland. He was searching for a slender, gray-haired old Jesuit. He found him on a pathway, strolling through a grove. He handed him a telegram. The old man thanked him, serene, eyes kindly, then turned and renewed his contemplation; continued his walk through a nature that he loved. Now and then he would pause to hear the song of a robin, to watch a bright butterfly hover on a branch. He did not open and read the telegram. He knew what it said. He had known. He had read it in the dust of the temples of Nineveh. He was ready.

He continued his farewells.

IV: "And let my cry come unto thee..."

"He who abides in love, abides in God, and God in him. . . ."
Saint Paul

one

In the breathing dark of his quiet office, Kinderman brooded above his desk.

He adjusted the desk-lamp beam a fraction. Below him were records, transcripts, exhibits; police files; crime-lab reports; scribbled notes. In a pensive mood, he had carefully fashioned them into a collage in the shape of a rose, as if to belie the ugly conclusion to which they had led him; that he could not accept.

Engstrom was innocent. At the time of Dennings' death, he had been visiting his daughter, supplying her with money for the purchase of drugs. He had lied about his whereabouts that night in order to protect her and to shield her mother, who believed Elvira to be dead and past all harm and degradation.

It was not from Karl that Kinderman had learned this. On the night of their encounter in Elvira's hallway, the servant remained obdurately silent. It was only when Kinderman apprised the daughter of her father's involvement in the Dennings case that Elvira volunteered the truth. There were witnesses to confirm it. Engstrom was innocent. Innocent and silent concerning events in Chris MacNeil's house.

Kinderman frowned at the rose collage. Something was wrong with the composition. He shifted a petal point—the corner of a deposition—a trifle lower and to the right.

Roses. Elvira. He had warned her grimly that failure to check herself into a clinic within two weeks would result in his dogging her trail with warrants until he had evidence to effect her arrest. Yet he did not really believe she would go. There were times when he stared at the law unblinkingly as he would the noonday sun in the hope it would temporarily blind him while some quarry made its escape.

Engstrom was innocent. What remained?

Kinderman, wheezing, shifted his weight. Then he closed his eyes and imagined he was soaking in a lapping hot bath. *Mental Closeout Sale!* he bannered at himself: *Moving to New Conclusions! Positively Everything Must Go!* For a moment he waited, unconvinced. Then, *Positively!* he added sternly.

He opened his eyes and examined afresh the bewildering data.

Item: The death of director Burke Dennings seemed somehow linked to the desecrations at Holy Trinity. Both involved witchcraft and the unknown desecrator could easily be Dennings' murderer.

Item: An expert on witchcraft, a Jesuit priest, had been seen making visits to the home of the MacNeils.

Item: The typewritten sheet of paper containing the text of the blasphemous altar card discovered at Holy Trinity had been checked for latent fingerprints. Impressions had been found on both sides. Some had been made by Damien Karras. But still another set had been found that, from their size, were adjudged to be those of a person with very small hands, quite possibly a child.

Item: The typing on the altar card had been analyzed and compared with the typed impressions on the unfinished letter that Sharon Spencer had pulled from her typewriter, crumpled up, and tossed at a wastepaper basket, missing it, while Kinderman had been questioning Chris. He had picked it up and smuggled it out of the house. The typing on this letter and the typing on the altar-card sheet had been done on the same machine. According to the report, however, the touch of the typists differed. The person who had typed the blasphemous text had a touch far heavier than Sharon Spencer's. Since the typing of the former, moreover, had not been "hunt and peck" but, rather, skillfully accomplished, it suggested that the unknown typist of the altar-card text was a person of extraordinary strength.

Item: Burke Dennings—if his death was not an accident— had been killed by a person of extraordinary strength.

Item: Engstrom was no longer a suspect.

Item: A check of domestic airline reservations disclosed that Chris MacNeil had taken her daughter to Dayton, Ohio. Kinderman had known that the daughter was ill and was being taken to a clinic. But the clinic in Dayton would have to be Barringer. Kinderman had checked and the clinic confirmed that the daughter had been in for observation. Though the clinic refused to state the nature of the illness, it was obviously a serious mental disorder.

Item: Serious mental disorders at times caused extraordinary strength.

Kinderman sighed and closed his eyes. The same. He was back to the same conclusion. He shook his head. Then he opened his eyes and stared at the center of the paper rose: a faded old copy of a national news magazine. On the cover were Chris and Regan. He studied the daughter: the sweet, freckled face and the ribboned ponytails, the missing front tooth in the grin. He looked out a window into darkness. A drizzling rain had begun to fall.

He went down to the garage, got into the unmarked black sedan and then drove through rain-slick, shining streets to the Georgetown area, where he parked on the eastern side of Prospect Street. And sat. For a quarter of an hour. Sat. Staring at Regan's window. Should he knock at the door and demand to see her? He lowered his head. Rubbed at his brow. *William F. Kinderman, you are sick! You are ill! Go home! Take medicine! Sleep!*

He looked up at the window again and ruefully shook his head. Here his haunted logic had led him.

He shifted his gaze as a cab pulled up to the house. He started the engine and turned on the windshield wipers.

From the cab stepped a tall old man. Black raincoat and hat and a battered valise. He paid the driver, then turned and stood motionless, staring at the house. The cab pulled away and rounded the corner of Thirty-sixth Street. Kinderman quickly pulled out to follow. As he turned the corner, he noticed that the tall old man hadn't moved, but was standing under street-light glow, in mist, like a melancholy traveler frozen in time. The detective blinked his lights at the taxi.

Inside, at that moment, Karras and Karl pinned Regan's arms while Sharon injected her with Librium, bringing the total amount injected in the last two hours to four hundred milligrams. The dosage, Karras knew, was staggering. But after a lull of many hours, the demonic personality had suddenly awakened in a fit of fury so frenzied that Regan's debilitated system could not for very long endure it.

Karras was exhausted. After his visit to the Chancery Office that morning, he returned to the house to tell Chris what had happened. Then he set up an intravenous feeding for Regan, went back to his room and fell on his bed. After only an hour and a half of sleep, however, the telephone had wrenched him awake. Sharon. Regan was still unconscious and her pulse had been gradually slipping lower. Karras had then rushed to the house with his medical bag and pinched Regan's Achilles tendon, looking for reaction to pain. There was none. He pressed down hard on one of her fingernails. Again no reaction. He was worried. Though he knew that in hysteria and in states of trance there was sometimes an insensitivity to pain, he now feared coma, a state from which Regan might slip easily into death. He checked her blood pressure: ninety over sixty; then pulse rate: sixty. He had waited in the room then, and checked her again every fifteen minutes for an hour and a half before he was satisfied that blood pressure and pulse rate had stabilized, meaning Regan was not in shock but in a state of stupor. Sharon was instructed to continue to check the pulse each hour. Then he'd returned to his room and his sleep. But again the telephone woke him up. The exorcist, the Chancery Office told him, would be Lankester Merrin. Karras would assist.

The news had stunned him. Merrin! the philosopher-paleontologist! the soaring, staggering intellect! His books had stirred ferment in the Church, for they interpreted his faith in the terms of science, in terms of a matter that was still evolving, destined to be spirit and joined to God.

Karras telephoned Chris at once to convey the news, but found that she'd heard from the Bishop directly. He had told her that Merrin would arrive the next day. "I told the Bishop he could stay at the house," Chris said. "It'll just be a day or so, won't it?" Before answering, Karras paused. "I don't know." And then, pausing again, said, "You mustn't expect too much." "If it works, I mean," Chris had answered. Her tone had been subdued. "I didn't mean to imply that it wouldn't," he reassured her. "I just meant that it might take time." "How long?" "It varies." He knew that an exorcism often took weeks, even months; knew that frequently it failed altogether. He expected the latter; expected that the burden, barring cure through suggestion, would fall once again, and at the last, upon him. "It can take a few days or weeks," he'd then told her. "How long has she got, Father Karras? . . ."

When he hung up the phone, he'd felt heavy, tormented. Stretched out on the bed, he thought of Merrin. *Merrin!* An excitement and a hope seeped through him. A sinking disquiet followed. He himself had been the natural choice for exorcist; yet the Bishop had passed him over. Why? Because Merrin had done this before?

As he closed his eyes, he recalled that exorcists were selected on the basis of "piety" and "high moral qualities"; that a passage in the gospel of Matthew related that Christ, when asked by his disciples the cause of their failure in an effort at exorcism, had answered them: ". . . because of your little faith."

The Provincial had known about his problem; so had the president, Karras reflected. Had either told the Bishop?

He had turned on his bed then, damply despondent; felt somehow unworthy; incompetent; rejected. It stung. Unreasonably, it stung. Then, finally, sleep came pouring into emptiness, filling in the niches and cracks in his heart.

But again the ring of the phone woke him, Chris calling to inform him of Regan's new frenzy. Back at the house, he checked Regan's pulse. It was strong. He gave Librium, then again. And again. Finally, he made his way to the kitchen, briefly joining Chris at the table for coffee. She was reading a book, one of Merrin's that she'd ordered delivered to the house. "Way over my head," she told him softly, yet she looked touched and deeply moved. "But there's some of it so beautiful—so great." She flipped back through pages to a passage she had marked, and handed the book across the table to Karras. He read:

. . . We have familiar experience of the order, the constancy, the perpetual renovation of the material world which surrounds us. Frail and transitory as is every part of it, restless and migratory as are its elements, still it abides. It is bound together by a law of permanence, and though it is ever dying, it is ever coming to life again. Dissolution does but give birth to fresh modes of organization, and one death is the parent of a thousand lives. Each hour, as it comes, is but a testimony how fleeting, yet how secure, how certain, is the great whole. It is like an image on the waters, which is ever the same, though the waters ever flow. The sun sinks to rise again; the day is swallowed up in the gloom of night, to be born out of it, as fresh as if it had never been quenched. Spring passes into summer, and through summer and autumn into winter, only the more surely, by its own ultimate return, to triumph over that grave towards which it resolutely hastened from its first hour. We mourn the blossoms of May because they are to wither; but we know that May is one day to have its revenge upon November, by the revolution of that solemn circle which never stops—which teaches us in our height of hope, ever to be sober, and in our depth of desolation, never to despair.

"Yes, it's beautiful," Karras said softly. His eyes were still on the page. The raging of the demon from upstairs grew louder.

"... *bastard* ... *scum* ... *pious hypocrite!*"

"She used to put a rose on my plate ... in the morning ... before I'd go to work."

Karras looked up with a question in his eyes. "Regan," Chris told him.

She looked down. "Yeah, that's right. I forget ... you've never met her." She blew her nose and dabbed at her eyes. "Want some brandy in that coffee, Father Karras?" she asked.

"Thanks, I don't think so."

"Coffee's flat," she whispered tremulously. "I think I'll get some brandy. Excuse me." She quickly left the kitchen.

Karras sat alone and sipped bleakly at his coffee. He felt warm in the sweater that he wore beneath his cassock; felt weak in his failure to have given Chris comfort. Then a memory of childhood shimmered up sadly, a memory of Ginger, his mongrel dog, growing skeletal and dazed in a box in the apartment; Ginger shivering with fever and vomiting while Karras covered her with towels, tried to make her drink warm milk, until a neighbor came by and saw it was distemper, shook his head and said, "Your dog needed shots right away." Then dismissal from school one afternoon . . . to the street . . . in columns of twos to the corner . . . his mother there to meet him . . . unexpected . . . looking sad . . . and then taking his hand to press a shiny half-dollar piece into it . . . elation . . . so much money! . . . then her voice, soft and tender, "Gingie die. . . ."

He looked down at the steaming, bitter blackness in his cup and felt his hands empty of comfort or of cure.

". . . pious bastard!"

The demon. Still raging.

"Your dog needed shots right away. . . ."

Quickly he returned to Regan's bedroom, where he held her while Sharon administered the Librium injection that now brought the total dosage up to five hundred milligrams.

Sharon was swabbing the needle puncture while Karras watched Regan, puzzled. The frenzied obscenities seemed to be directed at no one in the room, but rather at someone unseen—or not present.

He dismissed the thought. "I'll be back," he told Sharon.

Concerned about Chris, he went down to the kitchen, where again he found her sitting alone at the table. She was pouring brandy into her coffee. "Are you sure you wouldn't like some, Father?" she asked.

Shaking his head, he came over to the table and sat down wearily. He stared at the floor. Heard porcelain clicks of a spoon stirring coffee. "Have you talked to her father?" he asked.

"Yes. Yes, he called." A pause. "He wanted to talk to Rags."

"And what did you tell him?"

A pause. Then, "I told him she was out at a party."

Silence. Karras heard no more clicks. He looked up and saw her staring at the ceiling. And then he noticed it too: the shouts above had finally ceased.

"I guess the Librium took hold," he said gratefully.

Chiming of the doorbell. He glanced toward the sound; then at Chris, who met his look of surmise with a questioning, apprehensive lifting of an eyebrow.

Kinderman?

Seconds. Ticking. They waited. Willie was resting. Sharon and Karl were still upstairs. No one coming to answer. Tense, Chris got up abruptly from the table and went to the living room. Kneeling on a sofa, she parted a curtain and peered furtively through the window at her caller. *Thank God!* Not Kinderman. She was looking, instead, at a tall old man in a threadbare raincoat, his head bowed patiently in the rain. He carried a worn, old-fashioned valise. For an instant, a buckle gleamed in street-lamp glow as the bag shifted slightly in his grip.

The doorbell chimed again.

Who is that?

Puzzled, Chris got down off the sofa and walked to the entry hall. She opened the door only slightly, squinting out into darkness as a fine mist of rain brushed her eyes. The man's hat brim obscured his face. "Yes, hello; can I help you?"

"Mrs. MacNeil?" came a voice from the shadows. It was gentle, refined, yet as full as a harvest.

As he reached for his hat, Chris was nodding her head, and then suddenly she was looking into eyes that overwhelmed her, that shone with intelligence and kindly understanding, with serenity that poured from them into her being like the waters of a warm and healing river whose source was both in him yet somehow beyond him; whose flow was contained and yet headlong and endless.

"I'm Father Merrin."

For a moment she looked blank as she stared at the lean and ascetic face, at the sculptured cheekbones, polished like soapstone; then quickly she flung wide the door. "Oh, my gosh, please come *in!* Oh, come *in!* Gee, I'm . . . *Honestly!* I don't know where my . . ."

He entered and she closed the door.

"I mean, I didn't expect you until tomorrow!"

"Yes, I know," she heard him saying.

As she turned around to face him, she saw him standing with his head angled sideways, glancing upward, as if he were listening—no, more like *feeling*, she thought—for some presence out of sight . . . some distant vibration that was known and familiar. Puzzled, she watched him. His skin seemed weathered by alien winds, by a sun that shone elsewhere, somewhere remote from her time and her place.

What's he doing?

"Can I take that bag for you, Father? It must weigh a ton by now."

"It's all right," he said softly. Still feeling. Still probing. "It's like part of my arm: very old . . . very battered." He looked down with a warm, tired smile in his eyes. "I'm accustomed to the weight. . . . Is Father Karras here?" he asked.

"Yes, he is. He's in the kitchen. Have you had any dinner, incidentally, Father?"

He flicked his glance upward at the sound of a door being opened. "Yes, I had some on the train."

"Are you sure you wouldn't like something else?"

A moment. Then sound of the door being closed. He glanced down. "No, thank you."

"Gee, all of this rain," she protested, still flustered. "If I'd known you were coming, I could have met you at the station."

"It's all right."

"Did you have to wait long for a cab?"

"A few minutes."

"I take that, Father!"

Karl. He'd descended the stairs very quickly and now slipped the bag from the priest's easy grip and took it off down the hall.

"We've put a bed in the study for you, Father." Chris was fidgeting. "It's really very comfortable and I thought you'd like the privacy. I'll show you where it is." She'd started moving, then stopped. "Or would you like to say hello to Father Karras?"

"I should like to see your daughter first," said Merrin.

She looked puzzled. "Right now, you mean, Father?"

He glanced upward again with that distant attentiveness. "Yes, now—I think now."

"Gee, I'm sure she's asleep."

"I think not."

"Well, if—"

Suddenly, Chris flinched at a sound from above, at the voice of the demon, booming and yet muffled, croaking, like amplified premature burial.

"Merriiiiinnnnnn!"

Then the massive and shiveringly hollow jolt of a single blow against the bedroom wall.

"God almighty!" Chris breathed as she clutched a pale hand against her chest. Stunned, she looked at Merrin. The priest hadn't moved. He was still staring upward, intense and yet serene, and in his eyes there was not even a hint of surprise. It was more, Chris thought, like recognition.

Another blow shook the walls.

"Merriiiiinnnnnnnnnnn!"

The Jesuit moved slowly forward, oblivious of Chris, who was gaping in wonder; of Karl, stepping lithe and incredulous from the study; of Karras, emerging bewildered from the kitchen while the nightmarish poundings and croakings continued. He went calmly up the staircase, slender hand like alabaster sliding upward on the banister.

Karras came up beside Chris, and together they watched

from below as Merrin entered Regan's bedroom and closed the door behind him. For a time there was silence. Then abruptly the demon laughed hideously and Merrin came out. He closed the door and started down the hall. Behind him, the bedroom door opened again and Sharon poked her head out, staring after him, an odd expression on her face.

The Jesuit descended the staircase rapidly and put out his hand to the waiting Karras.

"Father Karras . . ."

"Hello, Father."

Merrin had clasped the other priest's hand in both of his; he was squeezing it, searching Karras' face with a look of gravity and concern, while upstairs the laughter turned to vicious obscenities directed at Merrin. "You look terribly tired," he said. "Are you tired?"

"Not at all. Why do you ask?"

"Do you have your raincoat with you?"

Karras shook his head and said, "No."

"Then here, take mine," said the gray-haired Jesuit, unbuttoning the coat. "I should like you to go to the residence, Damien, and gather up a cassock for myself, two surplices, a purple stole, some holy water and two copies of *The Roman Ritual*." He handed the raincoat to the puzzled Karras. "I believe we should begin."

Karras frowned. "You mean now? Right away?"

"Yes, I think so."

"Don't you want to hear the background of the case first, Father?"

"Why?"

Merrin's brows were knitted in earnestness.

Karras realized that he had no answer. He averted his gaze from those disconcerting eyes. "Right," he said. He was slipping on the raincoat and turning away. "I'll go and get the things."

Karl made a dash across the room, got ahead of Karras and pulled the front door open for him. They exchanged brief glances, and then Karras stepped out into the rainy night. Merrin glanced back to Chris. "You don't mind if we begin right away?" he asked softly.

She'd been watching him, glowing with relief at the feeling of decision and direction and command rushing in like a shout in sunlit day. "No, I'm glad," she said gratefully. "You must be tired, though, Father."

He saw her anxious gaze flick upward toward the raging of the demon.

"Would you like a cup of coffee?" she was asking. "It's fresh." Insistent. Faintly pleading. "It's hot. Wouldn't you like some, Father?"

He saw the hands lightly clasping, unclasping; the deep caverns of her eyes. "Yes, I would," he said warmly. "Thank you." Something heavy had been gently brushed aside; told to wait. "If you're sure it's no trouble . . ."

She led him to the kitchen and soon he was leaning against the stove with a mug of black coffee in his hand.

"Want some brandy in it, Father?" Chris held up the bottle.

He bent his head and looked down into the mug without expression. "Well, the doctors say I shouldn't," he said. And then he held out the mug. "But thank God, my will is weak."

Chris paused for a moment, unsure, then saw the smile in his eyes as he lifted his head.

She poured.

"What a lovely name you have," he told her. "Chris Mac-Neil. It's not a stage name?"

Chris trickled brandy into her coffee and shook her head. "No, I'm really not Esmerelda Glutz."

"Thank God for *that*," murmured Merrin.

Chris smiled and sat down. "And what's Lankester, Father? So unusual. Were you named after someone?"

"A cargo ship," he murmured as he stared absently and put the mug to his lips. He sipped. "Or a bridge. Yes, I suppose it was a bridge." He looked rueful. "Now, Damien," he went on, "how I wish I had a name like Damien. So lovely."

"Where does that come from, Father? That name?"

"Damien?" He looked down at his cup. "It was the name of a priest who devoted his life to taking care of the lepers on the island of Molokai. He finally caught the disease himself." He paused. "Lovely name," he said again. "I believe that with a first name like Damien, I might even be content with the last name Glutz."

Chris chuckled. She unwound. Felt easier. And for minutes, she and Merrin spoke of homely things, little things. Finally, Sharon appeared in the kitchen, and only then did Merrin move to leave. It was as if he had been waiting for her arrival, for immediately he carried his mug to the sink, rinsed it out and placed it carefully in the dish rack. "That was good; that was just what I wanted," he said.

Chris got up and said, "I'll take you to your room."

He thanked her and followed her to the door of the study. "If there's anything you need, Father," she said, "let me know."

He put his hand on her shoulder and squeezed it reassuringly. Chris felt a power and warmth flowing into her. Peace. She felt peace. And an odd sense of . . . safety? she wondered.

"You're very kind." His eyes smiled. "Thank you."

He removed his hand and watched her walk away. As soon as she was gone, a tightening pain seemed to clutch at his face. He entered the study and closed the door. From a pocket of his trousers, he slipped out a tin marked *Bayer Aspirin*, opened it, extracted a nitroglycerin pill and placed it carefully under his tongue.

Chris entered the kitchen. Pausing by the door, she looked at Sharon, who was standing by the stove, the palm of her hand against the percolator as she waited for the coffee to reheat.

Chris went over to her, concerned. "Hey, honey," she said softly. "Why don't you get a little rest?"

No response. Sharon seemed lost in thought. Then she

turned and stared blankly at Chris. "I'm sorry. Did you say something?"

Chris studied the tightness in her face, the distant look. "What happened up there, Sharon?" she asked.

"Happened where?"

"When Father Merrin walked in upstairs."

"Oh, yes . . ." Sharon frowned. She shifted her faraway gaze to a point in space between doubt and remembrance. "Yes. It was funny."

"Funny?"

"Strange. They only . . ." She paused. "Well, they only just stared at each other for a while, and then Regan—that thing— it said . . ."

"Said what?"

"It said, 'This time, you're going to lose.' "

Chris stared at her, waiting. "And then?"

"That was it," Sharon answered. "Father Merrin turned around and walked out of the room."

"And how did he look?" Chris asked her.

"Funny."

"Oh, Christ, Sharon, think of some other word!" snapped Chris, and was about to say something else when she noticed that Sharon had angled her head up, to the side, abstracted, as if she were listening.

Chris glanced upward and heard it too: the silence; the sudden cessation of the raging of the demon; yet something more . . . something . . . and growing.

The women flicked sidelong stares at each other.

"You feel it too?" asked Sharon quietly.

Chris nodded. The house. Something in the house. A tension. A gradual thickening of the air. A pulsing, like energies slowly building up.

The lilting of the door chimes sounded unreal.

Sharon turned away. "I'll get it."

She walked to the entry hall and opened the door. It was

Karras. He was carrying a cardboard laundry box. "Thank you, Sharon."

"Father Merrin's in the study," she told him.

Karras moved quickly to the study, tapped lightly and cursorily at the door and then entered with the box. "Sorry, Father," he was saying, "I had a little—"

Karras stopped short. Merrin, in trousers and T-shirt, kneeled in prayer beside the rented bed, his forehead bent low to his tight-clasped hands. Karras stood rooted for a moment, as if he had casually rounded a corner and suddenly encountered his boyhood self with an altar boy's cassock draped over an arm, hurrying by without a glance of recognition.

Karras shifted his eyes to the open laundry box, to speckles of rain on starch. Then slowly, with his gaze still averted, he moved to the sofa and soundlessly laid out the contents of the box. When he finished, he took off the raincoat and draped it carefully over a chair. As he glanced back toward Merrin, he saw the priest blessing himself and he hastily looked away, reaching down for the larger of the white cotton surplices. He began to put it on over his cassock. He heard Merrin rising, and then, "Thank you, Damien." Karras turned to face him, tugging down the surplice while Merrin came over in front of the sofa, his eyes brushing tenderly over its contents.

Karras reached for a sweater. "I thought you might wear this under your cassock, Father," he told Merrin as he handed it over. "The room gets cold at times."

Merrin touched the sweater lightly with his hands. "That was thoughtful of you, Damien."

Karras picked up Merrin's cassock from the sofa, and watched him pull the sweater down over his head, and only now, and very suddenly, while watching this homely, prosaic action, did Karras feel the staggering impact of the man; of the moment; of a stillness in the house, crushing down on him, choking off breath.

He came back to awareness with the feeling of the cassock being tugged from his hands. Merrin. He was slipping it on. "You're familiar with the rules concerning exorcism, Damien?"

"Yes, I am," answered Karras.

Merrin began buttoning up the cassock. "Especially important is the warning to avoid conversations with the demon. . . ."

"*The demon.*" He'd said it so matter-of-factly, thought Karras. It jarred him.

"We may ask what is relevant," said Merrin as he buttoned the collar of the cassock. "But anything beyond that is dangerous. Extremely." He lifted the surplice from Karras' hands and began to slip it over the cassock. "Especially, do not listen to anything he says. The demon is a liar. He will lie to confuse us; but he will also mix lies with the truth to attack us. The attack is psychological, Damien. And powerful. Do not listen. Remember that. Do not listen."

As Karras handed him the stole, the exorcist added, "Is there anything at all you would like to ask now, Damien?"

Karras shook his head. "No. But I think it might be helpful if I gave you some background on the different personalities that Regan has manifested. So far, there seem to be three."

"There is only one," said Merrin softly, slipping the stole around his shoulders. For a moment, he gripped it and stood unmoving as a haunted expression came into his eyes. Then he reached for the copies of *The Roman Ritual* and gave one to Karras. "We will skip the Litany of the Saints. You have the holy water?"

Karras slipped the slender, cork-tipped vial from his pocket. Merrin took it, then nodded serenely toward the door. "If you will lead, please, Damien."

Upstairs, by the door to Regan's bedroom, Sharon and Chris stood tense and waiting. They were bundled in heavy sweaters and jackets. At the sound of a door coming open, they turned and looked below and saw Karras and Merrin come down the hall to the stairs in solemn procession. Tall: how tall they were, thought Chris; and Karras: the dark of that rock-chipped face above the innocent, altar-boy white of the surplice. Watching them steadily ascending the staircase, Chris felt deeply and strangely moved. *Here comes my big brother to beat your brains in, creep!* It was a feeling, she thought, much like that. She could feel her heart begin to beat faster.

At the door of the room, the Jesuits stopped. Karras frowned at the sweater and jacket Chris wore. "You're coming in?"

"Well, I really thought I should."

"Please don't," he urged her. "Don't. You'd be making a great mistake."

Chris turned questioningly to Merrin.

"Father Karras knows best," said the exorcist quietly.

Chris looked to Karras again. Dropped her head. "Okay," she said despondently. She leaned against the wall. "I'll wait out here."

"What is your daughter's middle name?" asked Merrin.

"Teresa."

"What a lovely name," said Merrin warmly. He held her gaze for a moment, reassuring. Then he looked at the door, and again Chris felt it: that tension; that thickening of coiled darkness. Inside. In the bedroom. Beyond that door. Karras felt it too, she noticed, and Sharon.

Merrin nodded. "All right," he said softly.

Karras opened the door, and almost reeled back from the blast of stench and icy cold. In a corner of the room, Karl sat huddled in a chair. He was dressed in a faded olive green hunting jacket and turned expectantly to Karras. The Jesuit quickly flicked his glance to the demon in the bed. Its gleaming eyes stared beyond him to the hall. They were fixed on Merrin.

Karras moved forward to the foot of the bed while Merrin walked slowly, tall and erect, to the side. There he stopped and looked down into hate.

A smothering stillness hung over the room. Then Regan licked a wolfish, blackened tongue across her cracked and swollen lips. It sounded like a hand smoothing crumpled parchment. "Well, proud scum!" croaked the demon. "At last! At last you've come!"

The old priest lifted his hand and traced the sign of the cross above the bed, and then repeated the gesture toward all in the room. Turning back, he plucked the cap from the vial of holy water.

"Ah, yes! The holy urine now!" rasped the demon. "The semen of the saints!"

Merrin lifted up the vial and the face of the demon grew livid, contorted. "Ah, will you, bastard?" it seethed at him. "*Will* you?"

Merrin started sprinkling.

The demon jerked its head up, the mouth and the neck muscles trembling with rage. "Yes, sprinkle! Sprinkle, Merrin! Drench us! Drown us in your sweat! Your sweat is sanctified, Saint Merrin! Bend and fart out clouds of incense! Bend and show the holy rump that we may worship and adore it! *kiss* it! *lick* it, blessed—"

"*Be silent!*"

The words flung forth like bolts. Karras flinched and jerked his head around in wonder at Merrin, who stared commandingly at Regan. And the demon was silent. Was returning his stare. But the eyes were now hesitant. Blinking. Wary.

Merrin capped the holy-water vial routinely and returned it to Karras. The psychiatrist slipped it into his pocket and watched as Merrin kneeled down beside the bed and closed his eyes in murmured prayer. " 'Our Father . . .' " he began.

Regan spat and hit Merrin in the face with a yellowish glob of mucous. It oozed slowly down the exorcist's cheek.

" '. . . Thy kingdom come . . .' " His head still bowed, Merrin continued the prayer without a pause while his hand plucked a handkerchief out of his pocket and unhurriedly wiped away the spittle. " '. . . and lead us not into temptation,' " he ended mildly.

" 'But deliver us from evil,' " responded Karras.

He looked up briefly. Regan's eyes were rolling upward into their sockets until only the white of the sclera was exposed. Karras felt uneasy. Felt something in the room congealing. He returned to his text to follow Merrin's prayer:

" 'God and Father of our Lord Jesus Christ, I appeal to your holy name, humbly begging your kindness, that you may graciously grant me help against this unclean spirit now tormenting this creature of yours; through Christ our Lord.' "

"Amen," responded Karras.

Now Merrin stood up and prayed reverently: " 'God, Creator and defender of the human race, look down in pity on this your servant, Regan Teresa MacNeil, now trapped in the coils of man's ancient enemy, sworn foe of our race, who . . .' "

Karras glanced up as he heard Regan hissing, saw her sitting erect with the whites of her eyes exposed, while her tongue flicked in and out rapidly, head weaving slowly back and forth like a cobra's.

Once again Karras had a feeling of disquiet. He looked back at his text.

" 'Save your servant,' " prayed Merrin, standing and reading from the *Ritual*.

" 'Who trusts in you, my God,' " answered Karras.

" 'Let her find in you, Lord, a fortified tower.' "

" 'In the face of the enemy.' "

As Merrin continued with the next line, Karras heard a gasp from Sharon behind him, and turning quickly around, he saw her looking stupefied at the bed. Puzzled, he looked back. And was instantly electrified. *The front of the bed was rising up off the floor!*

He stared at it incredulously. Four inches. Half a foot. A foot. Then the back legs began to come up.

"*Gott in Himmel!*" Karl whispered in fear. But Karras did not hear him or see him make the sign of the cross on himself as the back of the bed lifted level with the front. *It's not happening!* he thought, as he watched, transfixed.

The bed drifted upward another foot and then hovered there, bobbing and listing gently as if it were floating on a stagnant lake.

"Father Karras?"

Regan undulating. Hissing.

"Father Karras?"

Karras turned. The exorcist was eyeing him serenely, and now motioned his head toward the copy of the *Ritual* in Karras' hands. "The response, please, Damien."

Karras looked blank and uncomprehending. Sharon ran from the room.

" 'Let the enemy have no power over her,' " Merrin repeated gently.

Hastily, Karras glanced back at the text and with a pounding heart breathed out the response: " 'And the son of iniquity be powerless to harm her.' "

" 'Lord, hear my prayer,' " continued Merrin.

" 'And let my cry come unto Thee.' "

" 'The Lord be with you.' "

" 'And with your spirit.' "

Merrin embarked upon a lengthy prayer and Karras again returned his gaze to the bed, to his hopes of his God and the supernatural hovering low in the empty air. An elation thrilled up through his being. *It's there! There it is! Right in front of me! There!* He looked suddenly around at the sound of the door opening. Sharon rushed in with Chris, who stopped, unbelieving, and gasped, "*Jesus Christ!*"

" 'Almighty Father, everlasting God . . .' "

The exorcist reached up his hand in a workaday manner and traced the sign of the cross, unhurriedly, three times on

Regan's brow while continuing to read from the text of the *Ritual:* " '. . . who sent your only begotten Son into the world to crush that roaring lion . . .' "

The hissing ceased and from the taut-stretched O of Regan's mouth came the nerve-shredding lowing of a steer.

" '. . . snatch from ruination and from the clutches of the noonday devil this human being made in your image, and . . .' "

The lowing grew louder, tearing at flesh and shivering through bone.

" 'God and Lord of all creation . . .' " Merrin routinely reached up his hand and pressed a portion of the stole to Regan's neck while continuing to pray: " '. . . by whose might Satan was made to fall from heaven like lightning, strike terror into the beast now laying waste your vineyard. . . .' "

The bellowing ceased. A ringing silence. Then a thick and putrid greenish vomit began to pump from Regan's mouth in slow and regular spurts that oozed like lava over her lip and flowed in waves onto Merrin's hand. But he did not move it. " 'Let your mighty hand cast out this cruel demon from Regan Teresa MacNeil, who . . .' "

Karras was dimly aware of a door being opened, of Chris bolting from the room.

" 'Drive out this persecutor of the innocent. . . .' "

The bed began to rock lazily, then to pitch, and then suddenly it was violently dipping and yawing, and with the vomit still pumping from Regan's mouth, Merrin calmly made adjustments and kept the stole firmly to her neck.

" 'Fill your servants with courage to manfully oppose that reprobate dragon lest he despise those who put their trust in you, and . . .' "

Abruptly, the movements subsided and as Karras watched, mesmerized, the bed drifted featherlike, slowly, to the floor and settled on the rug with a cushioned thud.

" 'Lord, grant that this . . .' "

Numb, Karras shifted his gaze. Merrin's hand. He could not see it. It was buried under mounded, steaming vomit.

"Damien?"

Karras glanced up.

" 'Lord, hear my prayer,' " said the exorcist gently.

Slowly, Karras turned to the bed. " 'And let my cry come unto Thee.' "

Merrin lifted off the stole, took a slight step backward, and then jolted the room with the lash of his voice as he commanded, " 'I cast you out, unclean spirit, along with every satanic power of the enemy! every specter from hell! every savage companion!' " Merrin's hand, at his side, dripped vomit to the rug. " 'It is Christ who commands you, who once stilled the wind and the sea and the storm! Who . . .' "

Regan stopped vomiting. Sat silent. Unmoving. The whites of her eyes gleamed balefully at Merrin. From the foot of the bed, Karras watched her intently as his shock and excitement began to fade, as his mind began feverishly to thresh, to poke its fingers, unbidden, compulsively, deep into corners of logical doubt: poltergeists; psychokinetic action; adolescent tensions and mind-directed force. He frowned as he remembered something. He moved to the side of the bed, leaned over, reached down to grasp Regan's wrist. And found what he'd feared. Like the shaman in Siberia, the pulse was racing at an unbelievable speed. It drained him suddenly of sun, and glancing at his watch, he counted the heartbeats, now, like arguments against his life.

" 'It is He who commands you, He who flung you headlong from the heights of heaven!' "

Merrin's powerful adjuration pounded off the rim of Karras' consciousness in resonant, inexorable blows as the pulse came faster now. And faster. Karras looked at Regan. Still silent. Unmoving. Into icy air, thin mists of vapor wafted from the vomit like a reeking offering. Karras felt uneasy. Then the hair on his arms began prickling up. With nightmare slowness, a fraction at a time, Regan's head was turning, swiveling like a manikin, creaking with the sound of some rusted mechanism, until the dread and glaring whites of those ghastly eyes were fixed on his.

" 'And therefore, tremble in fear, now, Satan . . .' "

The head turned slowly back toward Merrin.

" '. . . you corrupter of justice! you begetter of death! you betrayer of the nations! you robber of life! you . . .' "

Karras glanced warily around as the lights in the room began flickering, dimming, and then faded to an eerie, pulsing amber. He shivered. It was colder. The room was getting colder.

" '. . . you prince of murderers! you inventor of every obscenity! you enemy of the human race! you . . .' "

A muffled pounding jolted the room. Then another. Then steadily, shuddering through walls, through the floor, through the ceiling, splintering, throbbing at a ponderous rate like the beating of a heart that was massive and diseased.

" 'Depart, you monster! Your place is in solitude! Your abode is in a nest of vipers! Get down and crawl with them! It is God himself who commands you! The blood of . . .' "

The poundings grew louder, began to come ominously faster and faster.

" 'I adjure you, ancient serpent . . .' "

And faster . . .

" '. . . by the judge of the living and the dead, by your Creator, by the Creator of all the universe, to . . .' "

Sharon cried out, pressing fists against her ears as the poundings grew deafening and now suddenly accelerated and leaped to a terrifying tempo.

Regan's pulse was astonishing. It hammered at a speed too rapid to gauge. Across the bed, Merrin reached out calmly and with the end of his thumb traced the sign of the cross on Regan's vomit-covered chest. The words of his prayer were swallowed in the poundings.

Karras felt the pulse rate suddenly drop, and as Merrin

prayed and traced the sign of the cross on Regan's brow, the nightmarish poundings abruptly ceased.

" 'O God of heaven and earth, God of the angels and archangels . . .' " Karras could now hear Merrin praying as the pulse kept dropping, dropping. . . .

"Prideful bastard, Merrin! Scum! You will lose! She will die! The pig will die!"

The flickering haze grew gradually brighter. The demonic entity had returned and raged hatefully at Merrin. "Profligate peacock! Ancient heretic! I adjure you, turn and look on me! Now *look on me, you scum!*" The demon jerked forward and spat in Merrin's face, and then croaked at him, "*Thus* does your master cure the blind!"

" 'God and Lord of all creation . . .' " prayed Merrin, reaching placidly for his handkerchief and wiping away the spittle.

"Now follow his teaching, Merrin! *Do* it! Put your sanctified cock in the piglet's mouth and *cleanse* it, *swab* it with the wrinkled relic and she will be *cured,* Saint Merrin! A *miracle!* A—"

" '. . . deliver this servant of . . .' "

"*Hypocrite!* You care nothing at *all* for the *pig.* You care *nothing!* You have *made her a contest between us!*"

" '. . . I humbly . . .' "

"Liar! Lying bastard! Tell us, where is your humility, Merrin? In the desert? in the ruins? in the tombs where you fled to escape your fellowman? to escape from your inferiors, from the halt and the lame of mind? Do you speak to men, you pious vomit? . . ."

" '. . . deliver . . .' "

"Your abode is in a nest of peacocks, Merrin! your place is within yourself! Go back to the mountaintop and speak to your only equal!"

Merrin continued with the prayers, unheeding, as the torrent of abuse raged on. "Do you hunger, Saint Merrin? Here, I give to you nectar and ambrosia, I give to you the food of your God!" croaked the demon. It excreted diarrhetically, mocking, "For *this* is my body! Now consecrate *that*, Saint Merrin!"

Repelled, Karras focused his attention on the text as Merrin read a passage from Saint Luke:

" '. . . "My name is Legion," answered the man, for many demons had entered into him. And they begged Jesus not to command them to depart into the abyss. Now a herd of swine was there, feeding on the mountain-side. And the demons kept entreating Jesus to let them enter into them. And he gave them leave. And the demons came out from the man and entered into the swine, and the herd rushed down the cliff and into the lake and were drowned. And . . .' "

"Willie, I bring you good news!" croaked the demon. Karras glanced up and saw Willie near the door, stopping short with an armload of towels and sheets. "I bring you tidings of redemption!" it gloated. "Elvira is *alive!* She *lives!* She is . . ."

Willie stared in shock and now Karl turned and shouted at her, "No, Willie! No!"

". . . a *drug* addict, Willie, a hopeless—"

"Willie, do not listen!" cried Karl.

"Shall I tell you where she lives?"

"*Do not listen! Do not listen!*" Karl was rushing Willie out of the room.

"Go and visit her on *Mother's* Day, Willie! Surprise her! Go and—"

Abruptly the demon broke off and fixed its eyes on Karras. He had again checked the pulse and found it strong, which meant it was safe to give Regan more Librium. Now he moved to Sharon to instruct her to prepare another injection. "Do you want her?" leered the demon. "She is yours! Yes, the stable whore is yours! You may ride her as you wish! Why, she fantasizes nightly concerning you, Karras! She masturbates, dreaming of your great priestly . . ."

Sharon crimsoned and kept her eyes averted as Karras gave instructions for the Librium.

"And a Compazine suppository in case there's more vomiting," he added.

Sharon nodded at the floor and started stiffly away. As she walked by the bed with her head still lowered, Regan croaked at her, "*Slut!*" then jerked up and hit her face with a flung bolt of vomit, and while Sharon stood paralyzed and dripping, the Dennings personality appeared, rasping, "*Stable* whore! *Cunt!*"

Sharon bolted from the room.

The Dennings personality now grimaced with distaste, glanced around and asked, "Would someone crack a *window* open, please? It bloody *stinks* in this room! It's simply—!

"No no no, don't!" it then amended. "No, for *heaven's* sake, don't, or someone *else* might be bloody well dead!" And then it cackled, winked monstrously at Karras and vanished.

" ' It is He who expels you . . .' "

"*Does he*, Merrin? *Does* he?"

Now the demon returned and Merrin continued the adjurations, the applications of the stole and the constant tracings of the sign of the cross while it lashed him again obscenely. Too long, worried Karras: the fit was continuing far too long.

"Now the sow comes! The mother of the piglet!" mocked the demon.

Karras turned and saw Chris coming toward him with a swab and disposable syringe. She kept her head down as the demon hurled abuse, and Karras went to her, frowning.

"Sharon's changing her clothes," Chris explained, "and Karl's—"

Karras cut her short with "All right," and they approached the bed.

"Ah, yes, come see your handiwork, sow-mother! Come!"

Chris tried desperately not to listen, not to look, while Karras pinned Regan's unresisting arms.

"See the *puke!* See the murderous bitch!" the demon raged. "Are you pleased? It is *you* who have done it! Yes, *you* with your career before *anything*, your career before your *husband*, before *her*, before . . ."

Karras glanced around. Chris stood paralyzed. "Go ahead!" he ordered. "Don't listen! Go ahead!"

". . . your *divorce!* Go to priests, will you? Priests will not help!" Chris's hand began to shake. "She is *mad!* She is *mad!* The piglet is *mad!* You have driven her to *madness* and to *murder* and . . ."

"I *can't!*" Face contorted, Chris was staring at the quivering syringe. Shook her head. "I can't do it!"

Karras plucked it from her fingers. "All right, swab it! Swab the arm! Over here!" he told her firmly.

". . . in her *coffin*, you bitch, by . . ."

"Don't listen!" cautioned Karras again, and now the demon jerked its head around, its eyes bulging fury. "And *you*, Karras!"

Chris swabbed Regan's arm. "Now, get out!" Karras ordered her, flicking the needle into wasted flesh.

She fled.

"Yes, we *know* of your kindness to *mothers*, dear Karras!" croaked the demon. The Jesuit blenched and for a moment did not move. Then slowly he drew the needle out and looked into eyes that had rolled upward into their sockets. Out of Regan's mouth came a slow, lilting singing, almost chanting, in a sweet, clear voice like a choirboy's. " '*Tantum ergo sacramentum veneremur cernui . . .*' "

It was a hymn sung at Catholic benediction. Karras stood bloodlessly as it continued. Weird and chilling, the singing was a vacuum into which Karras felt the horror of the evening rushing with a horrible clarity. He looked up and saw Merrin with a towel in his hands. With weary, tender movements he wiped away the vomit from Regan's face and neck. " '. . . *et antiquum documentum . . .*' "

The singing. *Whose voice?* wondered Karras. And then fragments: *Dennings . . . The window . . .* Haunted, he saw Sharon come back in and take the towel from Merrin. "I'll finish that, Father," she told him. "I'm all right now. I'd like to change her and get her cleaned up before I give her the Compazine; all right? Could you both wait outside for a while?"

The two priests stepped into the warmth and the dimness of the hall and leaned wearily against the wall.

Karras listened to the eerie, muffled singing from within. After some moments, he spoke softly to Merrin. "You said —you said earlier there was only . . . one entity."

"Yes."

The hushed tones, the lowered heads, were confessional.

"All the others are but forms of attack," continued Merrin. "There is one . . . only one. It is a demon." There was a silence. Then Merrin stated simply, "I know you doubt this. But you see, this demon . . . I have met once before. And he is powerful . . . powerful. . . ."

A silence. Karras spoke again. "We say the demon . . . cannot touch the victim's will."

"Yes, that is so . . . that is so. . . . There is no sin."

"Then what would be the *purpose* of possession?" Karras said, frowning. "What's the point?"

"Who can know?" answered Merrin. "Who can really hope to know?" He thought for a moment. And then probingly continued: "Yet I think the demon's target is not the possessed; it is us . . . the observers . . . every person in this house. And I think—I think the point is to make us despair; to reject our own humanity, Damien: to see ourselves as ultimately bestial; as ultimately vile and putrescent; without dignity; ugly; unworthy. And there lies the heart of it, perhaps: in unworthiness. For I think belief in God is not a matter of reason at all; I think it finally is a matter of love; of accepting the possibility that God could love *us*. . . ."

Again Merrin paused. He continued more slowly and with a hush of introspection: "He knows . . . the demon knows where to strike. . . ." He was nodding. "Long ago I despaired of ever loving my neighbor. Certain people . . . repelled me. How could I love them? I thought. It tormented me, Damien; it led me to despair of myself . . . and from that, very soon, to despair of my God. My faith was shattered. . . ."

Karras looked up at Merrin with interest. "And what happened?" he asked.

"Ah, well . . . at last I realized that God would never ask of me that which I know to be psychologically impossible; that the love which He asked was in my *will* and not meant to be felt as emotion at all. Not at all. He was asking that I *act* with love; that I *do* unto others; and that I should do it unto those who repelled me, I believe, was a greater act of love than any other." He shook his head. "I know that all of this must seem very obvious, Damien. I know. But at the time I could not see it. Strange blindness. How many husbands and wives," he uttered sadly, "must believe they have fallen out of love because their hearts no longer race at the sight of their beloveds! Ah, dear God!" He shook his head; and then nodded. "There it lies, I think, Damien . . . possession; not in wars, as some tend to believe; not so much; and very seldom in extraordinary interventions such as here . . . this girl . . . this poor child. No, I see it most often in the little things, Damien: in the senseless, petty spites; the misunderstandings; the cruel and cutting word that leaps unbidden to the tongue between friends. Between lovers. Enough of these," Merrin whispered, "and we have no need of Satan to manage our wars; these we manage for ourselves . . . for ourselves. . . ."

The lilting singing could still be heard in the bedroom. Merrin looked up at the door and listened for a moment. "And yet even from this—from evil—will come good. In some way. In some way that we may never understand or ever see." Merrin paused. "Perhaps evil is the crucible of goodness," he brooded. "And perhaps even Satan—Satan, in spite of himself—somehow serves to work out the will of God."

He said no more, and for a time they stood in silence while Karras reflected. Another objection came to mind. "Once the demon's driven out," he probed, "what's to keep it from coming back in?"

"I don't know," Merrin answered. "I don't know. And yet it never seems to happen. Never. Never." Merrin put a hand to his face, tightly pinching at the corners of his eyes. "Damien . . . what a wonderful name," he murmured. Karras heard exhaustion in the voice. And something else. Some anxiety. Something like repression of pain.

Abruptly, Merrin pushed himself away from the wall, and with his face still hidden in his hand, he excused himself and hurried down the hall to the bathroom. What was wrong? wondered Karras. He felt a sudden envy and admiration for the exorcist's strong and simple faith. He turned toward the door. The singing. It had stopped. Had the night at last ended?

Some minutes later, Sharon came out of the bedroom with a foul-smelling bundle of bedding and clothing. "She's sleeping now," she said. She looked away quickly and moved off down the hall.

Karras took a deep breath and returned to the bedroom. Felt the cold. Smelled the stench. He walked slowly to the bedside. Regan. Asleep. At last. And at last, thought Karras, he could rest.

He reached down and gripped Regan's thin wrist, looking at the sweep-second hand of his watch.

"Why you do this to me, Dimmy?"

His heart froze.

"Why you do this?"

The priest could not move, did not breathe, did not dare to glance over to that sorrowful voice, did not dare see those eyes really there: eyes accusing, eyes lonely. His mother. His *mother!*

"You leave me to be priest, Dimmy; send me institution. . . ."

Don't look!

"Now you chase me away? . . ."

It's not her!

"Why you do this? . . ."

His head throbbing, heart in his throat, Karras shut his eyes tightly as the voice grew imploring, grew frightened, grew tearful. "You always good boy, Dimmy. Please! I am 'fraid! Please no chase me outside, Dimmy! *Please!*"

. . . not my mother!

"Outside *nothing!* Only *dark*, Dimmy! *Lonely!*" Now tearful.

"You're not my mother!" Karras vehemently whispered.

"Dimmy, *please!* . . ."

"You're not my—"

"*Oh*, for heaven's sake, Karras!"

Dennings.

"Look, it simply isn't fair to drive us out of here! Really! I mean, speaking for myself it's only justice I should be here! Little bitch! She took my body and I think it only right that I ought to be allowed to stay in hers, don't you think? Oh, for *Christ's* sake, Karras, *look* at me, now would you? Come along! It isn't very often I get out to speak my piece. Just turn around now."

Karras opened up his eyes and saw the Dennings personality.

"There, that's better. Look, she killed me. Not our *inn*keeper, Karras—*she!* Oh, yes, indeed!" It was nodding affirmation. "*She!* I was minding my business at the bar, you see, when I thought I heard her moaning. Upstairs. Well, now, I *had* to see what ailed her, after all, so up I went and don't you know she bloody took me by the *throat*, the little cunt!" The

314

voice was whiny now; pathetic. "Christ, I've never in my *life* seen such strength! Began to scream that I was diddling her mother or something, or that I caused the divorce. Some such thing. It wasn't clear. But I *tell* you, love, she pushed me out the bloody fucking *window!*" Voice cracking. High-pitched now. "She *killed* me! Fucking *killed* me! Now you think it's bloody *fair* to throw me *out?* Come along, now, Karras, answer me! You think it really fair? I mean, *do* you?"

Karras swallowed.

"Yes, or no," it prodded. "Is it fair?"

"How was . . . the head turned around?" asked Karras hoarsely.

Dennings shifted his gaze around evasively. "Oh, well, that was an accident . . . a freak. . . . I hit the steps, you know. . . . It was freaky."

Karras pondered, a dryness in his throat. Then he picked up Regan's wrist again, and glanced at his watch in a move of dismissal.

"Dimmy, please! Don' make me be alone!"

His mother.

"If instead of be priest, you was doctor, I live in nice house, Dimmy, not wit' da cockroach, not all by myself in da apartment! Then . . ."

He was straining to block it all out, but the voice began to weep again.

"Dimmy, *please!*"

"You're not my—"

"Won't you face the truth, stinking scum?" It was the demon. "You believe what Merrin tells you?" It seethed. "You believe him to be holy and good? Well, he is *not!* He is proud and unworthy! I will prove it to you, Karras! I will prove it by *killing the piglet!*"

Karras opened up his eyes. But still dared not look.

"Yes, she will die and Merrin's God will not save her,

Karras! You will not save her! She will die from Merrin's pride and your incompetence! *Bungler! You should not have given her the Librium!*"

Karras turned now and looked at the eyes. They were shining with triumph and piercing spite.

"Feel her pulse!" The demon grinned. "Go ahead, Karras! Feel it!"

Regan's wrist was still gripped in his hand, and now he frowned worriedly. The pulse beat was rapid and . . .

"Feeble?" croaked the demon. "Ah, yes. A trifle. For the moment, just a bit."

Karras fetched his medical bag and took out his stethoscope. The demon rasped, "Listen, Karras! Listen well!"

Karras listened. The heart tones sounded distant and inefficient.

"I will not let her sleep!"

Karras flicked up his glance to the demon. Felt chilled.

"Yes, Karras!" it croaked. "She will not sleep! Do you hear? *I will not let the piglet sleep!*"

As Karras stared numbly, the demon put its head back in gloating laughter. He did not hear Merrin come back into the room.

The exorcist stood by him at the side of the bed and studied his face. "What is it?" he asked.

Karras answered dully, "The demon . . . said he wouldn't let her sleep." He turned haunted eyes on Merrin. "Her heart's begun to work inefficiently, Father. If she doesn't get rest pretty soon, she'll die of cardiac exhaustion."

Merrin looked grave. "Can you give her drugs? Some medicine to make her sleep?"

Karras shook his head. "No, that's dangerous. She might go into coma." He turned as Regan clucked like a hen. "If her blood pressure drops any more . . ." He trailed off.

"What can be done?" Merrin asked.

"Nothing . . . nothing . . ." Karras answered. "But I don't

know—maybe new advances . . ." He said abruptly to Merrin, "I'm going to call in a cardiac specialist, Father."

Merrin nodded.

Karras went downstairs. He found Chris keeping vigil in the kitchen and from the room off the pantry he heard Willie sobbing, heard the sound of Karl's consoling voice. He explained the need for consultation, carefully not divulging the full extent of Regan's danger. Chris gave him permission, and Karras telephoned a friend, a noted specialist at the Georgetown University Medical School, awakening him and briefing him tersely.

"Be right there," said the specialist.

He was at the house in less than half an hour. In the bedroom he reacted with bewilderment to the cold and the stench and with horror and compassion to Regan's condition. She was now croaking gibberish. While the specialist examined her, she alternately sang and made animal noises. Then Dennings appeared.

"Oh, it's terrible," it whined at the specialist. "Just awful! Oh, I do hope there's something you can do! Is there something? We'll have no place to go, you see, otherwise, and all because . . . Oh, *damn* the stubborn devil!" As the specialist stared oddly while taking Regan's blood pressure, Dennings looked to Karras and complained, "What the hell are you doing! Can't you see the little bitch should be in hospital? She belongs in a madhouse, Karras! Now you *know* that! Really! Now let's stop all this cunting mumbo-jumbo! If she dies, you know, it's *your* fault! All *yours!* I mean, just because *he's* stubborn doesn't mean *you* should behave like a snot! You're a doctor! You should know better, Karras! Now come along; there's just a *terrible* shortage of housing these days. If we're—"

Back came the demon now, howling like a wolf. The specialist, expressionless, undid the sphygmomanometer wrapping. Then he nodded at Karras. He was finished.

They went out into the hall, where the specialist looked back at the bedroom door for a moment, and then turned to Karras. "What the hell's going on in there, Father?"

The Jesuit averted his face. "I can't say," he said softly.

"Okay."

"What's the story?"

The specialist's manner was somber. "She's got to stop that activity . . . sleep . . . go to sleep before the blood pressure drops. . . ."

"Is there anything I can *do*, Bill?"

The specialist looked directly at Karras and said, "Pray."

He said good night and walked away. Karras watched him, every artery and nerve begging rest, begging hope, begging miracles though he knew none could be. ". . . *You should not have given her the Librium!*"

He turned back to the room and pushed open the door with a hand that was heavy as his soul.

Merrin stood by the bedside, watching while Regan neighed shrilly like a horse. He heard Karras enter and looked at him inquiringly. Karras shook his head. Merrin nodded. There was sadness in his face; then acceptance; and as he turned back to Regan, there was grim resolve.

Merrin knelt by the bed. "Our Father . . ." he began.

Regan splattered him with dark and stinking bile, and then croaked, "You will *lose!* She will *die!* She will *die!*"

Karras picked up his copy of the *Ritual*. Opened it. Looked up and stared at Regan.

" 'Save your servant,' " prayed Merrin.

" 'In the face of the enemy.' "

In Karras' heart there was a desperate torment. *Go to sleep! Go to sleep!* roared his will in a frenzy.

But Regan did not sleep.

Not by dawn.

Not by noon.

Not by nightfall.

Not by Sunday, when the pulse rate was one hundred and forty, and ever threadier, while the fits continued unremittingly, while Karras and Merrin kept repeating the ritual, never sleeping, Karras feverishly groping for remedies: a restraining sheet to hold Regan's movements to a minimum; keeping everyone out of the bedroom for a time to see if lack of provocation might terminate the fits. It did not. And Regan's shouting was as draining as her movements. Yet the blood pressure held. But how much longer? Karras agonized. *Ah, God, don't let her die!* he cried repeatedly to himself. *Don't let her die! Let her sleep! Let her sleep!* Never was he conscious that his thoughts were prayers; only that the prayers were never answered.

At seven o'clock that Sunday evening, Karras sat mutely next to Merrin in the bedroom, exhausted and racked by the demonic attacks: his lack of faith; his incompetence; his flight from his mother in search of status. And Regan. His fault. *"You should not have given her the Librium. . . ."*

The priests had just finished a cycle of the ritual. They were resting, listening to Regan singing *"Panis Angelicus."* They rarely left the room, Karras once to change clothes and to shower. But in the cold it was easier to stay wakeful; in the stench that since morning had altered in character to the gorge-raising odor of decayed, rotted flesh.

Staring feverishly at Regan with red-veined eyes, Karras thought he heard a sound. Something creaked. Again. As he blinked. And then he realized it was coming from his own crusted eyelids. He turned toward Merrin. Through the hours, the exorcist had said very little: now and then a homely story of his boyhood; reminiscences; little things; a story about a duck he owned named Clancy. Karras worried about him. The lack of sleep. The demon's attacks. At his age. Merrin closed his eyes and let his chin rest on his chest. Karras glanced around at Regan, and then wearily stood up and moved over to the bed. He checked her pulse and then began to take a blood pressure reading. As he wrapped the black sphygmoman-ometer cloth around the arm, he blinked repeatedly to clear the blurring of his vision.

"Today Muddir Day, Dimmy."

For a moment, he could not move; felt his heart wrenched from his chest. Then he looked into those eyes that seemed not Regan's anymore, but eyes sadly rebuking. His mother's.

"I not good to you? Why you leave me to die all alone, Dimmy? Why? Why you . . ."

"*Damien!*"

Merrin clutching tightly at his arm. "Please go and rest for a little now, Damien."

"Dimmy, *please!* Why you . . ."

Sharon came in to change the bedding.

"Go, rest for a little, Damien!" urged Merrin.

With a lump rising dry to his throat, Karras turned and left the bedroom. Stood weak in the hall. Then he walked down the stairs and stood indecisively. Coffee? He craved it. But a shower even more, a change of clothing, a shave.

He left the house and crossed the street to the Jesuit residence hall. Entered. Groped to his room. And when he looked at his bed . . . *Forget the shower. Sleep. Half an hour.* As he reached for the telephone to tell Reception to awaken him, it rang.

"Yes, hello," he answered hoarsely.

"Someone waiting here to see you, Father Karras: a Mr. Kinderman."

For a moment, Karras held his breath and then, weakly, he answered, "Please tell him I'll be out in just a minute."

As he hung up the telephone, Karras saw the carton of Camels on his desk. A note from Dyer was attached. He read blearily:

A key to the Playboy Club has been found on the chapel kneeler in front of the votive lights. Is it yours? You can claim it at Reception.

Without expression, Karras set down the note, dressed in fresh clothing and walked out of the room. He forgot to take the cigarettes.

In Reception, he saw Kinderman at the telephone switchboard counter, delicately rearranging the composition of a vase full of flowers. As he turned and saw Karras, he was holding the stem of a pink camellia.

"Ah, Father! Father Karras!" glowed Kinderman, his expression changing to concern at the exhaustion in the Jesuit's face. He quickly replaced the camellia and came forward to meet Karras. "You look awful! What's the matter? That's what comes of all this *schle*ping around the track? Give it up! Listen, come!" He gripped Karras by the elbow and propelled him toward the street. "You've got a minute?" he asked as they passed through the entry doors.

"Barely," murmured Karras. "What is it?"

"A little talk. I need advice, nothing more, just advice."

"What about?"

"In just a minute," waved Kinderman in dismissal. "Now we'll walk. We'll take air. We'll enjoy." He linked his arm through the Jesuit's and guided him diagonally across Prospect Street. "Ah, now, *look* at that! Beautiful! Gorgeous!" He was pointing to the sun sinking low on the Potomac, and in the stillness rang the laughter and the talking-all-together of Georgetown undergraduates in front of a drinking hall near the corner of Thirty-sixth Street. One punched another one hard on the arm, and the two began wrestling amicably. "Ah, college, college . . ." breathed Kinderman ruefully, nodding as he stared. "I never went . . . but I wish . . . I wish . . ." He saw that Karras was watching the sunset. "I mean, seriously, you really look bad," he repeated. "What's the matter? You've been sick?"

When would Kinderman come to the point? Karras wondered. "No, just busy," he answered.

"Slow it down, then," wheezed Kinderman. "Slow. You know better. You saw the Bolshoi Ballet, incidentally, at the Watergate?"

"No."

"No, me neither. But I wish. They're so graceful . . . so cute!"

They had come to the Car Barn wall. Resting a forearm, Karras faced Kinderman, who had clasped his hands atop the wall and was staring pensively across the river. "Well, what's on your mind, Lieutenant?" asked Karras.

"Ah, well, Father," sighed Kinderman, "I'm afraid I've got a problem."

Karras flicked a brief glance up at Regan's shuttered window. "Professional?"

"Well, partly . . . only partly."

"What is it?"

"Well, mostly it's . . ." Hesitant, Kinderman squinted. "Well, mostly it's ethical, you could say, Father Karras . . . a question. . . ." The detective turned around and leaned his back against the wall. He frowned at the sidewalk. Then he shrugged. "There's just no one I could talk to about it; not my captain in particular, you see. I just couldn't. I couldn't tell him. So I thought . . ." His face lit with sudden animation. "I had an aunt . . . you should hear this; it's funny. She was terrified—terrified—for years of my uncle. Never dared to say a word to him. Wouldn't dare to raise her voice. Never! So whenever she got mad at him for something—for whatever—right away, she'd run quick to the closet in her bedroom, and then there in the dark—you won't believe this!—in the dark, by herself, and the moths and the clothes hanging up, she would curse—she would curse!—at my uncle for maybe twenty minutes! Tell exactly what she thought of him! Really! I mean, *yelling!* She'd come out, she'd feel better, she'd go kiss him on the cheek. Now what *is* that, Father Karras? That's good therapy or not!"

"It's very good," said Karras, smiling bleakly. "And I'm your closet now? Is that what you're saying?"

"In a way," said Kinderman. Again he looked down. "In a way. But more serious, Father Karras." He paused. "And the closet must speak," he added heavily.

"Got a cigarette?" asked Karras with shaking hands.

The detective looked up at him, blankly incredulous. "A condition like mine and I would *smoke?*"

"No, you wouldn't," murmured Karras, clasping hands atop the wall and staring at them. *Stop shaking!*

"Some doctor! God forbid I should be sick in some jungle and instead of Albert Schweitzer, there is with me only you! You cure warts still with frogs, Doctor Karras?"

"It's toads," Karras answered, subdued.

"You're not laughing today," worried Kinderman. "Something's wrong?"

Mutely Karras shook his head. Then, "Go ahead," he said softly.

The detective sighed and faced out to the river. "I was saying . . ." he wheezed. He scratched his brow with his thumbnail. "I was saying—well, let's say I'm working on a case, Father Karras. A homicide."

"Dennings?"

"No, no, purely hypothetical. You wouldn't be familiar with it. Nothing. Not at all."

Karras nodded.

"Like a ritual witchcraft murder, this looks," the detective continued broodingly. He was frowning, picking words slowly. "And let us say in this house—this hypothetical house—there are living five people, and that one must be the killer." With his hand, he made flat, chopping motions of emphasis. "Now

I *know* this. I *know* this—I know this for a *fact*." Then he paused, slowly exhaling breath. "But then the problem. . . . All the evidence—well, it points to a child, Father Karras; a little girl maybe ten, twelve years old . . . just a baby; she could maybe be my daughter." He kept his eyes fixed on the embankment beyond them. "Yes, I know: sounds fantastic . . . ridiculous . . . but true. Now there comes to this house, Father, a priest—very famous—and this case being purely hypothetical, Father, I learn through my also hypothetical genius that this priest has once cured a very special type illness. An illness which is mental, by the way, a fact I mention just in passing for your interest."

Karras felt himself turning grayer by the moment.

"Now also there is . . . satanism involved in this illness, it happens, plus . . . strength . . . yes, incredible strength. And this . . . hypothetical girl, let us say, then, could . . . twist a man's head around, you see. Yes, she could." He was nodding now. "Yes . . . yes, she could. Now the question . . ." He grimaced thoughtfully. "You see . . . you see, the girl is not responsible, Father. She's demented." He shrugged. "And just a child! A *child!*" He shook his head. "And yet the illness that she has . . . it could be dangerous. She could kill someone else. Who's to know?" He again squinted out across the river. "It's a problem. What to do? Hypothetically, I mean. Forget it? Forget it and hope she gets"—Kinderman paused —"gets well?" He reached for a handkerchief. "Father, I don't know . . . I don't know." He blew his nose. "It's a terrible decision; just awful." He was searching for a clean, unused section of handkerchief. "Awful. And I hate to be the one who has to make it." He again blew his nose and lightly dabbed at a nostril. "Father, what would be right in such a case? Hypothetically? What do you believe would be the right thing to do?"

For an instant, the Jesuit throbbed with rebellion, with a dull, weary anger at the piling on of weight. He let it ebb.

He met Kinderman's eyes and answered softly, "I would put it in the hands of a higher authority."

"I believe it is there at this moment," breathed Kinderman.

"Yes . . . and I would leave it there."

Their gazes locked. Then Kinderman pocketed the hand-kerchief. "Yes . . . yes, I thought you would say that." He nodded, then glanced at the sunset. "So beautiful. A sight." He tugged back his sleeve for a look at his wrist watch. "Ah, well, I have to go. Mrs. K. will be *schreiing* now: 'The dinner, it's cold!' " He turned back to Karras. "Thank you, Father. I feel better . . . much better. Oh, incidentally, you could maybe do a favor? Give a message? If you meet a man named Eng-strom, tell him—well, say, 'Elvira is in a clinic, she's all right.' He'll understand. Would you do that? I mean, if you should meet him."

Karras was puzzled. Then, "Sure," he said. "Sure."

"Look, we couldn't make a film some night, Father?"

The Jesuit looked down and murmured, "Soon."

" 'Soon.' You're like a rabbi when he mentions the Messiah: always 'Soon.' Listen, do me another favor, please, Father." The detective looked gravely concerned. "Stop this running round the track for a little. Just walk. Walk. Slow down. You'll do that?"

"I'll do that."

Hands in his pockets, the detective looked down at the sidewalk in resignation. "I know." He sighed wearily. "Soon. Always soon." As he started away, his head still lowered, he reached up a hand to the Jesuit's shoulder. Squeezed. "Elia Kazan sends regards."

For a time, Karras watched him as he listed down the street. Watched with wonder. With fondness. And surprise at the heart's labyrinthine turnings. He looked up at the clouds washed in pink above the river, then beyond to the west, where they drifted at the edge of the world, glowing faintly, like a promise remembered. He put the side of his fist against his lips and looked down against the sadness as it welled from his throat toward the corners of his eyes. He waited. Dared not risk another glance at the sunset. He looked up at Regan's window, then went back to the house.

Sharon let him in and said nothing had changed. She had a bundle of foul-smelling laundry in her hands. She excused herself. "I've got to get this downstairs to the washer."

He watched her. Thought of coffee. But now he heard the demon croaking viciously at Merrin. He started toward the staircase. Then remembered the message. Karl. Where was he? He turned to ask Sharon and glimpsed her disappearing down the basement steps. In a fog, he went to the kitchen.

No Karl. Only Chris. She was sitting at the table looking down at . . . an album? Pasted photographs. Scraps of paper. Cupped hands at her forehead obscured her from his view.

"Excuse me," said Karras very softly. "Is Karl in his room?"

She shook her head. "He's on an errand," she whispered huskily. Karras heard her sniffle. Then, "There's coffee there, Father," Chris murmured. "It ought to perc in just a minute."

As Karras glanced over at the percolator light, he heard Chris getting up from the table, and when he turned he saw her moving quickly past him with her face averted. He heard a quavery "Excuse me." She left the kitchen.

His gaze shifted to the album. He walked over and looked down. Candid photos. A young girl. With a pang, Karras realized he was looking at Regan: here, blowing out candles on a whipped-creamy birthday cake; here, sitting on a lakefront dock in shorts and a T-shirt, waving gaily at the camera. Something was stenciled on the front of the T-shirt: CAMP . . . He could not make it out.

On the opposite page a ruled sheet of paper bore the script of a child:

> If instead of just clay
> I could take all the prettiest things

Like a rainbow,
Or clouds or the way a bird sings,
Maybe then, Mother dearest,
If I put them all together,
I could *really* make a sculpture of you.

Below the poem: I LOVE YOU! HAPPY MOTHER'S DAY! The signature, in pencil, was *Rags*.

Karras shut his eyes. He could not bear this chance meeting. He turned away wearily and waited for the coffee to brew. With lowered head, he gripped the counter and again closed his eyes. *Shut it out!* he thought; *shut it all out!* But he could not, and as he listened to the thump of the percolating coffee, his hands began to tremble and compassion swelled suddenly and blindly into rage at disease and at pain, at the suffering of children and the frailty of the body, at the monstrous and outrageous corruption of death.

"*If instead of just clay . . .*"

The rage drained to sorrow and helpless frustration.

"*. . . all the prettiest things . . .*"

He could not wait for coffee. He must go . . . he must do something . . . help someone . . . try. . . .

He left the kitchen. As he passed by the living room, he looked in. Chris was on the sofa, sobbing convulsively, and Sharon was comforting her. He looked away and walked up the stairs, heard the demon roaring frenziedly at Merrin. ". . . would have *lost!* You would have *lost* and you *knew* it! You *scum*, Merrin! Bastard! Come *back!* Come and . . ."

Karras blocked it out.

"*. . . or the way a bird sings . . .*"

He realized as he entered the bedroom that he had forgotten to wear a sweater. He looked at Regan. The head was turned away from him, sideways, as the demon continued to rage.

"*. . . All the prettiest . . .*"

He went slowly to his chair and picked up a blanket, and

only then, in his exhaustion, did he notice Merrin's absence. On the way back to Regan to take a blood-pressure reading, he nearly stumbled over him. Limp and disjointed, he lay sprawled face down on the floor beside the bed. Shocked, Karras knelt. Turned him over. Saw the bluish coloration of his face. Felt for pulse. And in a wrenching, stabbing instant of anguish, Karras realized that Merrin was dead.

". . . saintly flatulence! *Die*, will you? *Die?* Karras, *heal* him!" raged the demon. "Bring him back and let us *finish*, let us . . ."

Heart failure. Coronary artery. "Ah, God!" Karras groaned in a whisper. "God, *no!*" He shut his eyes and shook his head in disbelief, in despair, and then, abruptly, with a surge of grief, he dug his thumb with savage force into Merrin's pale wrist as if to squeeze from its sinews the lost beat of life.

". . . pious . . ."

Karras sagged back and took a deep breath. Then he saw the tiny pills scattered loose on the floor. He picked one up and with aching recognition saw that Merrin had known. Nitroglycerin. He'd known. His eyes red and brimming, Karras looked at Merrin's face. ". . . *go and rest for a little now, Damien.*"

"Even *worms* will not eat your corruption, you . . ."

Karras heard the words of the demon and began to tremble with a murderous fury.

Don't listen!

". . . homosexual . . ."

Don't listen! Don't listen!

A vein stood out angrily on Karras' forehead, throbbing darkly. As he picked up Merrin's hands and started tenderly to place them in the form of a cross, he heard the demon croak, "Now put his *cock* in his hands!" and a glob of putrid spittle hit the dead man's eye. "The last rites!" mocked the demon. It put back its head and laughed wildly.

Karras stared numbly at the spittle, eyes bulging. Did not

move. Could not hear above the roaring of his blood. And then slowly, in quivering, side-angling jerks, he looked up with a face that was a purpling snarl, an electrifying spasm of hatred and rage. "*You son of a bitch!*" Karras seethed in a whisper that hissed into air like molten steel. "You bastard!" Though he did not move, he seemed to be uncoiling, the sinews of his neck pulling taut like cables. The demon stopped laughing and eyed him with malevolence. "You were losing! You're a loser! You've *always* been a loser!" Regan splattered him with vomit. He ignored it. "Yes, you're very good with children!" he said, trembling. "Little girls! Well, come on! Let's see you try something bigger! Come on!" He had his hands out like great, fleshy hooks, beckoning slowly. "Come on! Come on, loser! Try *me!* Leave the girl and take me! Take *me!* Come into . . ."

It was barely a minute later when Chris and Sharon heard the sounds from above. They were in the study and, dry-eyed, Chris sat in front of the bar while Sharon, behind it, was mixing them a drink. As she set the vodka and tonic on the bar, both the women glanced up at the ceiling. Stumblings. Sharp bumps against furniture. Walls. Then the voice of . . . the demon? The demon. Obscenities. But another voice. Alternating. Karras? Yes, Karras. Yet stronger. Deeper.

"No! I won't let you hurt them! You're *not going to hurt them!* You're coming with . . ."

Chris knocked her drink over as she flinched at a violent splintering, at the breaking of glass, and in an instant she and Sharon were racing from the study, up the stairs, to the door of Regan's bedroom, bursting in. They saw the shutters of the window on the floor, ripped off their hinges! And the window! The glass had been totally shattered!

Alarmed, they rushed forward toward the window, and as they did, Chris saw Merrin on the floor by the bed. She stood rooted in shock. Then she ran to him. Knelt. She gasped. "Oh, my God!" she whimpered. "Sharon! Shar, come here! Quick, come—"

Sharon screamed from the window, and as Chris looked up bloodlessly, gaping, she ran again toward the door.

"Shar, what *is* it?"

"Father Karras! Father Karras!"

She bolted from the room in hysteria, and Chris got up and ran trembling to the window. She looked below and felt her heart dropping out of her body. At the bottom of the steps on busy M Street, Karras lay crumpled amid a gathering crowd.

She stared horrified. Paralyzed. Tried to move.

"Mother?"

A small, wan voice calling tearfully behind her. Chris gulped. Did not dare to believe or— "What's happening, Mother? Oh, please! Please come here! Mother, please! I'm *afraid!* I'm a—"

Chris turned quickly and saw the tears of confusion, the pleading, and suddenly she was racing to the bed, weeping, "Rags! Oh, my baby, my baby! Oh, Rags!"

Downstairs, Sharon lunged from the house and ran frantically to the Jesuit residence hall. She asked urgently for Dyer. He came quickly to Reception. She told him. He turned pale.

"Called an ambulance?"

"Oh, my God, I didn't think!"

Swiftly Dyer gave instructions to the switchboard operator, then he raced from the hall, followed closely by Sharon. Crossed the street. Down the steps.

"Let me through, please! Coming through!" As he pushed through the bystanders, Dyer heard murmurs of the litany of indifference. "What happened?" "Some guy fell down the steps." "Did you . . . ?" "Musta been drunk. See the vomit?" "Come on, we'll be late for the . . ."

Dyer at last broke through, and for a heart-stopping instant felt frozen in a timeless dimension of grief, in a space where the air was too painful to breathe. Karras lay crumpled and twisted, on his back, with his head in the center of a growing pool of blood. He was staring vacantly, jaw slack. And now his eyes shifted numbly to Dyer. Leaped alive. Seemed to glow with an elation. Some plea. Something urgent.

"Come on, back now! Move it back!" A policeman. Dyer knelt and put a light, tender hand like a caress against the bruised, gashed face. So many cuts. A bloody ribbon trickled down from the mouth. "Damien . . ." Dyer paused to still the quaver in his throat, and in the eyes saw that faint, eager shine, the warm plea.

He leaned closer. "Can you talk?"

Slowly Karras reached his hand to Dyer's wrist. Staring fixedly, he clutched it. Briefly squeezed.

Dyer fought back the tears. He leaned closer and put his mouth next to Karras' ear. "Do you want to make your confession now, Damien?"

A squeeze.

"Are you sorry for all of the sins of your life and for having offended Almighty God?"

A squeeze.

Now Dyer leaned back and as he slowly traced the sign of the cross over Karras, he recited the words of absolution: "*Ego te absolvo . . .*"

An enormous tear rolled down from a corner of Karras' eye, and now Dyer felt his wrist being squeezed even harder, continuously, as he finished the absolution: ". . . *in nomine Patris, et Filii, et Spiritus Sancti. Amen.*"

Dyer leaned over again with his mouth next to Karras' ear. Waited. Forced the swelling from his throat. And then murmured, "Are you . . . ?" He stopped short as the pressure on his wrist abruptly slackened. He pulled back his head and saw the eyes filled with peace; and with something else: something mysteriously like joy at the end of heart's longing. The eyes were still staring. But at nothing in this world. Nothing here.

331

Slowly and tenderly, Dyer slid the eyelids down. He heard the ambulance wail from afar. He began to say, "Good-bye," but could not finish. He lowered his head and wept.

The ambulance arrived. They put Karras on a stretcher, and as they were loading him aboard, Dyer climbed in and sat beside the intern. He reached over and took Karras' hand.

"There's nothing you can do for him now, Father," said the intern in a kindly voice. "Don't make it harder on yourself. Don't come."

Dyer held his gaze on that chipped, torn face. He shook his head.

The intern looked up to the ambulance rear door, where the driver was waiting patiently. He nodded. The ambulance door went up with a click.

From the sidewalk, Sharon watched stunned as the ambulance slowly drove away. She heard murmurs from the bystanders.

"What happened?"

"Who knows, buddy? Who the hell knows?"

The wail of the ambulance siren lifted shrill into night above the river until the driver remembered that time no longer mattered. He cut it off. The river flowed quiet again, reaching toward a gentler shore.

epilogue

Late June sunlight streamed through the window of Chris's bedroom. She folded a blouse on top of the contents of the suitcase and closed the lid. She moved quickly toward the door. "Okay, that's all of it," she said to Karl, and as the Swiss came forward to lock the suitcase, she went out into the hall and toward Regan's bedroom. "Hey, Rags, how ya comin'?"

It was now six weeks since the deaths of the priests. Since the shock. Since the closed investigation by Kinderman. And still there were no answers. Only haunting speculation and frequent awakenings from sleep in tears. The death of Merrin had been caused by coronary artery disease. But as for Karras . . . "Baffling," Kinderman had wheezed. Not the girl, he'd decided. She'd been firmly secured by restraining straps and sheet. Obviously, Karras had ripped away the shutters, leaping through the window to deliberate death. But why? Fear? An attempt to escape something horrible? No. Kinderman had quickly ruled it out. Had he wished to escape, he could have gone out the door. Nor was Karras in any case a man who would run.

But then why the fatal leap?

For Kinderman, the answer began to take shape in a statement by Dyer making mention of Karras' emotional conflicts: his guilt about his mother; her death; his problem of faith; and when Kinderman added to these the continuous lack of sleep for several days; the concern and the guilt over Regan's imminent death; the demonic attacks in the form of his mother; and finally, the shock of Merrin's death, he sadly concluded that Karras' mind had snapped, had been shattered by the burden of guilts he could no longer endure. Moreover, in investigating Dennings' death, the detective had learned from his readings on possession that exorcists frequently became possessed, and through just such causes as might here have been present: strong feelings of guilt and the need to be punished, added to the power of autosuggestion. Karras had been ripe. And the sounds of struggle, the priest's altered voice heard by both Chris and Sharon, these seemed to lend weight to the detective's hypothesis.

But Dyer had refused to accept it. Again and again he returned to the house during Regan's convalescence to talk to Chris. He asked over and over again if Regan was now able to recall what had happened in the bedroom that night. But the answer was always a headshake; or a no; and finally the case was closed.

Now Chris poked her head into Regan's bedroom; saw her daughter with two stuffed animals in her clutch, staring down with a child's discontent at the packed, open suitcase on her bed. "How are you coming with your packing, honey?" Chris asked her.

Regan looked up. A little wan. A little gaunt. A little dark beneath the eyes. "There's not enough room in this thing!" She frowned.

"Well, you can't take it all, now, sweetheart. Leave it, and Willie will bring the rest. Come on, baby; hurry or we'll miss our plane."

They were catching an afternoon flight to Los Angeles, leaving Sharon and the Engstroms to close up the house. Then Karl would drive the Jaguar cross-country back home.

"Oh, okay." Regan pouted mildly.

"That's my baby." Chris left her and went quickly down the stairs. As she got to the bottom, the door chimes rang. She opened the door.

"Hi, Chris." It was Father Dyer. "Just came by to say so long."

"Oh, I'm glad. I was just going to call you myself." She stepped back. "Come on in."

"No, that's all right, Chris; I know you're in a hurry."

She took his hand and drew him in. "Oh, please! I was just about to have a cup of coffee."

"Well, if you're sure . . ."

She was. They went to the kitchen, where they sat at the table, drank coffee, spoke pleasantries, while Sharon and the Engstroms bustled back and forth. Chris spoke of Merrin: how awed and surprised she had been at seeing the notables and foreign dignitaries at his funeral. Then they were silent together while Dyer stared down into his cup, into sadness. Chris read his thought. "She still can't remember," she said gently. "I'm sorry."

Still downcast, the Jesuit nodded. Chris glanced to her breakfast plate. Too nervous and excited, she hadn't eaten. The rose was still there. She picked it up and pensively twisted it, rolling it back and forth by the stem. "And he never even knew her," she murmured absently. Then she held the rose still and flicked her eyes at Dyer. Saw him staring. "What do you think really happened?" he asked softly. "As a nonbeliever. Do you think she was really possessed?"

She pondered, looking down, still toying with the rose. "Well, like you say . . . as far as God goes, I am a nonbeliever. Still am. But when it comes to a devil—well, that's something else. I could buy that. I do, in fact. I do. And it isn't just what happened to Rags. I mean, generally." She shrugged. "You come to God and you have to figure if there is one, then he must need a million years' sleep every night or else he tends to get irritable. Know what I mean? He never talks. But the devil keeps advertising, Father. The devil does lots of commercials."

For a moment Dyer looked at her, and then said quietly, "But if all of the evil in the world makes you think that there might be a devil, then how do you account for all the *good* in the world?"

The thought made her squint as she held his gaze. Then she dropped her eyes. "Yeah . . . yeah," she murmured softly. "That's a point." The sadness and shock of Karras' death settled down on her mood like a melancholy haze. Yet through it, she saw a speckled point of light, and tried to focus on it, remembering Dyer as he had walked her to her car at the cemetery after Karras' funeral. "*Can you come to the house for a while?*" she'd asked him. "*Oh, I'd like to, but I can't miss the feast,*" he replied. She looked puzzled. "*When a Jesuit dies,*" he explained to her, "*we always have a feast. For him it's a beginning, so we celebrate.*"

Chris had another thought. "You said Father Karras had a problem with his faith."

Dyer nodded.

"I can't believe that," she said. "I've never seen such faith in my life."

"Taxi here, madam."

Chris came out of her reverie. "Thanks, Karl. Okay." She

and Dyer stood up. "No, you stay, Father. I'll be right down. I'm just going upstairs to get Rags."

He nodded absently and watched her leave. He was thinking of Karras' puzzling last words, the shouts overheard from below before his death. There was something there. What was it? He didn't know. Both Chris's and Sharon's recollections had been vague. But now he thought once again of that mysterious look of joy in Karras' eyes. And something else, he suddenly remembered: a deep and fiercely shining glint of . . . triumph? He wasn't sure, yet oddly he felt lighter. Why lighter? he wondered.

He walked to the entry hall. Hands in his pockets, he leaned against the doorway and watched as Karl helped stow luggage in the cab. It was humid and hot and he wiped his brow, then turned at the sound of footsteps coming down the staircase. Chris and Regan, hand in hand. They came toward him. Chris kissed his cheek. Then she held her hand to it, probing his eyes tenderly.

"It's all right," he said. Then he shrugged. "I've got a feeling it's all right."

She nodded. "I'll call you from L.A. Take care."

Dyer glanced down at Regan. She was frowning at him, as at a sudden remembrance of forgotten concern. Impulsively, she reached up her arms to him. He leaned over and she kissed him. Then she stood for a moment, still staring at him oddly. No, not at him: at his round Roman collar.

Chris looked away. "Come on," she said huskily, taking Regan's hand. "We'll be late, hon. Come on."

Dyer watched as they moved away. Returned Chris's wave. Saw her blow a kiss, then pile quickly after Regan into the cab. And as Karl climbed in front beside the driver, Chris waved again through the window. The taxi pulled away. Dyer walked over to the curb. Watched. Soon the cab turned a corner and was gone.

From across the street, he heard a squeal of brakes. He

looked. A police car. Kinderman emerging. The detective moved slowly around the car and waddled toward Dyer. He waved. "I came to say good-bye."

"You just missed them."

Kinderman stopped in his tracks, crestfallen. "They're gone?"

Dyer nodded.

Kinderman looked down the street and shook his head. Then he glanced up at Dyer. "How's the girl?"

"She seemed fine."

"Ah, that's good. Very good. Well, that's all that's important." He looked away. "Well, back to business," he wheezed. "Back to work. Bye, now, Father." He turned and took a step toward the squad car, then stopped and turned back to stare speculatively at Dyer. "You go to films, Father Dyer? You like them?"

"Oh, sure."

"I get passes." He hesitated for a moment. "In fact, I've got a pass for the Crest tomorrow night. You'd like to go?"

Dyer had his hands in his pockets. "What's playing?"

"*Wuthering Heights.*"

"Who's in it?"

"Heathcliff, Jackie Gleason, and in the role Catherine Earnshaw, Lucille Ball. You're happy?"

"I've seen it," said Dyer without expression.

Kinderman stared limply for a moment. Looked away. "Another one," he murmured. Then he stepped to the sidewalk, hooked an arm through Dyer's and slowly started walking him down the street. "I'm reminded of a line in the film *Casablanca,*" he said fondly. "At the end Humphrey Bogart says to Claude Rains: 'Louie—I think this is the beginning of a beautiful friendship.'"

"You know, you *look* a little bit like Bogart."

"You noticed."

In forgetting, they were trying to remember.

author's note

I have taken a few liberties with the current geography of Georgetown University, notably with respect to the present location of
the Institute of Languages and Linguistics. Moreover, the house on
Prospect Street does not exist, nor does the reception room of the
Jesuit residence hall as I have described it.

The fragment of prose attributed to Lankester Merrin is not my
creation, but is taken from a sermon of John Henry Newman entitled "The Second Spring."

acknowledgments

My special thanks to Herbert Tanney, M.D.; Mr. Joseph E. Jeffs, Librarian, Georgetown University; Mr. William Bloom; and Mrs. Ann Harris, my editor at Harper & Row, for their invaluable assistance and generosity in the preparation of this work. I would also like to thank the Rev. Thomas V. Bermingham, S.J., Vice-Provincial for Formation of the New York Province of the Society of Jesus, for suggesting the subject matter of this novel; and Mr. Marc Jaffe of Bantam Books for his singular (and lonely) faith in its eventual worth. To these mentions I would like to add Dr. Bernard M. Wagner of Georgetown University, for teaching me to write, and the Jesuits, for teaching me to think.

ABOUT THE AUTHOR

William Peter Blatty was born in New York in 1928 and was educated at Jesuit schools and at Georgetown University. After taking an M.A. in English literature at George Washington University, he served as an editor with the U.S. Information Agency in Lebanon and was Policy Branch Chief of the U.S. Air Force Psychological Warfare Division in Washington, D.C. He now lives in Beverly Hills, California, has published four previous books, and is the author of numerous screenplays.

The idea for *The Exorcist* first came to him in 1950. Since then, Mr. Blatty has read every book in English on the subject. He spent almost a year writing the novel. He is particularly intrigued by the fact that psychiatrically we know no more about the phenomenon of possession, its nature and causes, than we did in 1921. In spite of scientific advances since then, the subject remains ultimately speculative.

71 72 73 10 9 8 7 6